P9-DIB-443

Materials and Structure of Music

VOLUME ONE

Materials

William Christ

Richard DeLone

Vernon Kliewer

Lewis Rowell

Indiana University

William Thomson

State University of New York, Buffalo

and Structure of Music

THIRD EDITION

Prentice-Hall, Inc., Englewood Cliffs, New Jersey 07632

Library of Congress Cataloging in Publication Data

Main entry under title:

Materials and structure of music.

Includes index.
1. Music—Theory. I. Christ, William.
MT6.M347 1979 781 79-10594
ISBN 0-13-560417-6

Materials and Structure of Music, Vol. I, 3/E
Christ/DeLone/Kliewer/Rowell/Thomson

Printed in the United States of America

10 9 8 7 6 5 4 3 2 1

Editorial/production supervision by Fred Bernardi
Interior design by Mark A. Binn
Page layout by Jenny Marcus
Cover design by Mark A. Binn
Manufacturing buyer: Ed Leone

PRENTICE-HALL INTERNATIONAL, INC., *London*
PRENTICE-HALL OF AUSTRALIA PTY. LIMITED, *Sydney*
PRENTICE-HALL OF CANADA, LTD., *Toronto*
PRENTICE-HALL OF INDIA PRIVATE LIMITED, *New Delhi*
PRENTICE-HALL OF JAPAN, INC., *Tokyo*
PRENTICE-HALL OF SOUTHEAST ASIA PTE. LTD., *Singapore*
WHITEHALL BOOKS LIMITED, *Wellington, New Zealand*

Contents

Preface

Materials and Structure of Music has been revised for the second time with two paramount goals in mind: 1) to retain basic ingredients—content, procedure, and format—that have made the two volumes useful, and yet 2) to perform major renovations on their presentation, which in earlier editions was at times diffuse and labored. We have added as well as subtracted content. Most notable perhaps is the infusion of musical examples from non-western repertories, consistent with our goal to reveal principles of musical structure, illustrating their most evident manifestations from the broadest sampling of music available to us.

The wisdom and experience of many others have played a significant role in the reorganization of this new edition, and from our teaching colleagues and critics we have gained insights that motivated our rearrangements, our reductions, and our additions. To all of these we extend our sincerest thanks for their thoughtfulness and concern.

Materials and Structure of Music

Chapter One

Introduction to Basic Properties and Notation

As performers, listeners, and composers, musicians deal with patterns of organized sound. Musical sound has four properties: *pitch,* which may be described as high or low; *intensity,* described as loud or soft; *timbre,* or tone quality; and *duration.* In this chapter we shall review some of the important characteristics of two of these properties, pitch and duration.

We often respond to music by tapping our feet, dancing, or snapping our fingers. In doing so we are carried along by a characteristic of rhythm called *pulse*. Rhythmic pulse can be compared to the ticking of a watch or the throbbing of a heartbeat. Rhythmic pulsations, like heartbeats, indicate "aliveness," and music comes alive through rhythm. We respond most easily to rhythmic pulse when it is periodic.

Rhythmic pulses (or beats) are usually grouped (or *metered*) so that one of a series is an accent, or "more important," pulse. These groupings are usually made in the form of twos or threes or fours. Any grouping is possible, however, and units of five, seven, or more beats per group occur in Western music. Beats, then, are regular pulsations, like the ticks of a metronome, which have a precise speed (or *tempo*). In the three melodies shown next, twelve periodic beats have been grouped differently: first in twos, next in threes, and last in alternate groupings of twos and threes. Perform the melodies at a moderate tempo and note that it is through the accented (strong) beats, as indicated below each melody, that we perceive each successive group.

Ex. 1–1.

The term *meter* designates the characteristic, or "normal," grouping of beats in a composition. A *metric accent* is produced by our perception of strong beats, which we usually expect to find at the beginning of each group or measure. Unaccented beats are called *weak beats.* In Ex. 1–1a the ordering of beats is *strong–weak* (*S–w*), and the pattern in Ex. 1–1b is *S–w–w.* The irregularity of Ex. 1–1c results from alternate groupings of *S–w* and *S–w–w.*

Basic Durations and the Beat

A beat is understood to last until a next beat occurs. But if we imagine beats as brief pulsations or ticks, then it is difficult to understand one beat as continuing until the next beat begins. However, if we regard the beat as only the beginning of a regularly recurring time span, then we can describe the *total time span* from one beat to the next as a *basic duration*. Furthermore, the various durations used in a composition can be related to the *basic duration*. Meter, then, is an *ordering of basic durations* into groups of two, three, or four units per measure, or whatever pattern the composer may wish to establish. Basic duration refers to the time span from one beat to the next, and this unit is represented in notation by one of the note-values shown in Ex. 1–2 for simple meters.

Ex. 1–2. Basic duration signs (note-values).

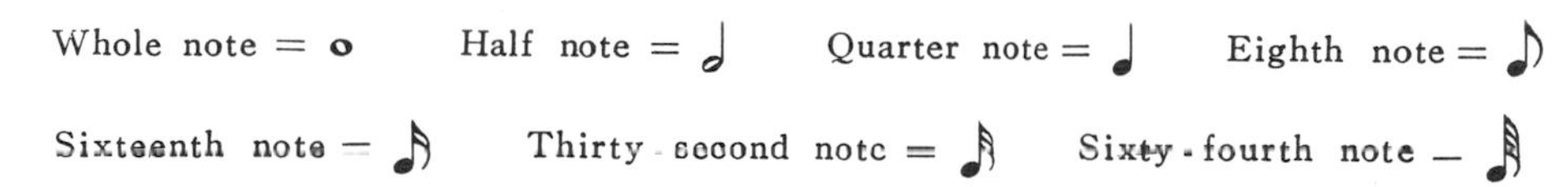

The relationship between the concepts of *beat* and *basic duration* can be graphically shown as follows:

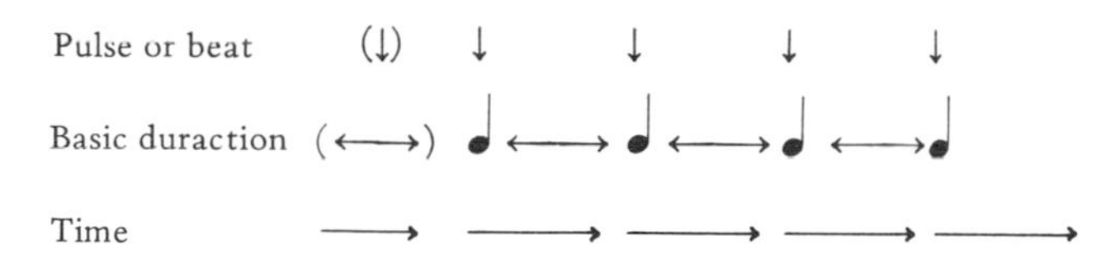

We have noted several processes that are involved in creating meter: first, a pulse at a particular tempo must be established; and second, the successive beats must be organized into periodic groups, each of which begins with a strong (or "mentally" accented) pulse. Meter is thus one of the most basic experiences of rhythm, and as listeners we have become strongly conditioned to expect the regular accents of some regular pattern such as *strong–weak* that we call *metric rhythm*.

The feeling of accent can be communicated by various musical means—length, separation, loudness, sharpness of attack, delay, choice of pitch, or timbre—anything, in fact, that marks an individual sound for our attention. Musical accents, then, can be *dynamic* (created by loudness of attack), *agogic* (created by a longer duration), *articulatory* (created by the way in which a note is begun or separated from preceding notes), or *tonal* (created by the particular pitch chosen).

Agogic accents—those contrasts of duration which communicate the meter to the listener—are illustrated in the melody of Ex. 1–3a. Both the distribution of long and short notes and the pitch line itself (which is grouped by threes) reinforce our perception of a triple meter.

Ex. 1–3a. Beethoven: Symphony No. 3, I.

In fact, the actual meter signature for the melody in Ex. 1–3a is $\frac{3}{4}$.

Syncopation

When conflicting accents occur in music, we call the resulting effect *syncopation*. A typical kind of syncopation occurs when the beginnings of long durations (the agogic accents) do not coincide with the metric accents, as illustrated in Ex. 1–3b. By renotating the melody from Ex. 1–3a in $\frac{2}{4}$ meter, a conflict is created between the implicit triple meter of the melody and the metric accents(*S–w*) suggested by the new meter signature.

Ex. 1–3b. Renotation of Ex. 1–3a.

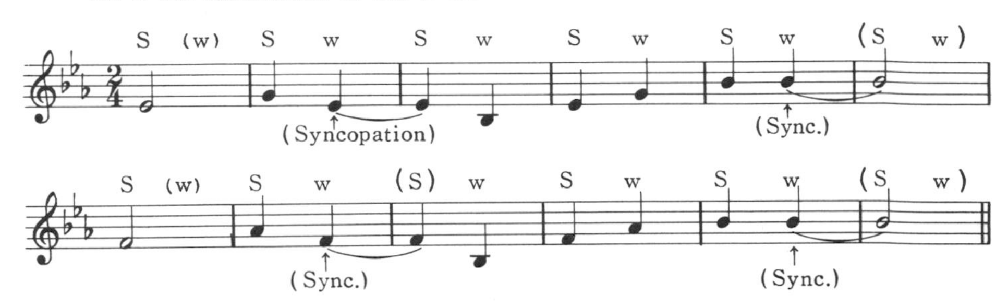

Other factors, too—particularly the placement of high or low notes, or the emphasis created by dynamic accents such as *f* or *szf*, or > — frequently reinforce or agree with metric accents. When they do not, syncopation results.

In Ex. 1–4 dynamic accents (*f*) reinforce the meter for the first four measures; however, this regular pattern of accents is broken by syncopation, which is introduced by dynamic accents and the bass pattern on the third beat of measure 5 and the second beat of measure 6. The particular pattern of displacement used here is called *hemiola*, a term used to signify the conflict of a duple pattern with a triple pattern.

Ex. 1–4. Mozart: Sonata in F Major, K. 332, I.

So far we have discussed various aspects of rhythm without defining the term itself. In its broadest sense, rhythm means the articulation of time (in music, the articulation of time by sound). It is crucial to remember that any aspect of music that possesses duration—such as successions of pitches that constitute a melody, the duration of a single chord, the time span occupied by a clarinet solo, or the total duration of a large section of a symphonic movement—creates rhythm. It is the coordinate activity of both short and long events that produces the total effect of rhythm in music.

Meter Signatures and Conducting Patterns

The rate at which basic durations occur is usually indicated by a word such as *Allegro* (fast) or *Adagio* (slow) or other descriptive words. Since the meanings of these terms, which are generally chosen from Italian, French, German, or English, are not precise, composers also often assign a metronome marking. The metronome is a clock-like instrument that divides the minute into a precise number of beats ranging from thirty to two-hundred. By indicating a metronome speed (M.M. = 120, or M.M. = 80),* the composer can set the desired tempo accurately for performers.

The number of basic durations per measure is shown as the upper part of the *meter signature*. The lower part, a number such as 2, 4, or 8, represents the *basic duration*. For example, the number 2 represents a half note; 4, a quarter note; and 8, an eighth note. Meter signatures whose upper numbers are 1, 2, 3, or 4 are called *simple* meters. The prevailing note values in simple meters normally represent divisions or multiples of the basic duration by two, four, or eight. The conductor's beat patterns for duple, triple, and quadruple-simple meters are shown in the following diagram of simple meters.

	Duple	Triple	Quadruple
Usual Number of Beats per Measure	2	3	4
Common Basic Durations	𝅗𝅥 ; ♩ ; ♪	𝅗𝅥 ; ♩ ; ♪	𝅗𝅥 ; ♩ ; ♪
Grouping of Strong (S) and weak (w) beats	S w	S w w	S w S w
Conducting Patterns	1 2	1 2 3	1 2 3 4

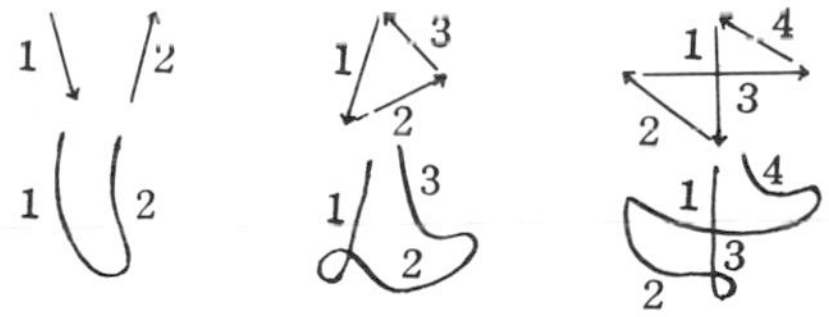

An interpretation of the meter signature often depends on the tempo. For example, a fast triple-simple measure such as $\frac{3}{4}$, *Allegro*

* M. M. is an abbreviation for *Maelzel's metronome*.

molto, may be interpreted or conducted "in one," with one main pulsation (divided by threes) per measure. And a duple or quadruple meter may be performed "in one," or "in two." By the same token, an extremely slow measure in a simple meter may be divided into twice as many beats as are indicated by the signature, when this facilitates the performance.

Compound Meter

We have noted that the common divisions and multiples of the basic duration in simple meters are duple. Since in a simple meter the division of the basic duration by three (the triplet) is not a usual one, it is generally shown by writing a 3 above the beam ♩♩♩ (3), or by a bracketed 3 above the stems ♪♪♪ (3) if a beam is not used. In contrast to simple meters, triple divisions of the basic duration are common to *compound meters.* In compound meters, the basic duration is a *dotted note,* as shown here:

Basic Durations in Compound Meters	and their	*Normal Divisions*
♩.	$(\frac{6}{8}, \frac{12}{8}, \frac{9}{8})$	♪♪♪
♪.	$(\frac{6}{16}, \frac{12}{16}, \frac{9}{16})$	𝅘𝅥𝅯𝅘𝅥𝅯𝅘𝅥𝅯
𝅗𝅥.	$(\frac{6}{4}, \frac{12}{4}, \frac{9}{4})$	♩♩♩
𝅘𝅥𝅯.	$(\frac{6}{32}, \frac{12}{32}, \frac{9}{32})$	𝅘𝅥𝅰𝅘𝅥𝅰𝅘𝅥𝅰

Compound meters, like simple meters, can be duple, triple, or quadruple, depending on the number of basic durations within each measure. However, the traditional signatures for compound meters do not follow the same logic. Ideally, the family of compound meters could be shown as $\frac{2,\ 3,\ \text{or}\ 4}{x}$ with the upper numbers signifying the number of beats per measure and × representing any of the basic durations available: e.g. $\frac{2}{♩.}$ rather than $\frac{6}{8}$, or $\frac{3}{𝅗𝅥.}$ rather than $\frac{9}{4}$.

Practically, however, we must use the traditional compound meter signatures, which are actually a representation of the first (or primary) *division* of the basic duration. For example, a common compound meter signature is 6/8. This signature would seem to denote a meter of six basic durations per measure, each of them equal to an eighth note. While such an interpretation can be practical at a very slow tempo, the general practice is to perform compound meters so that one recognizes a larger note value as the basic duration. In this case, 6/8 meter would be felt as two pulses per measure, the basic duration would be a dotted quarter note, and the three eighth notes represent the first division of the beat. Read the melody in Ex. 1–5 and note the rhythmic analysis given underneath.

Ex. 1–5.

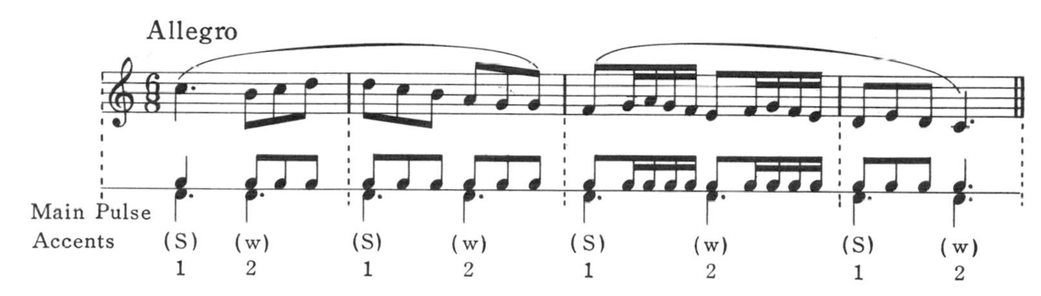

Note the grouping of each measure into *two* main pulses (duple). The eighth notes divide each basic duration by three and are in fact a division of the basic beat rather than a primary level of accent. Only those eighths that fall as the first or fourth of a measure correspond with the accents of the measure.

Applying the same reasoning to other compound meters, note that 9/8 is a triple-compound meter, easily grasped as 3/♩., and 12/8 is a quadruple meter that represents 4/♩.. In fact, any dotted note can serve as the basic duration for a compound meter. The following table presents a comparison of the most common simple and compound meters.

Primary Division of the beat	Simple meters: Duple	Triple	Quadruple	Compound meters: Duple	Triple	Quadruple
𝅘𝅥𝅯	2/8 = 2/♪	3/8 = 3/♪	4/8 = 4/♪	6/16 = 2/♪.	9/16 = 3/♪.	12/16 = 4/♪.
	Basic duration = ♪			Basic duration = ♪.		
♪	2/4 = 2/♩	3/4 = 3/♩	4/4 = 4/♩	6/8 = 2/♩.	9/8 = 3/♩.	12/8 = 4/♩.
	Basic duration = ♩			Basic duration = ♩.		
♩	2/2 = 2/𝅗𝅥	3/2 = 3/𝅗𝅥	4/2 = 4/𝅗𝅥	6/4 = 2/𝅗𝅥.	9/4 = 3/𝅗𝅥.	12/4 = 4/𝅗𝅥.
	Basic duration = 𝅗𝅥			Basic duration = 𝅗𝅥.		

Subdivisions of the Basic Duration

Although the primary division of the pulse in a compound meter is usually triple, the *subdivisions* of the basic duration (divisions of the primary division) are generally *duple.* Triple subdivisions of the basic duration are *irregular,* as are triple divisions of the beat in simple meter. The first four measures of the melody in Ex. 1–6 contain regular (duple) subdivisions of the basic duration, while the second four measures illustrate both regular and irregular subdivisions. An analysis of the rhythmic content of the example shows:

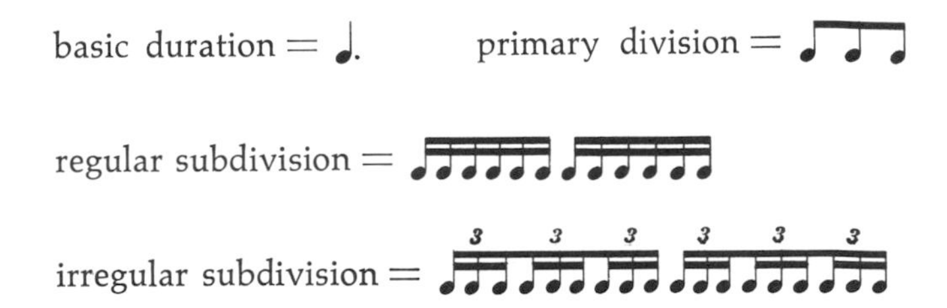

Ex. 1–6.

Moderato

Notation of Rhythm

Notating rhythm involves the use of the following symbols:

1. a note-head 𝅗 , • that is written on the line or space of the chosen pitch.
2. a note-stem | (for all durations except whole notes) that is formed by a straight line that joins the note-head at the left or right, depending upon the location of the note-head on the staff. The general rule for single notes is this: if the note-head is on the middle line of the staff or higher, the stem is attached to the left and points down; otherwise the stem is attached to the right of the note-head and points up. This convention is often disregarded when notating chords or when groups of notes are beamed together;
3. a flag ⟩ ⟩ that joins the note-stem at the farthest point from the note-head. Double, triple, or quadruple flags are also used, depending

on the duration of the note. Flags are frequently replaced by beams ♪ ♪ = ♫. Beamed notes are associated primarily with instrumental notation; flagged notes are more characteristic in vocal music, where the flags help to indicate the separate syllables of a text, as shown in Ex. 1–7.

Ex. 1–7. Schubert: *Frühlingssehnsucht.*

Flags are always used for isolated notes or where single durations of an eighth note or less are preceded or followed by quarter, half, or whole notes (or their equivalent rests). See Ex. 1–8.

Ex. 1–8.

Beams help the reader to group note patterns according to basic durations. In the first group of patterns shown in Ex. 1–9, the location of beats has been obscured by illogical beaming.

Ex. 1–9.

In Ex. 1–10 the same patterns are beamed more logically, in groups that reveal the meter's beat structure.

Ex. 1–10.

A general guide for notation is to avoid beaming more than six notes together, unless more are needed to fill one basic duration; and further, beams begin *on the beat* unless the notes they join are preceded by a rest sign.

Ex. 1–11.

When possible, avoid mixing flagged and beamed notes, except in notating vocal music.

Ex. 1–12.

Rests

Absence of tone is indicated by *rests,* and each of the basic durations discussed earlier has an equivalent rest symbol. Rest equivalents for each basic duration are shown as Ex. 1–13.

Ex. 1–13. Basic durations and their rest equivalents.

Note-value	Rest	Name
		Breve (or double whole-note)
		Whole note
		Half note
		Quarter note
		Eighth note
		Sixteenth note
		Thirty-second note
		Sixty-fourth note

Rests may be used in the same situations as their corresponding note-values, with the following exceptions:

1. Rests are never tied 𝄽⁀𝄽.
2. Combinations of two different rests usually are preferable to a single dotted rest.
3. Half-note rests are not used in $\frac{3}{4}$ meter (𝄽 𝄽 ♩ is preferable to 𝄼 ♩).
4. The whole-note rest is used to indicate a full measure's rest in any meter except when the whole note is equal to less than a complete measure's duration (as in $\frac{12}{8}$).
5. The notation of rests, like that of notes, should help the reader keep track of the beats in each measure.

Ex. 1–14 clarifies the use of rests.

Ex. 1–14.

(a) $\frac{3}{4}$ 𝄼 ♩ | 𝅗𝅥. ‖ better written 𝄽 𝄽 ♩ | 𝅗𝅥. ‖

(b) $\frac{3}{8}$ 𝄽 𝄾 | ♩. ‖ better written 𝄼 | ♩. ‖

(c) $\frac{4}{4}$ more clearly written

Augmentation Dots, Ties, and Slurs

The *augmentation* dot (·), placed immediately after a note-head (𝅗𝅥.), extends the duration of the note by one half of its normal duration. This means that 𝅗𝅥⁀♩ could also be written as 𝅗𝅥., but augmentation dots are not used if they would prolong a note into the next measure ($\frac{3}{4}$ ♩ 𝅗𝅥.). In such a situation, and where a continuation of sound between two notes of the same pitch is sought, *ties* are used. The *tie* is a curved line that connects two notes of *identical* pitch:

The tie should not be confused with the *slur,* which is used to indicate a smooth connection of two notes of *different* pitch:

Ex. 1–15 illustrates several notational signs and principles of clear notating.

Ex. 1–15. Beethoven: Sonata for Violin and Piano, Op. 23, II.

Notation of Pitch

Pitch results from the sustained, periodic vibrations of a flexible body such as a string or a column of air. Pitches are named by the first seven letters of the alphabet, *A B C D E F G.* These letter names represent the different lines and spaces on the five-line staff: .
However, this staff is meaningless until a *clef sign* is notated at its left edge; a clef serves as a "locater" of one specific pitch. For example, the *treble clef* is actually an elaborate script G that places the pitch g^1 on the second line of the staff.

Ex. 1–16. Notes on the staff in the treble clef.

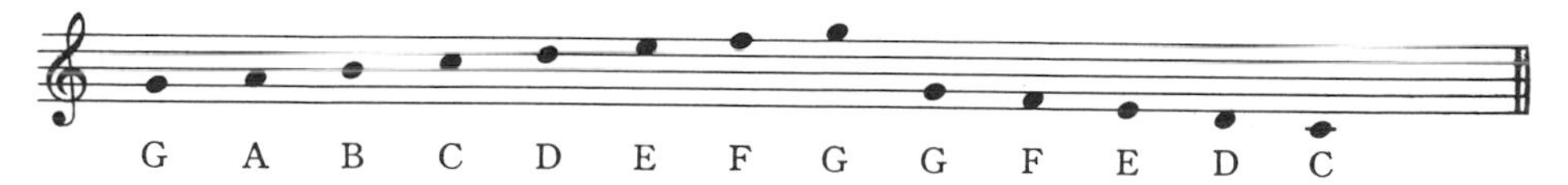

The *bass clef* specifies the note *F* for the fourth line of the staff, as shown in Ex. 1–17.

Ex. 1–17. Notes on the staff in the bass clef.

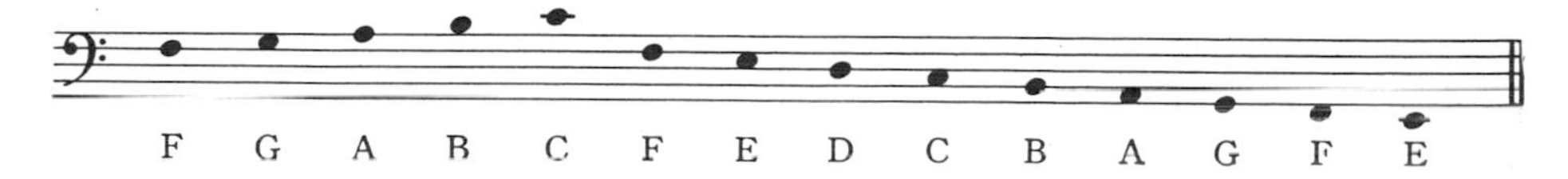

The question may arise why we need more than one clef. If our musical system were limited to only seven or so pitches, there would be no such need. However, our capabilities of hearing are such that a broad range of pitches has been used in most music. Consequently, a number of clefs are used, each employed to represent pitches in particular areas of the pitch spectrum, or *gamut.*

The gamut of pitches most used in music is shown in Ex. 1–18, which illustrates the "Great" staff.

Ex. 1–18. The "Great" staff.

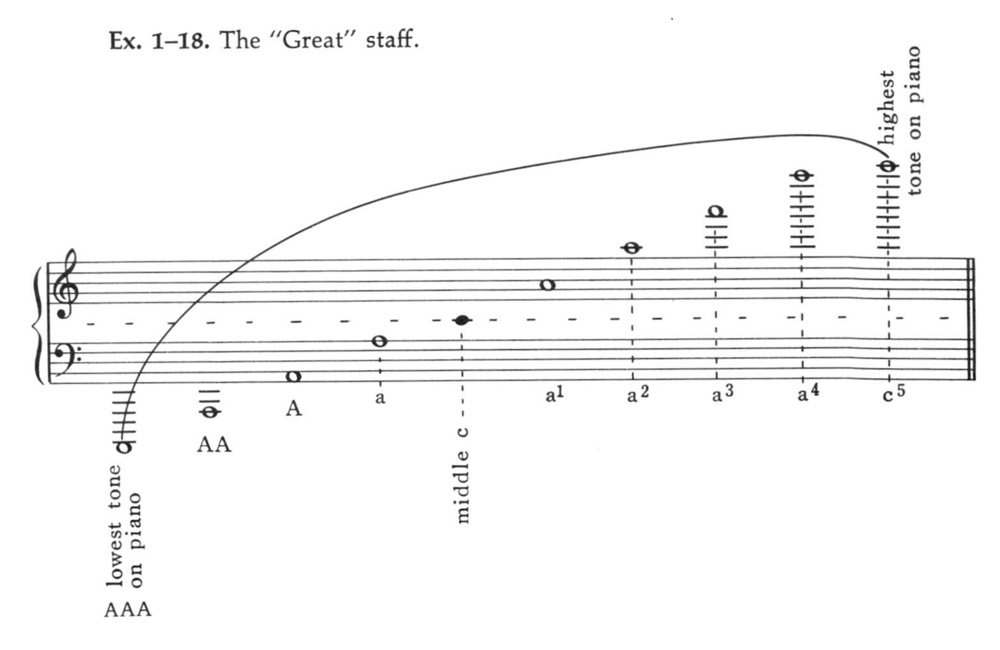

The midpoint of the great staff, which links the treble and bass clefs, is a broken line that represents middle C, or c^1. Added line segments above or below either staff are called *ledger lines,* and they are used to notate pitches that lie beyond the staff lines of a particular clef.

Although treble and bass are the most frequently used clefs, others are needed for the notation of some music. They are known as the *C clefs,* since they locate middle C, and can be placed upon any line of the staff. Of these, the alto and tenor clefs are by far the most frequent and—as their names imply—are used to notate parts for alto and tenor instruments such as the viola, cello, trombone, and bassoon.

Ex. 1–19. The movable C clefs.

Musicians have developed a useful terminology for pinpointing the various pitches of the gamut. This amounts to grouping the notes of the pitch spectrum into seven-note segments, called "octave segments." Each segment begins with a *C* and includes all possible pitches between *C* and the *B* seven notes above. This nomenclature is illusrtrated in Ex. 1–20.

Ex. 1–20. The octave segments of the pitch spectrum.

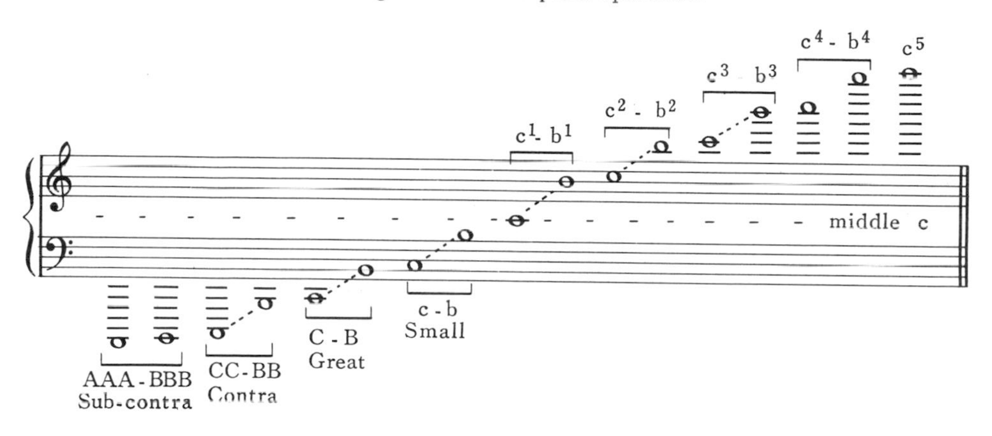

Pitch Class

It is useful to distinguish between *pitch* and *pitch class:* specific pitches are usually referred to by their correct octave name–c^1, D, e^4, etc. However, musicians often have occasion to refer to pitches in the aggregate—all *D*s or all *F*s. In this case *D* or *F* stands for the pitch class of that same letter name and represents all octave duplicates of that pitch. When we say "That song is in the key of *D*," we actually mean pitch class *D* rather than any particular pitch *D*.

Accidentals

Any of the notes of the gamut may be preceded by accidentals. Sharps (♯) or flats (♭), double sharps (𝄪) or double flats (𝄫) are placed immediately before the note-head and indicate slight pitch modifications. Sharps indicate a raising of the natural note by one half step, while flats indicate that the natural note is to be lowered a half step. Similarly, double sharps indicate a raising of the note by two half steps, and double flats are used to lower the note by two half steps.

Natural signs (♮) are used to cancel previous sharps or flats. Proper use of all accidentals may be found in Ex. 1–21.

Ex. 1–21. Correct use of accidentals.

In measures 8 and 9 of Ex. 1–21, the same pitch is spelled in two different ways: *A-flat* and *G-sharp*. These notes are said to be *enharmonic*. A composer's choice of which enharmonic spelling to use is generally influenced by the musical context; as a general rule, simpler spellings are preferred.

Accidentals are understood to continue throughout the measure in which they appear without being rewritten. Therefore, all of the notated F's appearing in Ex. 1–22 should be performed as *F-sharps*.

Ex. 1–22.

Furthermore, accidentals govern only those notes that occur on the pitch level at which they are introduced; they do not affect pitches in different octaves. A more precise notation of Ex. 1–23a is shown in Ex. 1–23b.

Ex. 1–23.

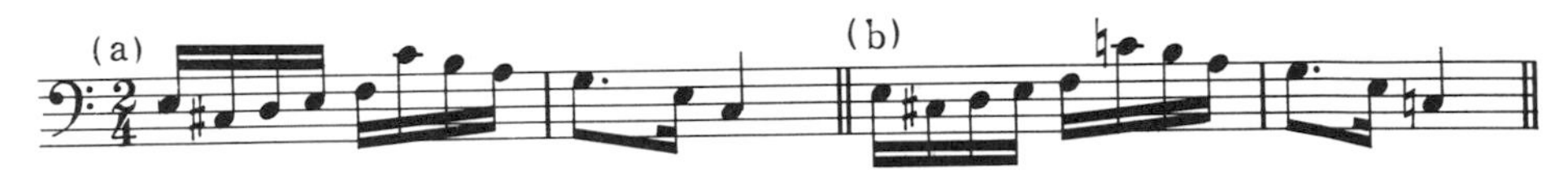

Intervals

An interval is the unit formed by two pitches, whether they are sounded simultaneously (a *harmonic* interval) or successively (a *melodic* interval). The generic name of an interval describes its size numerically—in terms of the total number of letter names encompassed by its two pitches. Thus a *fourth* is an interval that spans four different letter names of the staff; for example, c^1 up to f^1 spans four letter names: c^1, d^1, e^1, and f^1. Although these generic names are useful, musicians usually prefer to describe intervals by the more specific names described presently.

Whole Steps and Half Steps

The *half step* is the smallest difference of pitch formally recognized in Western music. The *half step* interval is easily observed by locating adjacent white keys on the piano that are not separated by a black key. The relation between these pairs of keys, *E-F* and *B-C*, is called a *half step*, a *minor second* (m2), or *semitone*. The relation between pairs of white keys separated by black keys is a whole step, or major second (M2).

Although the numerical name of an interval describes the number of different lines and spaces spanned, and this is easily relatable to the positions of two notes on the staff, it does not account for the *exact size* of the interval. This can be checked by comparing the sound and total number of whole and half steps in each of the following intervals, both of which are fourths: (1) (2). The first of these two intervals is one half step smaller than the second, since it consists of a total of two and a half steps (or five semitones), while the second interval spans three whole steps (or six semitones). To describe intervals more accurately, musicians use the terms *perfect, major, minor, augmented,* and *diminished.* The abbreviations for these are shown below:

Perfect——P
Major——M
minor——m

Augmented——A or (+)
diminished——d or (°)

The term *perfect* is applied only to unisons (primes), fourths, fifths, and octaves, while the words *major* and *minor* are applied only to seconds, thirds, sixths, and sevenths. *Augmented* and *diminished* are applied to certain modifications of any type of interval. As a synopsis of the preceding discussion, the following chart may prove useful for reference.

Perfect Intervals: octave (8ve), unison (prime), fifth, fourth
become *augmented* when enlarged by a half step
become *diminished* when reduced by a half step

Major Intervals
become *augmented* when enlarged by a half step
become *minor* when reduced by a half step

Minor Intervals
become *major* when enlarged by a half step
become *diminished* when reduced by a half step

(Major and Minor Intervals:) seventh, sixth, third, second

In spelling intervals we recognize two types of half steps; they are the same in sound but enharmonic in notation. The *diatonic* half step is found between notes that have adjacent letter names (such as *E–F* and *C*-sharp–*D*). The *chromatic* half step occurs between two different notes with the same letter name: *E–E-sharp, B–B-flat*. In spelling the intervals in the previous chart, enlargements and reductions by half step are always by the *chromatic* half step; otherwise the generic name of the interval would not remain the same.

Naming Intervals

Two processes are necessary for the precise identification of any interval. First a generic classification must be made, based on the number of letter names spanned. This is easily done by noting the relative positions of two notes in terms of lines and/or spaces on the staff. These are illustrated in Ex. 1–24.

Ex. 1–24.

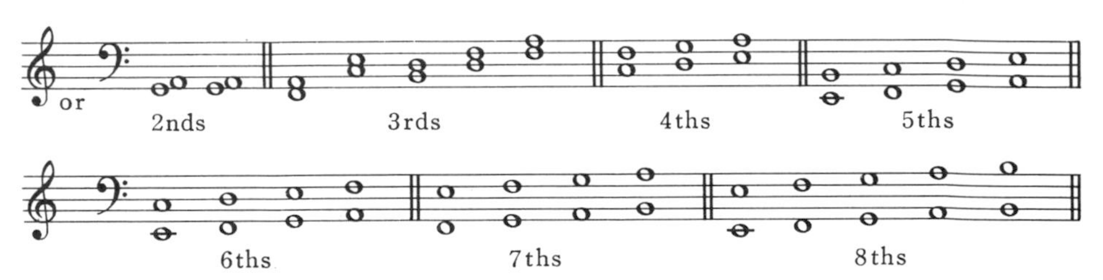

Note that seconds are notated on adjacent lines and spaces; thirds span two lines or two spaces; fourths span two lines and a space or two spaces and a line; fifths span three lines or three spaces; sixths span three spaces and a line or three lines and a space; sevenths span four lines or four spaces; and octaves span four lines and a space or four spaces and a line.

Having determined the generic classification of an interval (as shown in Ex. 1–24), a more precise description, such as *perfect, major, minor, augmented,* or *diminished,* can be made on the basis of the number of whole and half steps involved. This is illustrated in Ex. 1–25.

Ex. 1–25. Major and minor

M2 = 1 m2 = ½ M3 = 2 m3 = 1½ M6 = 4½ or P5 plus 1 m6 = 3 whole steps plus 2 halfs or P5 plus ½

M7 = 5½, or 2½ plus 3, or P8 minus ½ m7 = 2½ plus 2½ or P8 minus 1

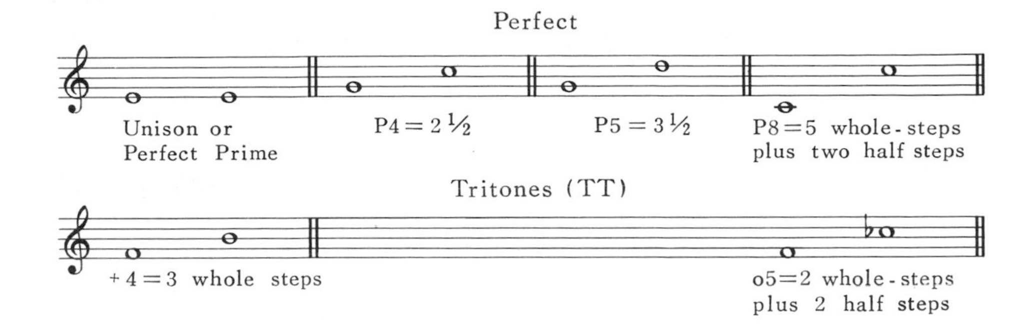

Exercises

Additional materials are contained in *Materials and Structure of Music I, Workbook,* Chapter 1.

1. Practice drawing treble and bass clef signs.
2. Identify the names of notes written in both clefs, indicating the specific octave (contra, small, 1, 2, etc.) of each note.
3. Locate the different note and rest symbols in a composition.
4. Name the equivalents of different notes in smaller denominations of note-values. For example, how many sixteenths equal a dotted half note?
5. Correctly rebeam patterns of incorrectly beamed notes.
6. Transcribe a vocal melody of many individually flagged notes into correct instrumental notation.
7. Compose eight measures of rhythm in $\frac{2}{4}$ meter, trying to avoid the repetition of any measure's pattern.
8. Make a neat copy of Ex. 1–7.
9. Play any note on the piano (within your voice range) and sing fourths above and below the note played. Apply the same procedure to the practice of other intervals.
10. Write the following intervals above and below g^1:
    P5, M3, m7, °4, +6, m3, M2, P8, °5, M6, °7, M7, +8, +4.
11. Transcribe Example 1–6 into $\frac{6}{16}$ and $\frac{6}{4}$ meters.

Chapter Two

Tonality

Our discussion of meter in Chapter 1 showed that most music can be grouped into regular units of time, or "metered." These groupings of weak and strong beats form a framework within which tones are organized into rhythms. The total range of pitches we use in music can be ordered in a similar way within still another kind of framework: *tonality*.

Rhythmic Causes of Tonality

If music were made from only one continuously repeated pitch, such an organizing scheme would not arise; melody would derive its charm from rhythmic play alone. In fact, some music does contain a severely limited set of pitches, its attraction arising primarily from rhythm. The two melodies of Ex. 2–1 illustrate such a condition.

Ex. 2–1a. Taulipang melody (after Hornbostel). From Curt Sachs, *The Rise of Music in the Ancient World* (New York: W. W. Norton & Company, Inc.)

Ex. 2–1b. Uitoto Indian melody (after Bose). From Curt Sachs, *The Rise of Music in the Ancient World* (New York: W. W. Norton & Company, Inc.)

In each of these melodies one pitch is emphasized so extensively (*A* in melody 2–1a, *C* in melody 2–1b) that it becomes a point of focus around which the other pitches are decorative.

In the melody of Ex. 2–1a the pitch *A* is stressed, for it is both the beginning and ending pitch, as well as the pitch of longest duration. The numerous *G-sharps* clearly perform a decorative role in a relationship with their more basic neighbors, the a^1s.

The melody of Ex. 2–1b is organized with *C* as its tonic. *C* is heard first and last, and it is heard more often than its two associates, *B* and *A*. In other words, *C* is dwelt upon as a kind of home base, a frequent point of departure and return during the course of the melodic unfolding.

These examples are simpler than most of the melodies we associate with our Western musical heritage. By our standards they are a bit dull in terms of pitch resources, and they move within a pitch range that is narrowly restricted. (The wider melody of Ex. 2–1b covers a span of only a minor third, a^1–c^2.) Nonetheless, the more complicated melodies of our own musical tradition reveal identical principles of organization. Note the repetitions and other kinds of emphases that create the tonality of the melodies in Ex. 2–2.

Ex. 2–2a. German folk song (tonic = *G*).

Ex. 2–2b. Irish folk song (tonic = *D*).

Ex. 2–2c. Gregorian chant (tonic = *D*).

Pitch Causes of Tonality

The melody of Ex. 2–3 begins and ends with the same pitch, f^1. But unlike the simpler melodies we have seen thus far, this melody does not confirm its first and last pitch by frequent repetitions, nor does the tonic have excessively greater durations than other pitches. And yet, the melody does not require a full playing to project to us that *F* is indeed its tonic.

Ex. 2–3. Mozart: Sonata in F, K. 332, I.

This leads us to the conclusion that something about tones in a melody—in addition to accents, or durations, or repetitions, or positions as first or last, or lowest or highest—can project this sense of pitch focus, or tonality, in melody. This further source of tonality lies in the pitch intervals formed between the tones of a melody. In their movement in time, the various pitches create a *tonal framework*, a kind of floor and ceiling within which the melodic parts all sound as related elements of the tonal design. Some pitches are basic to this framework, like the beams of a house; other tones are important in forming the decorative overlay.

In the Mozart melody of Ex. 2–3 the longer and metrically stressed notes seem more important to the overall contour of the whole melody. The first pitch, f^1, is the beginning of the pattern. It performs the vital function of "leading the listener" into the melodic organization. Here the composer's problem is similar to that of the painter who wishes to compose an effective picture: both must immediately attract attention and, at the same time, ensure that this first attraction is the beginning of understanding, of a sense of *structure*.

To achieve this immediate goal, a painter usually organizes color and line in ways that establish focal points within the canvas. Regardless of which area of the painting we look at first, we are always led into the picture plane (if it is a sucessful painting!) by the arrangements of lines and forms and colors. A clear illustration of this attention-focusing can be seen in the reproduction shown in Ex. 2–4.

Ex. 2–4. *The Last Supper,* Leonardo da Vinci. European Art Color, Peter Adelberg, N.Y.C.

DIRECTIONAL FORCES OF MAIN LINES

In music, the composer ushers the listener into a structure of tones—the *auditory* "picture plane"—by beginning his music with patterns that establish a clear frame. Melodies that begin with a downbeat most frequently begin with the pitch that is tonic, while melodies that begin with an upbeat frequently begin with some other pitch, then move to the tonic without much delay, usually on the first strong beat.[1]

Regardless of the relation of the first pitch to the melody's tonality, the first few pitches usually make clear all or a part of the pitch framework that will serve for the remainder of that melody.

Ex. 2–5a. *The Star-Spangled Banner.*

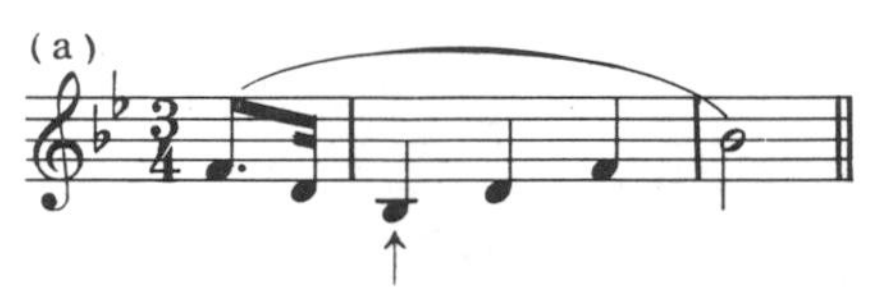

Ex. 2–5b. *Comin' Round the Mountain.*

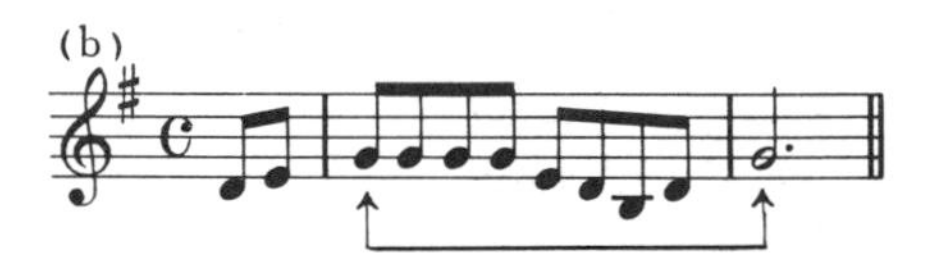

Ex. 2–5c. Italian folk song.

The pitch framework of a melody has still another facet. Notice that the metric stress we associate with the f^2 of measure 5 in the Mozart melody (Ex. 2–3) invites us to accept this pitch as an important point of arrival. It acts as the basic high point of melodic motion. Though the g^2 of measure 3 actually is higher, it is rhythmically less forceful, a mere upper neighbor to the more important f^2 that finally arrives in measure 5.

Ex. 2–6. Mozart: Sonata in F, K. 332, I.

[1] Our discussion pertains only to melodies that are *tonal* (that is, have tonality). Some melodies do not have this property.

The pitch f^1 forms the bottom of this pitch framework, and so the Mozart melody is essentially a pitch line that forms a path from f^1 up to f^2, then returns to its original point of departure as shown in Ex. 2–3. Its framework of activity is the octave, . This residual framework, combined with the importance of *F* as the first and last pitches of the whole melody, projects a tonality that unmistakably bears *F* as its central pitch class, its tonic. We shall refer to the framework, formed by the tonic, the highest and the lowest *structural* pitches (both of which may also be the tonic pitch) as the *tonality frame.* As we shall find, only three different pitch classes participate in the tonality frames of tonal music. Most important, of course, is the *tonic* (1). Another is the *dominant* (5), which is a perfect fifth above (or perfect fourth below) the tonic note. And last is the *mediant* (3), which is a major third or a minor third above the tonic note.

In many melodies only the tonic participates in the frame. In other melodies one or both of the other pitches flesh out the melodic structure, but the tonic is always a part—the central part—of any melody's tonality frame.

Pitch Roots

The particular way pitches are organized in a melody can confirm or deny a particular pitch as tonic. Just as the words "I am going home" take on a quite different meaning when rearranged into the order "Am I going home?," so the tonality of a melody is affected by the way its pitches are interspersed. Although both melody *a* and *b* of Ex. 2–7 contain the same pitches, they have different "tonal meanings." Because of the way they are organized, *C* is tonic for the first melody and *F* the tonic for the second.

Ex. 2–7. Melodies of same pitches but different tonics.

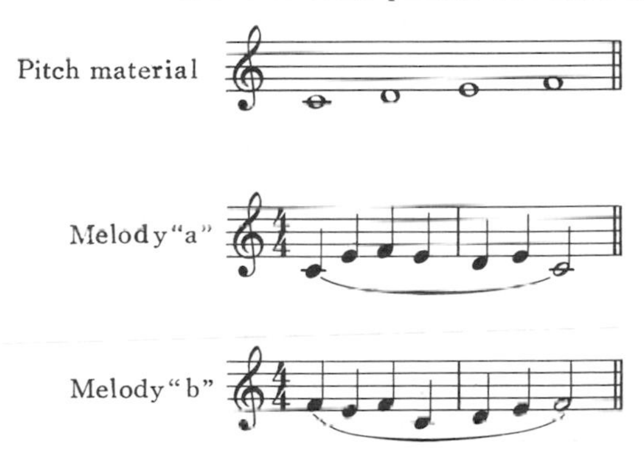

Furthermore, meter affects tonality by imposing a sense of accent on some pitches. By reorganizing the pitch successions used in Ex. 2–7, we can create different focal points through metric and durational changes alone.

Ex. 2–8. Effect of meter and duration on tonality.

Interval Quality

In addition to these causes of pitch significance, the particular intervals formed between pitches affect tonality.

The octave has the unusual quality of sounding like the same pitch duplicated at different high-low levels. It is this peculiar effect that leads us to repeat note names of pitches of the musical staff, so that the thirteenth note of any chromatic series always has the same name as the first. For instance, if at the piano we begin with any key and play every successive white and black key, the thirteenth key will always have the same note name as the beginning key.

Other intervals share this quality of pitch identity in lesser degrees than the octave; the octave is the only interval to bear notes of the same name.

Ex. 2–9. Octaves.

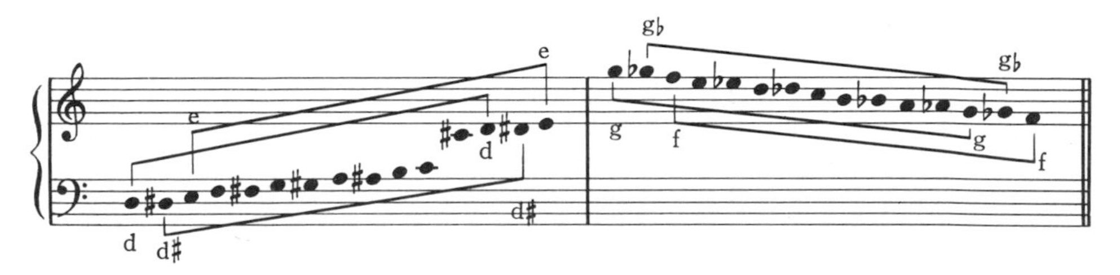

A clear representation of the decreasing mutual identity of pitches is found in the *overtone,* or *harmonic, series.* This natural order of pitches functions as a part of our hearing process, and it operates as a part of the tone production of almost all musical instruments. When we hear a tone, we recognize only its most prominent characteristic, for the "tone" is actually composed of several different elements. In a sense, we hear only a *generalized tone,* for the less obvious features of its constitution escape our attention.[2]

[2] With training one can learn to recognize some of these other parts of a tone (*its overtones*) that lie higher in pitch than the note by which we name it.

A tone *D*, for example, when played on most musical instruments, is really only the most prominent part of a scheme of pitches that follows the pattern of overtones illustrated in Ex. 2–10, the *natural harmonic series.*

Ex. 2–10. Harmonic series on *D.*

Fewer or more parts (or *partials,* as these pitch constellations are called) are present in the makeup of a tone, depending upon what instrument produces it. A violin normally produces a tone that contains more partials above its fundamental pitch than a saxophone or a flute. But the pattern is duplicated in a greater or lesser fashion by any musical instrument.[3] Except for unusual cases, we recognize only the lowest (or *fundamental*) as *the pitch* of the tone. These additional members of the harmonic series affect the qualitative aspects of instrumental and vocal tone, controlling the *tone color* or *timbre* by their presence or absence and relative strength.

This pattern of pitches in the harmonic series is imposed upon our every experience of musical tone. Its particular formation (the way the various parts are ordered in relation to one another) has many interesting parallels in the world of sound. The harmonic series of a single tone is itself a kind of "pitch framework," for the fundamental of the series serves as a nucleus, or *tonic,* for all of its accompanying parts.

We have already noted the unique quality of the octave, the way its separate parts fit together in a relationship that suggests a mutual identity; for this reason the two parts even bear identical note names. The second interval that occurs in the harmonic series after the octave, the *perfect fifth,* shares this mutual identity of its parts to a lesser degree. It is not difficult to hear this interval as two separate pitches, even when played simultaneously. But next to the octave, the fifth is the simplest of all pitch relationships. It is not so simple as to sound like a single tone, but it is simple enough to create a strong effect of tonal focus, this quality causing its lower tone to act as the fundamental pitch, or "root", of the interval.

[3] Only pure tones contain one simple pitch element, and they are quite rare in music. Called *sine waves,* they are easily produced by an electronic sound generator.

Ex. 2–11. Root pitch in the perfect fifth.

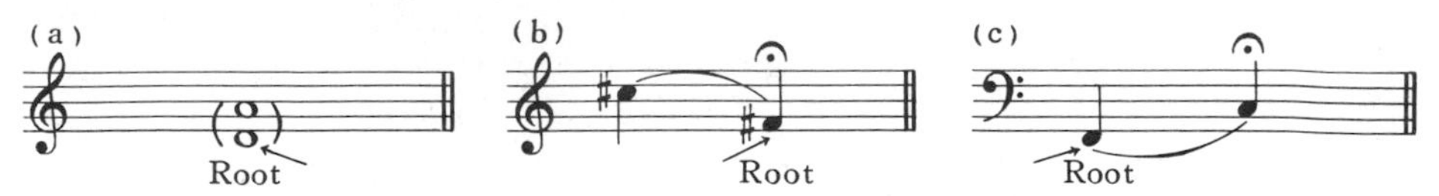

The first five partials of the harmonic series project five different intervals, including the perfect octave and the perfect fifth.

Ex. 2–12. First five partials and intervals.

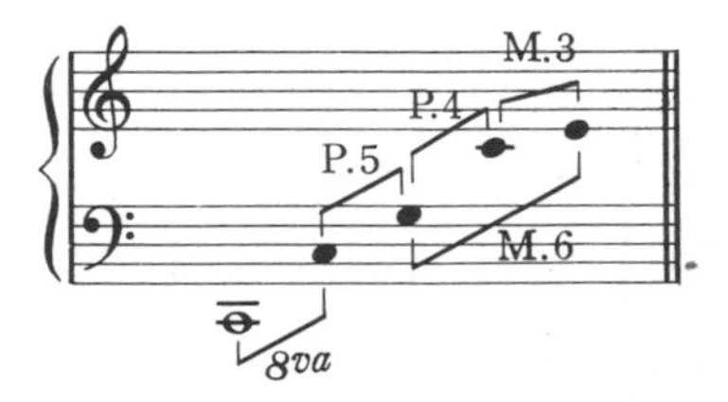

Since the fundamental pitch of the harmonic series is the focal point for the whole pattern, *the root pitch for any one of these intervals is the fundamental pitch of its series.* This means that if we hear one of these intervals apart from any extraneous sounds, our orientation tends to be around the fundamental of the series to which the interval belongs. Whether the interval is melodic (successive tones) or harmonic (simultaneous tones), each of these intervals implies a root.

Interval Inversion

The intervals in Ex. 2–13 are arranged in pairs according to their *inversion properties.* Note that turning each interval upside down produces its inversion complement: the inversion of the perfect fifth is the perfect fourth; the inversion of the major third is the minor sixth; and the inversion of the major sixth is the minor third. Each interval of the inverted pairs shares the same root pitch.

Ex. 2–13. Interval roots.

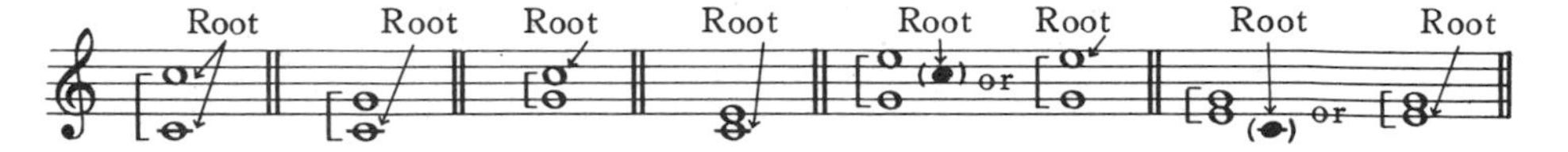

This root effect is more apparent for the octave, the perfect fifth, and the perfect fourth than for any other intervals. Implied within the harmonic series itself is a set of weakening relationships to a fundamental pitch; the higher in the series an interval appears, the weaker is its root effect.[4] The roots of intervals that lie above the fifth partial become increasingly negligible. For this reason, melodies that span a range of less than a perfect fifth or perfect fourth rely most heavily on rhythm—repetition, duration, and accent—to produce an effect of pitch focus.

As you can see in Ex. 2–13, even the major sixth and minor third are subject to two possible root interpretations. As isolated intervals, the first root possibility shown is the more probable, but emphasis in a melody on either tone can impart a significance that may outweigh the interval effect alone.

The Harmonic Triad

Western music has for the most part consisted of chords comprising fifths, fourths, thirds, and sixths in a way that creates a larger harmonic unit than the mere interval. Called *triad*, this unit can consist (as we shall see in Chapter 12) of any three different pitch classes. Four kinds of triads are of special importance, however, because they represent harmonic content and melodic configuration in most of our traditional music.

These special kinds of triads are called *major, minor, diminished,* and *augmented*. The name of each is derived from the principal intervals which form them. Each is illustrated below with notations that make clear their most salient features.

Ex. 2–14. The four basic triads of tonal music.

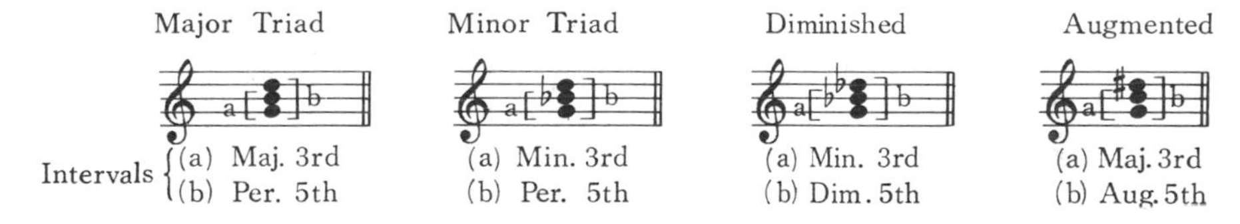

We shall return for a more detailed study of these four triad types in Chapter 12. For the present we shall confine our attention to the way two of these—the major and the minor—play principal roles in tonal music.

Interval Quality and Melodic Organization

Returning to the Mozart melody of Ex. 2–3, we now can see other reasons for the importance of *F* as the tonic. Looking back at that example, you will find that from the melody's first skip, tones trace a pattern that reinforces *F*. Each new pitch of the first two measures con-

[4] Other intervals, such as seconds, sevenths, and tritones, occur between higher partials in the harmonic series.

firms this relationship to *F* as root tone, therein establishing the *F* major triad (*F–A–C*) as the tonal basis for the entire melody.

Ex. 2–15. Analysis of Ex. 2–3, first two measures.

These inner relationships within the pitch framework of f^1–c^2 preestablish the basis for this melody's pitch organization. After the first two measures any digressions (such as the *B-flats* and *E*'s of measures 3 and 4) are heard as secondary in their relationships to the *F* major triad. And then the return of *F* in the seventh measure is like the closing of a full circle; it comes as the return and reconfirmation of the fundamental pitch from which the melody originated.

Other melodies reveal similar characteristics to lesser or to greater degrees. The relative simplicity or complexity of any melody is determined largely by the clarity with which its pitches have been organized in relation to a tonic pitch. Some simple songs—hymns, communal songs, children's play songs—are even more tenacious than the Mozart melody in projecting a tonic. ("My Country, 'tis of Thee" is a good example.)

Take some time to hear and study the melodies of Ex. 2–16. Each illustrates less definite tonality than the Mozart melody. The melody of Ex. 2–16a is slightly ambiguous because the initial *C* is not reinforced by interval relations with other pitches or by repetitions. After early emphasis (repetition at the octave and the fifth–fourth formed with *G* in between), no pattern conclusively confirms *C* as tonic.

Ex. 2–16a. Hindemith: *Theme and Four Variations.* © 1947 by B. Schott's Soehne, Mainz. Reprinted by permission.

The next melody (Ex. 2–16b) represents a slightly different condition. In it we can find two plausible tonics, *B-flat* and *F*. The numerous soundings of *F* draw our attention to it as a possible reference pitch, but *B-flat* also is very much in evidence. *B-flat* is the intended tonality (we discover this from the harmonies!), but the patterns of the first few measures of melody alone do not decisively establish this pitch as tonic.

Ex. 2–16b. J. S. Bach: Fugue in B-flat Major (*Well-tempered Clavier,* Book I).

Melody 2–16c is similar to 2–16b, for again there is some question about pitch focus. Is the tonic *B-flat* or is it *E-flat*? Heard along with Mozart's accompaniment there would be little question, for *E-flat* dominates the first measure. But removed from its accompaniment, this short melody dwells on *B-flat* to such an extent that even the perfect fourths of *B-flat–E-flat* (measures 1 and 3) do not convince us that *E-Flat* is tonic. Only with the entrance of *A-flat,* and its resolution to *G* in the final pattern, does *B-flat* become an improbable tonic. Once we have heard this melody through measures 3 and 4 it is easier to hear the beginning tones within a framework that has *E-flat* as its tonic.

Ex. 2–16c. Mozart: Sonata in E-flat Major, K. 282, I.

When rhythms and intervals both emphasize a particular pitch, a sense of organization results where aimless, random successions of tones might otherwise prevail. (The effect of tonal randomness can be engaging in some music.) Tonality provides just one of several ways tones can be organized into meaningful patterns. (Meter is one other.) We shall learn about other agents of musical structure as our study progresses, but of all those in music, tonality is perhaps the most intrinsic to musical tone.

We can isolate five simple questions that are pertinent to any decision about the tonality of a melody. Your study of any particular melody should begin with the answers to each of these questions.

1. Does the melody seem to have pitch focus or is this property absent? (An affirmative answer makes the next four questions relevant.)
2. What is the last pitch, and what is the first pitch of rhythmic importance (because of metric position or greater duration or both)?
3. Is any pitch prominent because of its frequent occurrence, its several repetitions, or its relatively greater durations and stress?
4. What intervals occur during the first patterns of pitch motion, and what is their common or most emphasized root?
5. Does the contour of the melody appear to form a frame of activity that is separated by an octave or a perfect fifth, or by another interval that forms a clear tonality frame?

Many melodies incorporate at least three of the above strategies for establishing a tonic, others no more than two, and still others all four. It is the basic problem of the performer and the listener to recognize the various clues of pitch ordering, these to serve as guides for musical understanding.

Three melodies of relatively simple pitch structure are shown below, each accompanied by an analysis of its tonality frame. Sing or play each melody, then see how you can justify the tonality frame shown for it.

Ex. 2–17a. Pergolesi.

Ex. 2–17b. Hungarian folk song.

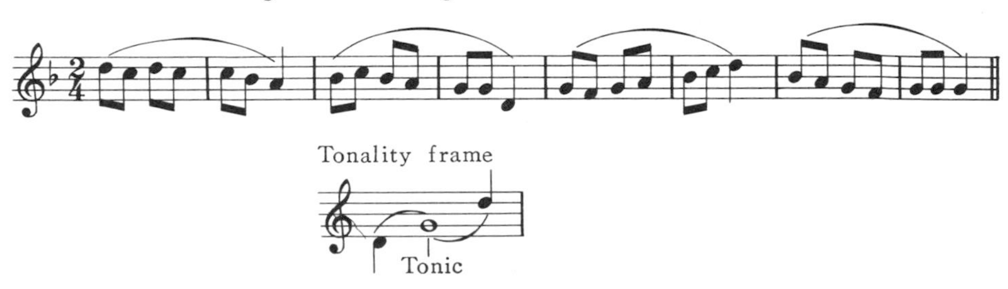

Ex. 2–17c. Scotch folk song: *My Bonnie Lies Over the Ocean.*

Exercises

See Chapter 2 of *Materials and Structure of Music I, Workbook* for more detailed work.

1. Using only the given prescription, write a short melody that fulfills each of the following:

   (a) Tonality, *F*; Meter, $\frac{3}{4}$; Pitches:

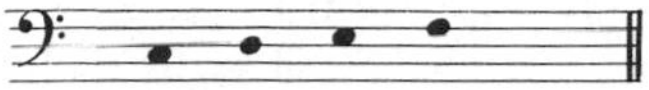

   (b) Tonality, *A*; Meter, C; Pitches:

   (c) Tonality, *E-flat*; Meter, $\frac{2}{4}$; Pitches:

2. In a collection of folk songs or a sight-singing text, sing various melodies, then analyze from each melody its tonality frame.

Chapter Three

Key, Mode, and Scale

Closely related to the tonality framework discussed in Chapter 2 are the keys of traditional music. Although pitch focus can be produced with tones in many different ways, the music of Western tradition has developed its own characteristic methods.

We commonly speak of a composition as being "in the key of *C* major" or "in the key of *b-flat* minor." In such statements we express a relationship between particular pitches of focus (*C* and *B-flat*, respectively) and particular collections of notes (major and minor scales). In other words, *key* combines the factors of tonic and scale.

Scale Structure and Derivation

Many different kinds of scales can be found in music. There are Hungarian scales, pentatonic scales, whole-tone scales, chromatic scales, gapped scales, symmetrical scales, and so on. Each is a unique combination of notes that sets it off from any other. Any one of these scales can form the basis for the pitch patterns of music. For the present we shall confine our attention to only a few types.

If we extract all of the notes from the Mozart melody quoted in Chapter 2 (Ex. 2–3), then order them in succession following the tonic pitch of the melody (*F*), the result is the *scale* that serves as the pitch basis for this melody; it represents the pitches that are used to fill in the span between the outer limits of the tonality frame, f^1 to f^2.

Ex. 3–1. Mozart: Sonata in F, K. 332, I.

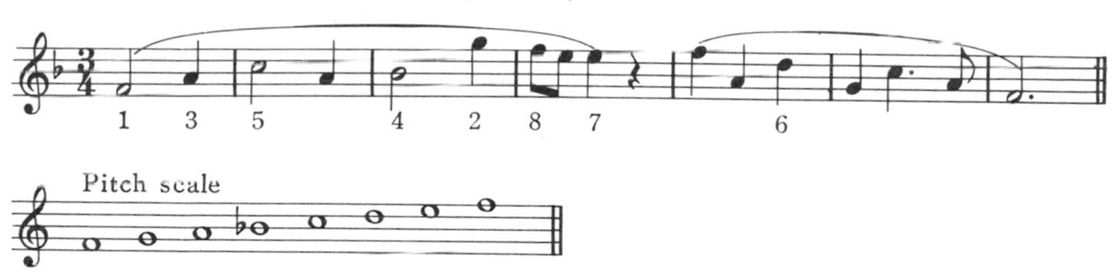

The result of this abstraction is what we call the *major scale of F*.

Any series of pitches that duplicates the same pattern of successive intervals—$1–1–\frac{1}{2}–1–1–1–\frac{1}{2}$—is a major scale. (The number 1 represents a whole step, $\frac{1}{2}$ represents a half step.) The note combinations of Ex. 3–2 contain five patterns which are major, five which are not.

Ex. 3–2. Major and non-major scales.

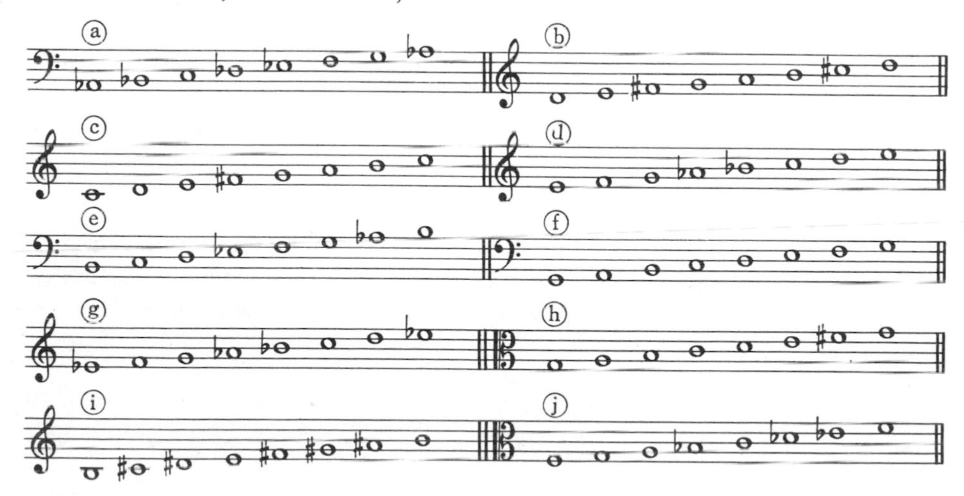

We can transpose[1] each of the scales shown in Ex. 3–2 so that the pattern of intervals remains the same but the initial note is always *C*. In this way the similarities and the differences in the various arrangements become more apparent.

Ex. 3–3. Modifications of the scales shown in Ex. 3–2.

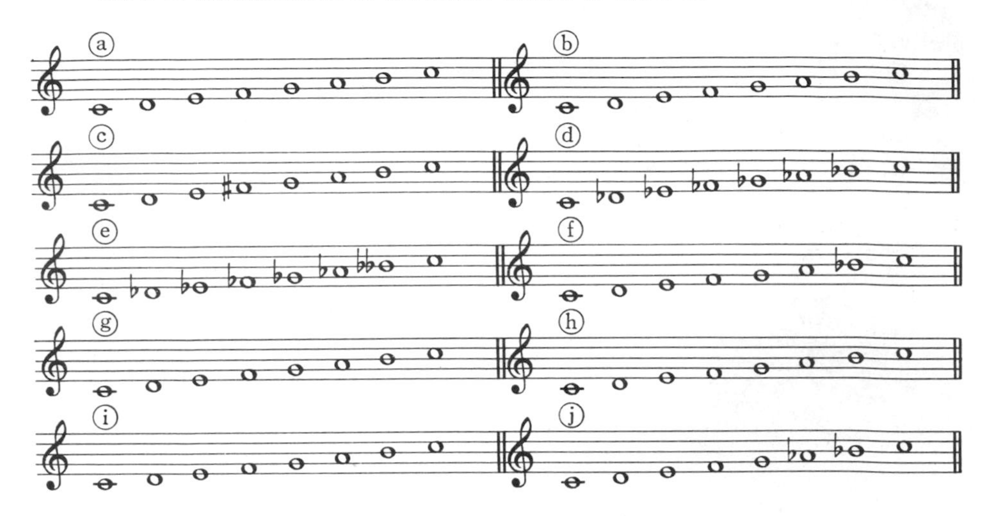

Each of the scales in Ex. 3–3 is a C scale, although half do not qualify as major scales.

Certain arrangements of pitches have been most favored by composers during the past several hundred years, and for this reason we shall pay particular attention to these. We might note in passing that both our musical staff, with its alternating lines and spaces, and the black and white key pattern of the piano have a simple relationship with the *C* major scale pattern.

Ex. 3–4.

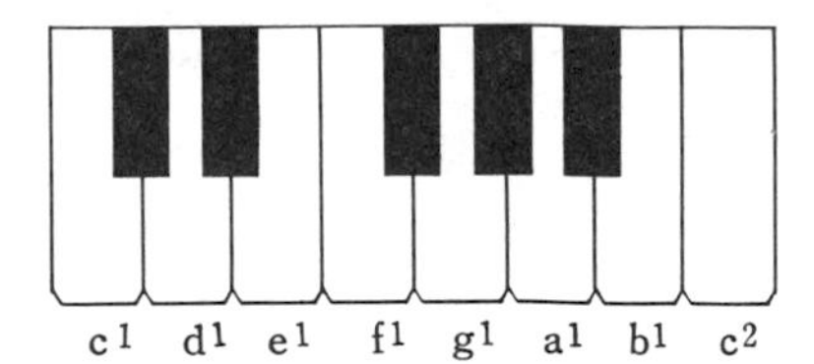

Thus a scale of all successive notes beginning on *C* and extending up or down an octave *automatically* creates a major scale pattern on the staff of any clef; playing the successive white keys of the piano from *C* to *c* automatically results in the *C* major pattern.

[1] *Transpose* literally means "to change position." In music it refers to a change of pitch level. Thus any series of notes can be transposed if the series is kept intact but changed to a higher or lower pitch register.

The Diatonic Scale Systems and Modes

If we begin a scale on any note other than *C*, and if we use only unaltered notes, different kinds of scales are produced. As in major, there will still be a pair of minor seconds at some two points within the series, but they will no longer fall between the 3–4 and 7–8 notes, where they fell in the major pattern. Shifting the location of these two smaller intervals within the series of natural notes determines the scale form.

Ex. 3–5.

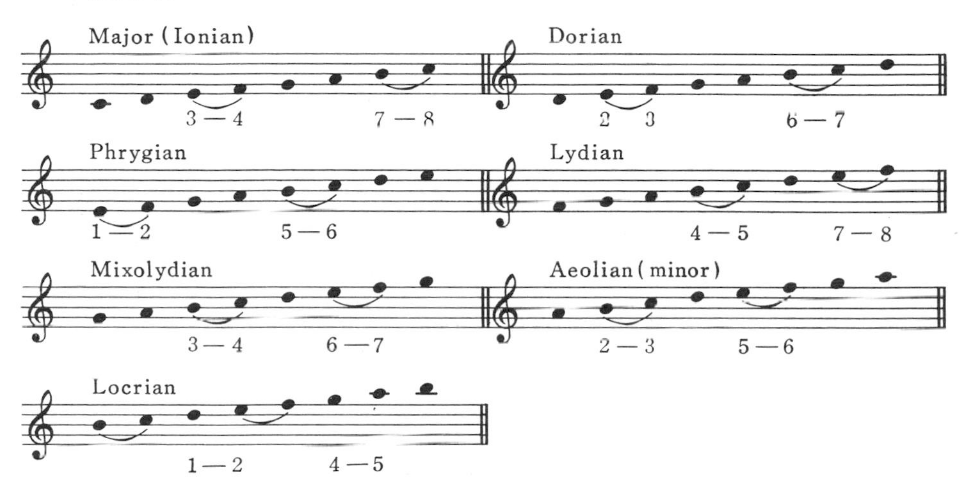

Each of these different arrangements of seven notes is called a *scale*, or *mode*.[2] If we again use *C* as a common tonic, we can see more readily how changes of mode are brought about with the relocation of the two half steps in relation to the tonic note.

Ex. 3–6.

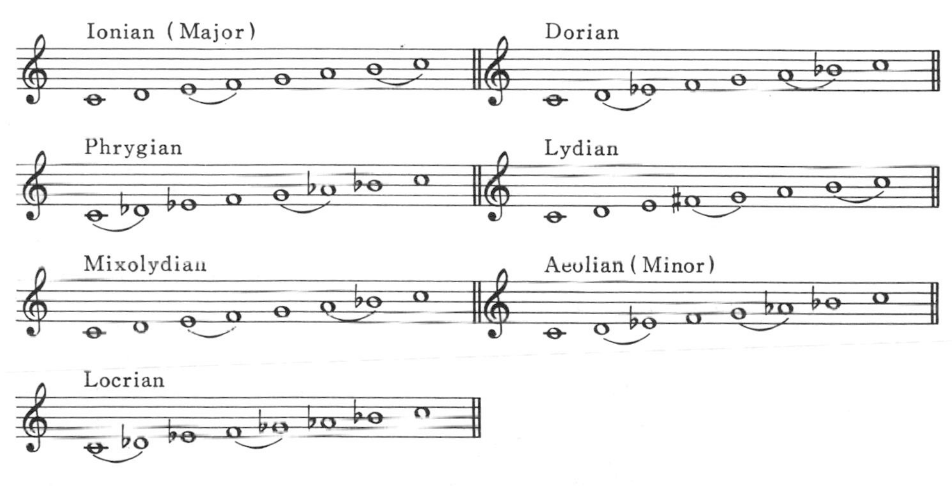

[2] The word *mode* is derived from the same word root as *mood*. Each of the traditional mode names is of Greek origin: *Ionian, Dorian, Phrygian, Lydian, Mixolydian, Aeolian,* and *Locrian*. In most instances the word *mode* is interchangeable with *scale*.

Since scales 1 and 6 of Ex. 3–6 are better known as *major* and *minor*, we shall henceforth drop their impressive Greek names in favor of the more familiar names.

It is significant that six of the seven modes contain a perfect fifth interval between their tonics and their fifth scale degrees (their dominants). As we can recall from our study of the tonality framework in Chapter 2, the diminished fifth is not one of the intervals that produces a strong root effect. For this reason, the Locrian mode (which contains a diminished fifth between 1 and 5) is rarely found as the pitch basis for a composition.

Each of the melodies of Ex. 3–7 is labeled according to the mode its pitches form. Sing or play each, making certain to produce all pitches accurately in order to recreate the true modal character. Note also the tonality frame for each melody.

Ex. 3–7a. Greek: Epitaph of Seikelos.

Ex. 3–7b. United States: Folk song.

Ex. 3–7c. Spain: Chant to the Virgin.

Scale Alterations

Composers and folk singers don't always limit their melodies just to the pitches of any one of these scales. In this sense, scales or modes are really basic patterns that sometimes represent the full pitch complement of a melody and sometimes do not. In many melodies it is impossible to represent melodic content by a single seven-note (*heptatonic*) scale. For instance, the melody in Ex. 3–8 seems to be Aeolian—or natural minor—in its first five measures, but notice that the sixth and seventh scale degrees are raised by a semitone in measure 6.[3]

Ex. 3–8. Dufay: *Le jour s'endort.*

By raising these notes one semitone (particularly the *C* to *C*-sharp) the melody leads with even greater force to the tonic pitch *D*. Because of this strong melodic tendency of the melodic half step below the tonic pitch, this seventh scale degree is called *leading tone*.

[3] Melodies which contain only the pitches of a single seven-tone scale are called *diatonic*. Thus the Dufay melody here is not, strictly speaking, diatonic.

Two modes contain the leading-tone relationship between their seventh and eighth notes: major and Lydian. To contain the leading tone, the remaining modes would require the raising (by a sharp or natural as needed) of the seventh scale member. Without this change their seventh degrees are called *subtonics,* to distinguish them from the semitone step of the leading tone—tonic relation.

Different Forms of Minor Scales

When the seventh degree of the Dorian mode is raised by one half step, a pattern very similar to the major mode results. It is different from major only in that its lower half step falls between 2 and 3 rather than between 3 and 4.

Ex. 3–9.

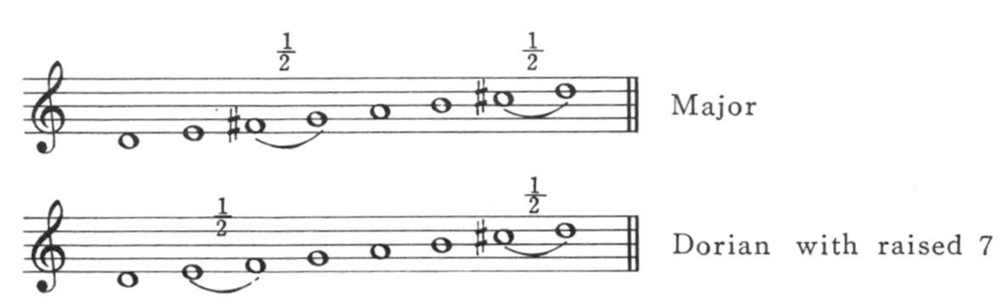

This scale is better known by still another name: *melodic minor.* It shares the minor second placement between pitches 2 and 3 of the Aeolian mode, but it is different in that its other minor second occurs between 7 and 8 rather than 5 and 6.[4] This whole scale, then, consists of the interval succession of 1–½–1–1–1–1–½.

A third kind of minor scale results if the seventh note of the natural minor pattern (Aeolian) is raised a semitone to create a leading tone. This new pattern differs from the other modes in that it contains three minor-second intervals rather than the usual two. Such an arrangement leaves an unusual interval, the augmented second, between 6 and 7.

Ex. 3–10.

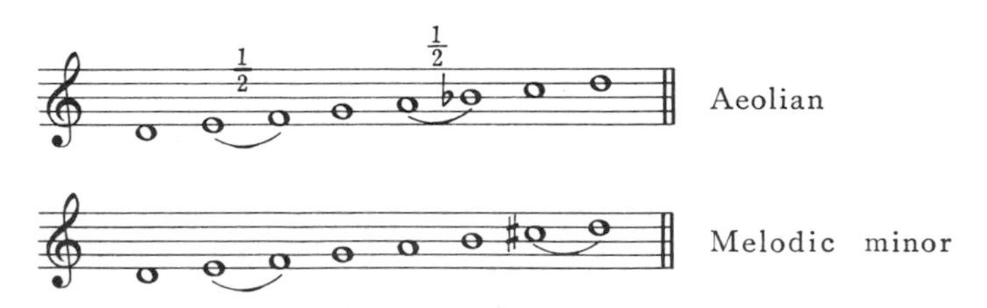

[4] One tradition regards melodic minor as actually consisting of two different scale patterns, one the ascending form (as shown in Ex. 3.9), the other what we shall call *natural minor.*

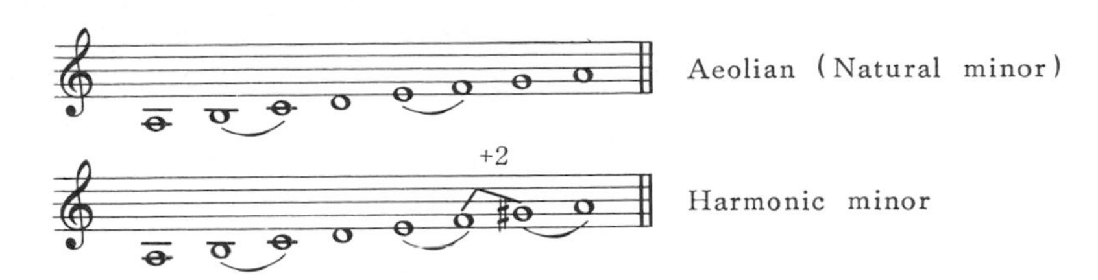

This fourth scale of Ex. 3–10 is called *harmonic minor.* Along with the melodic and natural patterns, it occurs frequently in the music most familiar to us.

It is important to remember that each of the modes derives its unique character from the particular intervals formed between its pitches, both successively and between any two members that are not adjacent. For this reason it is helpful to note in each scale type the most significant intervals, those which in actual melody impart its characteristic *modality.* Study next the statements which best differentiate the various modes, regarding these as direct clues for determining the particular mode of any melody.

Ex. 3–11.

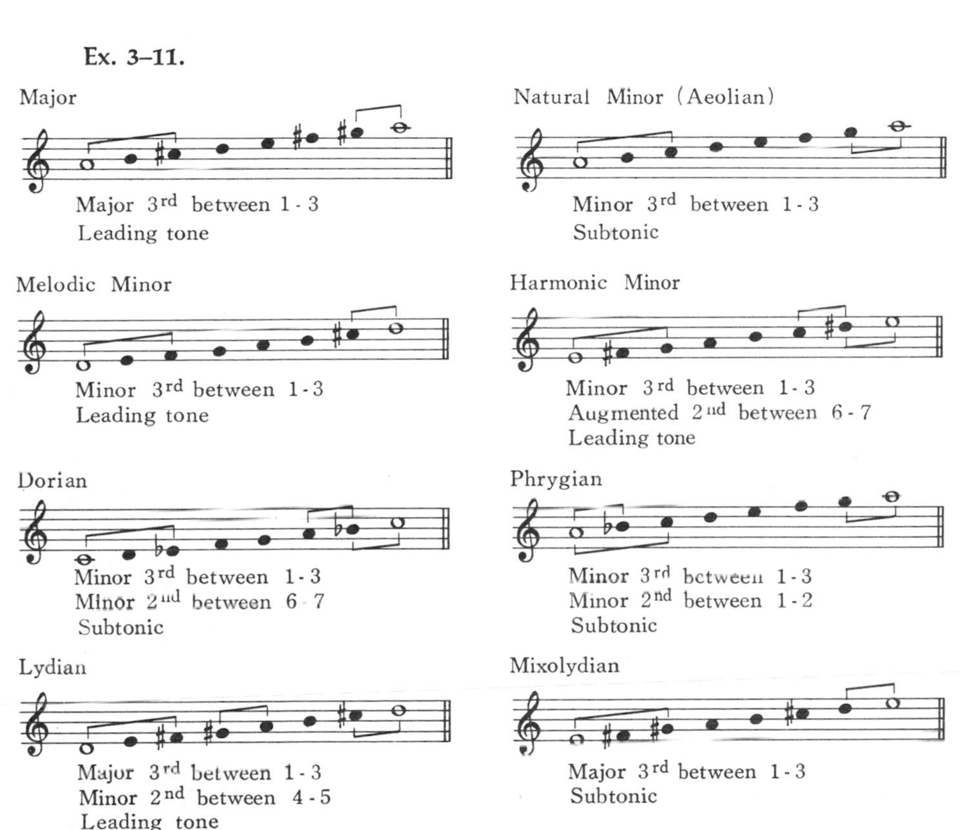

Names of Scale Degrees

In addition to the *tonic,* which is the central tone of any scale, the tones of all scales are named in a way that classifies their particular functions within the total scale system. This gives us an additional name for reference. Ex. 3–12 shows a C major scale and the various symbols commonly used to represent each degree.

Ex. 3–12.

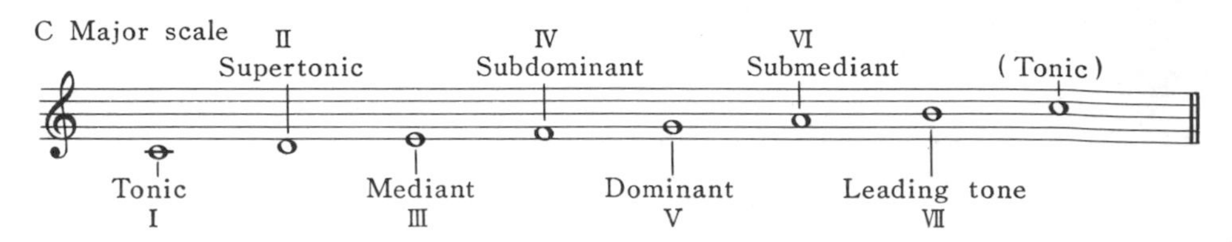

This set of names is applied to every scale or mode, no matter what its structure, except when the seventh degree is called *subtonic* rather than leading tone.

The name for each scale degree is derived from its functional relationship to tonic. The set of definitions that follows explains the distinction of each name as it relates to the scale set.

Tonic: Tone of focus for the scale
Dominant: The tone a fifth *above* (or fourth *below*) the tonic

Mediant: The tone between (the "medium" or "halfway" tone) the *tonic* and its *dominant*

Subdominant: The tone a fifth *below* (or fourth *above*) the tonic (the *under-dominant*)

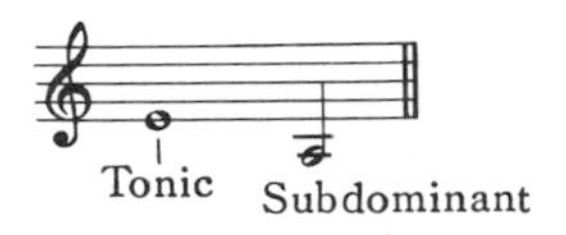

Submediant: The tone between (the "medium" or "halfway" tone) the *tonic* and its *subdominant*

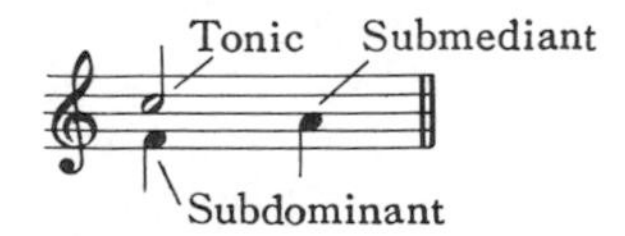

Supertonic: The next tone above *tonic*
Leading tone: The tone a semitone below tonic
Subtonic: The tone (when present) a whole step below tonic

Each of these names is a normal part of the musician's vocabulary. We shall use them even more when we deal with chords. At that time we shall use both the numerical distinction (such as I (for one) and V (for five) and the functional name, such as *tonic chord* (or pitch) and *dominant chord* (or pitch).

Key Signatures

Our system of music notation developed concurrently with our major-minor scale systems.[5] One effect these scales have had on our notation has been the development of a shorthand method for previewing the pitches encountered in a composition. This is the main function of the *key signature* that appears at the beginning of most compositions. These collections of sharps or flats (or their absence) indicate the alterations of the natural note system that must be made to achieve the desired pitches. Without sharps or flats the musical staff represents a set of notes that renders a major scale possible only from *C*, a natural minor scale only from *A*.

Ex. 3–13.

Since the lines and the spaces of the staff have built-in half steps and whole steps, untransposed modes result from successions of unaltered pitches. A beginning on any note other than *C* or *A* will produce one of the following modes; Dorian, Phrygian, Lydian, Mixolydian, or Locrian. (See Ex. 3–5.)

A composer writing a composition for soprano voice based on the natural minor scale could, by pitch alterations, shift the intervals of the unaltered *C* scale so that minor results. The required alterations are those which produce minor seconds where they occur in the pattern of natural minor, between 2–3 and 5–6.

[5] Most of our current notation practices were established during the seventeenth and eighteenth centuries. Earlier music requires considerable deciphering to be made readable by modern performers.

Ex. 3–14.

As a convenience to the composer and the performer the three flats (*B-flat*, *E-flat*, and *A-flat*) required to make this shift of pattern can be indicated as a "signature" at the beginning of the line after the clef sign. This relieves the composer of inserting necessary alterations every time these notes occur within the melody.

Ex. 3–15.

In the same way, the key signature of three flats can be used to produce the major scale from a scale that begins on the note *E-flat*.

The order in which flats or sharps are placed in a key signature follows a set pattern; it is based on the sequence of pitch changes required to produce relocations of the scale.

Using the unaltered mode based on *F*, one alteration is needed to create the major scale: the lowering of *B* to *B-flat*. Since this is the first flat demanded in the notational system, it is always the first flat to the right of the clef sign of any signature containing flats. Ex. 3–16 shows the successive alterations required to produce major scales from the natural notes of the musical staff.

Ex. 3–16.

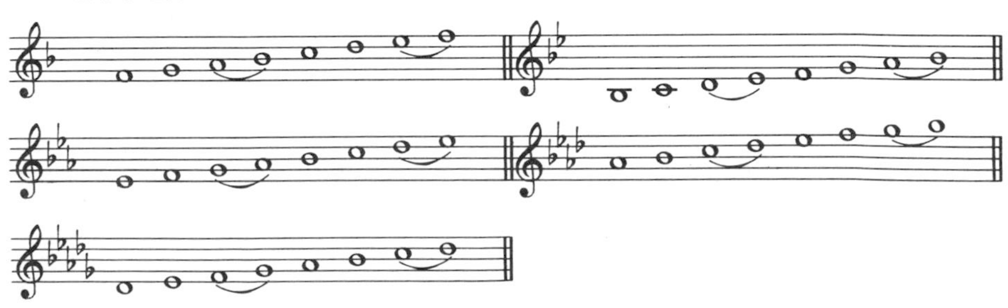

Notice that after *B-flat* is introduced, *E-flat* follows; *A-flat* is next, then *D-flat* and *G-flat*. A progressive series by fours is established that can be represented as:

BCD EFG ABC DEF GAB etc.
1 2 3 4 5

With the addition of sharps for the creation of major scales, the series follows a sequence by fives. The first sharp alteration required is *F-sharp*, the second *C-sharp*, the third *G-sharp*, and so on.

Ex. 3–17.

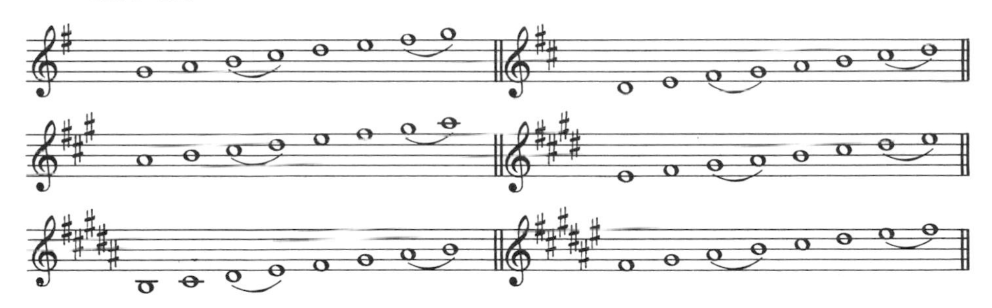

This series of pitch alterations has historical significance as the *circle of fifths*, which is the scheme shown next. It represents the system of keys for our major-minor tonal systems.

Ex. 3–18. Circle of fifths.

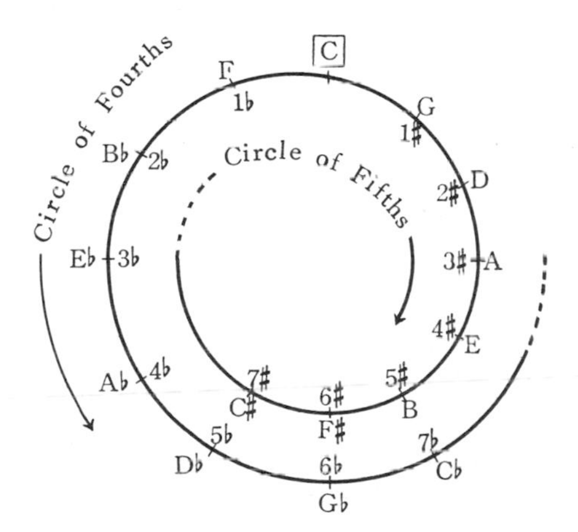

Two scales that have the same tonic but do not contain identical pitches on every scale degree are called *parallel scales*. For intsance, the keys of *b-flat* minor and *B-flat* major are parallel keys. On the other hand, two scales (or keys) that contain identical pitches but do not have the same tonic are called *relative scales*. Thus *g* minor and *B-flat* major are relatives, and *D* major is the relative major of *b* minor.

Ex. 3–19.

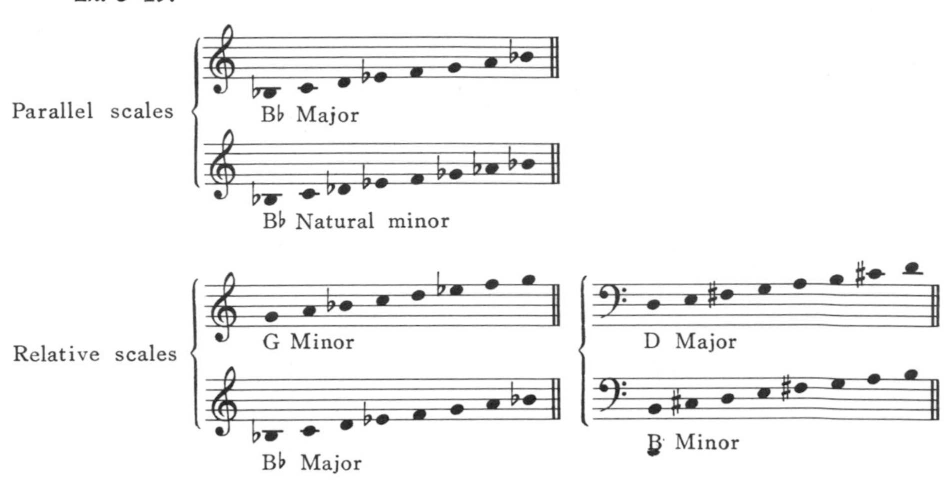

Since double sharps (𝄪) and double flats (♭♭) are not used in key signatures, the system of keys normally is extended no further than seven sharps (for *C-sharp* major or *a-sharp* minor) and seven flats (for *C-flat* major or *a-flat* minor). But the progression by fifths can be continued until the original pitch, spelled enharmonically as *B-sharp*, is reached.

The key signatures of our music are usually derived from the diatonic scale structures. As a result, music based on the pitch resources of some other scale does not readily fit our traditional signatures. A composition that makes free use of the twelve tones of the chromatic scale gains little of practical use from a key signature. If used, the composer and the performer are kept busy staying abreast of alterations and, ultimately, their frequent cancellation.

Ex. 3–20. Chopin: Waltz in A-flat Major, Op. 64, No. 3.

Compositions based on scales unlike the traditional modes might conceivably use unfamiliar signatures. The melody in Ex. 3–21 incorporates such a scale, and the composer used a special key signature that indicates to the performer the pitch materials to be expected within the composition.

Ex. 3–21. Bartok: *Cradle Song.* (Violin Duets, No. 11). Copyright 1933 by Universal Edition, Vienna. Renewed 1960. Copyright & Renewal assigned to Boosey & Hawkes Inc., for the U.S.A. Reprinted by permission.

Non-Western Scales

The key signatures of our music can be misleading when they are applied in the notation of music that originates outside the major–minor tradition. The melody in Ex. 3–22 bears a key signature of one sharp, and yet it certainly is not in the key of *G major* or *e minor*.

Ex. 3–22. Kengyo (Japanese, nineteenth century).

If we examine this melody's pitch structure, we find that its notes form a pentatonic (five-note) scale, and its tonality frame consists of a tonic of *B*. Example 3–23 illustrates these basic materials. They are remote from *G* major or *e* minor.

Ex. 3–23. Tonality frame and scale of Kengyo's melody.

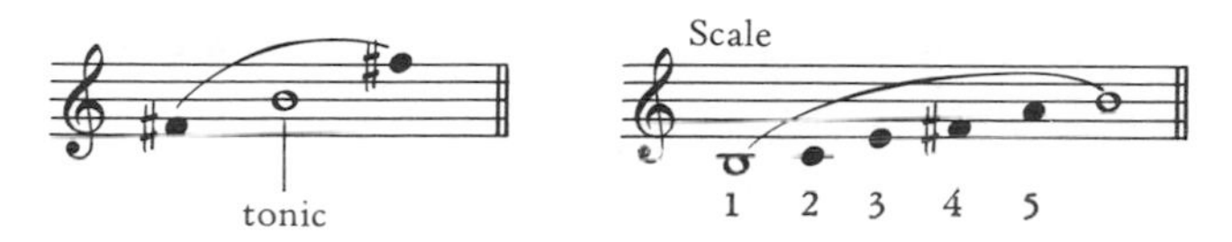

A similar yet still quite different kind of pitch organization prevails in Example 3–24. Here the absence of any key signature can suggest to us the key of *C* major or *a* minor. Hearing the melody convinces us, however, that these would be farfetched descriptions for the melody. In fact, the tonic is *F*, and the scale is again pentatonic.

Ex. 3–24. Chinese Melody (Southern opera).

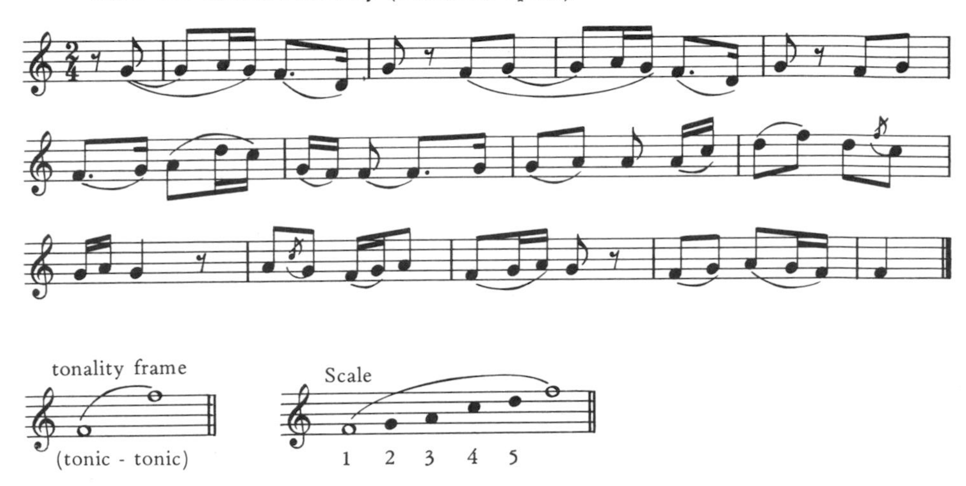

A further examination of non-Western melodies (and even many from our own west-European tradition) would divulge scales quite different from the major and minor patterns. And this leads us to the conclusion that key signatures are useful parts of our musical notation, but they must be viewed as less than conclusive as indicators of musical structure. They are especially misleading when they appear in the notation of melodies whose pitch materials do not correspond with the major or minor scales.

Modulation and Mutation

Our foregoing discussion of keys, modes, and scales must be amplified somewhat to account for the pitch organization of many melodies we hear and play. For the sake of variety, more than one tonality framework is often used within a single composition.

The word *modulation* refers to this shifting from one pitch focus, or tonic, to another. Thus we can say that a modulation, or change of key, occurs at section Y of Ex. 3–25, the initial tonic of *C* replaced by the new tonic of *G*.

Sections X and Y both utilize simple scale materials within their respective boundaries, each incorporating only four different pitches. It is the new focus on *G*, following the focus on *C*, that constitutes the modulation, or *change of key*.

Ex. 3–25. Russian folk song.

Change of mode alone does not achieve the same result as a change of tonic. On the contrary, we can best describe the pitch organization of Ex. 3–26 by noting that a common tonic, *F*, persists throughout. The change of mode from minor to major at section Y represents *mutation* rather than modulation. In this case, mutation refers to scale change as distinct from tonic change. In this example the contrast is affected by a change to the parallel major scale.

Ex. 3–26. Swedish folk song.

X

Y

X

Y

Pitch frames
(minor)

(major)

Modulation usually is closely allied with the sectional divisions—the phrases of musical form—which we shall discuss later in Chapters 4 and 5. For the present, however, we can observe that the melody of

Ex. 3–25 illustrates this formal division by shifting tonics halfway through. In a similar way, Ex. 3–26 is sectionalized by the change of mode—the *mutation*—that occurs after measure 8.

It is this shift from the old tonic to the new that makes modulation an element of variety, for only the relation of the original tonality to another establishes a condition of change. Either one without the other would represent merely one particular tonality, and thus provide no contrast.

In establishing a new pitch focus, the same techniques of repetition, duration, metric placement, and strong interval embellishment are used. The melodies that follow incorporate these various methods of establishing a new tonic. It is interesting to see that several techniques can be combined, as in Ex. 3–27, to create an immediate and unmistakable shift of pitch focus.

It would be unrealistic, however, to regard all shifts of pitch emphasis, no matter how brief, as key changes. In this sense we are dealing with an organizational matter that is subject to relative judgments. Pitch focus is itself a product of the way we hear tone patterns, so it is reasonable to assume that one person's response might be slightly different from another's. For instance, one person might regard the Y section of Example 3–29 as an interesting *diversion* within the tonality of *D*; yet another might hear the passage as a definite modulation to the new tonic of *A*.

Ex. 3–29. German chorale: *Valet will ich dir geben.*

As a general rule, we can judge melodies as modulating if the apparent shift of tonic is confirmed by at least one consecutive part of the melody.[6] Thus the melody of Ex. 3–30 does not contain a change of key; the emphasis on *E-flat* in the bracketed section represents emphasis on the dominant note within the tonality of *A-flat*. On the other hand, the melody of Ex. 3–31 modulates, for the emphasis continues long enough for the new tonality frame to be established clearly in the listener's mind.

Ex. 3–30. Beethoven: *Trio in E-flat Major,* Op. 1, No. 1, II.

[6] We shall make our definition more precise in Chapter Five by regarding the *phrase*, with its attendant cadence, as the defining unit for modulation.

Ex. 3–31. Zumsteeg: *Frohlich.*

Some melodies use a shifting scheme of tonics, each new section creating a new reference point. These *transitory modulations* (or *tonal regions*) usually occur between sections of clear tonal focus, the shifts of tonics creating a tonal contrast with the definite, unchanging pitch frameworks of the beginning and ending sections. Once again, it is quite possible to hear such melodies as organized around a single tonic, the changing pitch frames representing changing stress upon different pitches belonging to the single overall tonality. In cases where a beginning and ending are clearly grounded in a single tonality, it is perhaps more accurate to favor the latter interpretation.

Ex. 3–32. Froberger: *Gigue*

The melody in Ex. 3–32 contains a beginning section based within the tonality frame of e^1–e^2. The leading tone—tonic (d^2-*sharp*–e^2) pattern in measure 8 is the final substantiation of this tonic before a change occurs, in the section marked X. This second section revolves around the pitch frame of g^2–g^1, with emphasis on the fifth (d^2). From measure 15–17 d^2 and f^2-*sharp* are emphasized by repetition and by the leading tone created by the sharped *c*. Measures 18 and 20 relate these two pitches (d^2 and f^2-*sharp*) to a new pitch frame based on a tonic of *B*. Thus section Y brings a new tonic to the fore, followed by a return (section Z) to the beginning tonality frame of e^1–e^2. We can digest this tonal movement into a simple diagram.

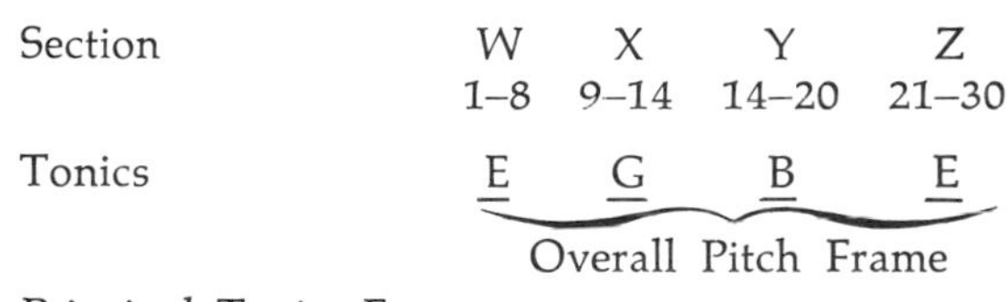

Principal Tonic: E

Exercises

See Chapter 3 of the *Materials and Structure of Music I, Workbook* for more detailed work.

1. Look in a collection of melodies (for sight singing, perhaps) and find examples of Dorian, Aeolian (or natural minor), Phrygian, Mixolydian, and Lydian scales. Copy the total melody and then show the pitch frame and scale in notation after the melody.
2. Write a melody according to each of the following prescriptions:
   (a) Six measures long, range *d*–d^1 in bass clef, tonic *D*, in Mixolydian mode.
   (b) Four measures long, range *g*–g^1, tonic *C*, in major mode.
   (c) Four measures long, range e^1–e^2, tonic *E*, in Phrygian mode.
3. Find examples of melodies which begin and end clearly in the same key but which contain a modulation to another tonic within interior parts.

4. Write a melody eight measures long that emphasizes *F* as beginning and ending tonic, but stresses *C* at some point within.
5. Transpose relatively simple melodies in major or minor keys to new pitch levels. (For example, transpose at sight a melody in the key of *B-flat* major to *E-flat* major.) Play at the piano. Practice the same procedure with other instruments.
6. Practice writing every possible major scale, beginning with *C* and ending with *B* as tonics.
7. Practice spelling scales orally.
8. Write the proper key signatures for all major and minor scales.

Chapter Four

Melodic Cadences

The normal flow of our lives is marked by periods of intensity separated by relaxation. This ebb and flow helps us achieve maximum efficiency, whether we are reading a book or engaged in more strenuous activities.

Even our speech reflects patterns of rise and fall, slow and fast, motion and rest, hard accent and soft accent, all of which, when combined, transmit more effectively what we wish to communicate; these patterns create the *cadence* of our phrases and sentences. The result is an organization of sounds into meaningful language. In a similar way, cadences in music provide pauses amidst activity that give form to the unfolding of tonal ideas.

Melodies are heard as patterns of tones grouped around certain structural rallying points. The cadence is a point in melody that provides momentary pause to the onward flow of musical pattern or, at the melody's end, signals permanent conclusion. It separates one melodic unit from another; it is, therefore, a sign for the listener of relative degrees of closure.

Cadence Types

Like the speech effects represented in language by commas and colons and periods, the cadence is a *heard* signal that helps us organize our world of tones into comprehensible forms.

The cadences of music are named according to the roles they play in tonal organization. In regard to melody alone we shall discuss only two basic types: the *terminal cadence,* denoting a partial or total cessation of melodic activity; and the *progressive cadence,* marking a break in flow but with the suggestion of continuation. Compared with the punctuation marks of language, the terminal cadence resembles the period, while the progressive type is more like the break in a sentence marked by a comma.

The Beethoven melody in Ex. 4–1 contains each of these cadential types, progressive at the midway point in measure 4, terminal at the end.

Ex. 4–1. Beethoven: Symphony No. 9, IV.

Rhythm and pitch combine to produce the cadence effect. Although each of the two segments of the melody in Ex. 4–1 closes with the same rhythm (♩. ♪ 𝅗𝅥), the two cadences create different expectations because of the roles played by their cadence pitches within the melody's tonality. The *E* of measure 4 does not create an effect of repose. Since it is foreign to the *D–A* frame established in measures 1–3, it sets the stage for continued activity. By contrast, the *D* of measure 8, as the tonic, provides an effect of closure.

In addition to the increased note durations in measures 4 and 8, another aspect of rhythm confirms the arrested motion at these two cadence points. Notice that the pitch contour of this melody consists of a two-measure arch that rises gently in measure 2, falling to a low point at the beginning of measure 3.

The same contour is repeated in measures 3 and 4, creating a balanced melodic shape, a musical statement modeled from the repetition of a two-measure unit. The continuation of this pattern into measure 4, combined with the longer durations (dotted quarter and half), implies that the close of a definite musical section has been reached. While these rhythmic groupings create the cadential *caesura*—the pause effect—it is the *pitch* of the cadence tone that determines the kind of punctuation.

It is interesting and informative to experiment with other pitches as cadential tones in the middle of the Beethoven melody, to observe the punctuative effects produced by different relations. Since the second four measures duplicate the first four (excepting the cadence pattern itself), separation of the two by a terminal cadence produces a monotonous, disjunct effect, as illustrated in melody *a* of Ex. 4–2.

Ex. 4–2.

With the exception of *D* and *F-sharp*, the alternate cadence pitches perform about the same role as *E* of the original. They imply, in varying degrees, the continuation of melodic flow. However, all would not be successful choices for this melody because some, such as *F-sharp* and *G*, destroy the two-measure contour established in measures 1 and 2.

Cadence Location

Cadences frequently lie at equally spaced locations within a melody, thus giving a simple continuity to the flow of tones. But not all melodies follow the same four-measure pattern of Ex. 4–1, and some melodies are notably free of regular phrase lengths.

Melodies *a* and *b* of Ex. 4–3 have balanced pattern lengths; but melodies *c*, *d*, and *e* deviate from this regularity of formation. The last three examples are interesting because their cadences establish unbalanced melodic units as the basis for melodic form.

Ex. 4–3a. American folk song.

Ex. 4–3b. Bartók: "Staccato and Legato" (*Mikrokosmos,* Vol. V). Copyright 1940 by Hawkes & Son (London) Ltd., Renewed 1967. Reprinted by permission of Boosey & Hawkes Inc.

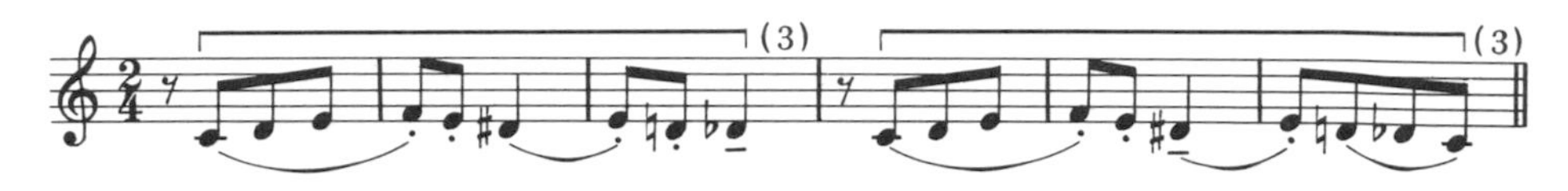

Ex. 4–3c. German folk song.

Ex. 4–3d. Brahms: Variations on a Theme of Haydn, theme.

Ex. 4–3e. Cambodian royal funeral chant.

The patterns that span the distance from one cadence to the next are called *phrases.* This unit of melodic form will be discussed in greater detail in Chapter 5, but no discussion of the melodic cadence is clear without some attention to it. We might turn to language again for comparison to note that the melodic phrase is similar to the clause or phrase of the sentence. And like its language counterpart, the musical phrase usually can be reduced further into smaller units. In music these smaller units are called *motives.* For instance, in the Brahms-Haydn melody (Ex. 4–3d) the five-measure phrase units can be reduced to two-part units, the first unit of three measures, the second of two. In this case the divisions are represented by *different* patterns rather than by the repetition of a single motive. A break occurs between the patterns of measures 3 and 4 which, in a limited sense, is a cadence; only after hearing the continuation of measures 6–11 can the listener decide that the phrases are five measures long. The combination of the two phrases results in a ten-measure section.[1]

Perfect and Imperfect Terminal Cadences

As we noticed earlier, it is the particular cadence pitch that determines the cadential effect. A strong progressive cadence forcefully suggests continuation, while a strong terminal cadence unquestionably marks finality. The tonic as cadence pitch most appropriately fulfills this latter function, while its scale relatives a third or fifth above also, under many circumstances, can imply closure to a limited degree.

The third cadence of the Brahms–Haydn melody in Ex. 4–3d is an *imperfect terminal cadence.* Such a cadence does not create as strong a tonal close: it has the characteristics of a terminal cadence, a result of the melodic proximity (same measure) of the tonic *B flat.* It also has the characteristics of continuation, the result of the melodic rise to d^2. Even so, this close is heard as a weak terminal cadence.

This cadence is a close on a scale degree other than tonic but in which the tonic is clearly perceived as the root of the closing melodic figure. It is for this reason (the root effect) that the third and fifth scale degrees can be the ultimate pitches of an imperfect terminal cadence: the tonic exerts the strongest root effect in relation to these two degrees.

The cadences of the melody in Ex. 4–4 are similar. Here there are two based on *A*, the perfect fifth above tonic *D*. In measure 4 the *A* acts

[1] This combination of two phrases separated by a progressive cadence and ending with a terminal cadence is sometimes called a *period.*

as a point of brief rest. It fits into the frame of *D*-tonality (since the tonic, *D*, is also the root of the relation *D–G*), so it does not demand resolution to the same extent as other pitches, such as *E*, *C-sharp*, or *G*. Compare the relative intensification of this cadence when these other pitches are substituted for *A*.

Ex. 4–4.

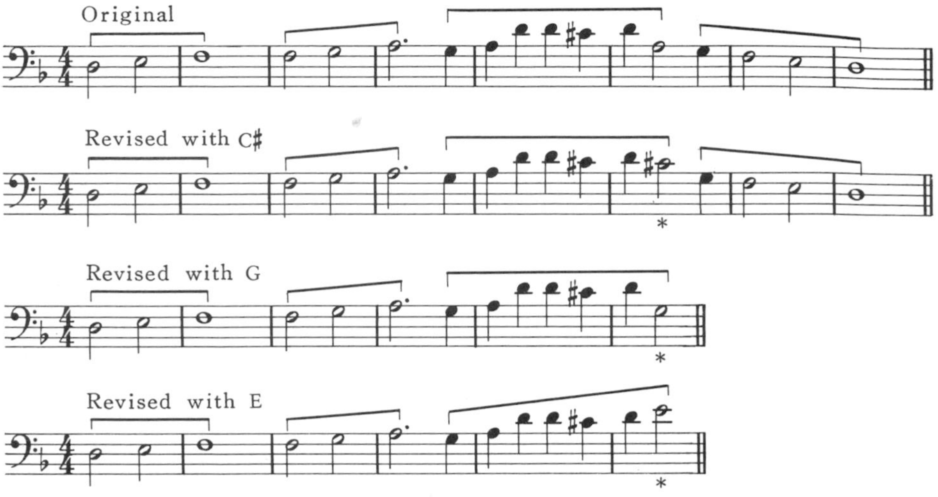

Original

Revised with C♯

Revised with G

Revised with E

In a later chapter we shall discuss the ways chords and melodic activity in other parts can emphasize or weaken the cadential effect of a particular pitch. This is one of the ways chords can add variety and alter the function of pitches within a melody. Without chordal underpinnings a melody must depend on rhythm and pitch relations alone to create the nuances of cadence.

Transient-Terminal Cadences

If melodies always hovered within a single tonality frame and scale, the fore-going discussion of cadences would suffice for all music. But since many melodies fluctuate in their obedience to a single pitch focus,[2] some cadences momentarily create the effect of closure, and yet they do not meet the other specifications demanded by our definition of the *terminal cadence.*

The middle portion of the melody in Ex. 4–5 pauses momentarily on *D*, a tone made prominent by its leading tone, *c-sharp*. If the initially established tonality were *D*, this would be a simple terminal cadence. But since *G* is the tonic of the tonality frame (g^1–d^2), the pause on *D* does not represent a *perfect terminal cadence.*

[2] See the earlier section of Chapter 3 that deals with modulation.

Ex. 4–5. German chorale: *Ermuntre dich, mein schwacher Geist.*

We shall call such a cadence *transient-terminal.* Only if the motion to the cadential *D* is interpreted as a modulation from the tonality of *G* to the tonality of *D* can it be associated with full termination.

Transient-terminal cadences can occur on any degree of a scale except tonic. The *dominant* (V) is one of the most common, as illustrated in Ex. 4–5. Other pitch degrees that frequently function in this way are the *subdominant* (IV), the *mediant* (III), and the *submediant* (VI).

Each of the melodies in Ex. 4–6 contains at least one transient-terminal cadence. Of particular importance to melodic structure is the way each of these "temporary tonics" is established as a pitch of emphasis, either by association with its leading tone, with pitches a fifth or third above, or by its successive repetitions.

Ex. 4–6a. German chorale: *Valet will ich dir geben.*

Ex. 4–6b. Irish folk song.

Ex. 4–6c. Dunstable: *Sancta Maria.*

Ex. 4–6d. Handel: Air with Variations, Var. 3.

A more detailed discussion and classification of cadence patterns must wait until harmonic features can be added to the rhythm and pitch elements that create the cadential effect. The present limitation of basic types to the progressive, the terminal (both perfect and imperfect), and the transient-terminal suffices for a comprehension of the usual patterns found in melody.

In summary, these melodic cadential patterns may be ranked according to the relative degree of closure they create:

1. Terminal cadence: signals termination.
2. Progressive cadence: signals continuation.
3. Transient-terminal cadence: shares qualities with both the terminal and the progressive cadences; strong close on scale degree other than tonic, but simultaneously signals continuation back to tonic or confirmation of the new tonic in next phrase.

Cadences and Musical Style

Since the cadence is a fundamental determinant of musical form, it is not surprising to find that composers consistently have made use of individualized cadence patterns in their music. Stereotyped formulas can be found, used repeatedly by one composer or by a group of composers who share a common musical heritage. These cadential clichés run the gamut from the strong terminal cadences in music of the eighteenth and nineteenth centuries to the actual suppression of cadential effect in some works of the twentieth century.

We mentioned earlier that the cadence acts as a signal in musical form. Like the other signs of everyday life—the green light, the siren, the waved hand, the raised eyebrow—the melodic cadence can function as a clear, absolute signal, or, at the other extreme, as a weak symbol or hint of musical organization. Music literature contains melodies whose cadences operate at both of these extremes, as well as at levels in between.

It is not difficult to follow the melodic structure of some fourteenth-century music, for instance, because many of the outlining cadences use a specific scale formula, 7–6–1, as their pitch content.

Ex. 4–7a. Ciconia: *Et in terra pax.*

Ex. 4–7b. Landini: *Amor dal tuo suggétto.*

Ex. 4–7c. Machaut: *Mes esperis.*

Although the name "Landini cadence" (after the fourteenth-century Italian composer) has been coined for this pattern, it was actually used as the common property of many earlier and later composers.

In music of the sixteenth century the fusion of a set rhythm and pitch formula provides the cadential basis for many compositions, particularly the choral sacred music of Palestrina. Ex. 4–8 shows this pattern, a rhythmic syncopation combined with the 7–1 scale degrees, both as a terminal and as a transient-terminal cadence.

Ex. 4–8a. Palestrina: *Missa Vestiva i colli,* Kyrie.

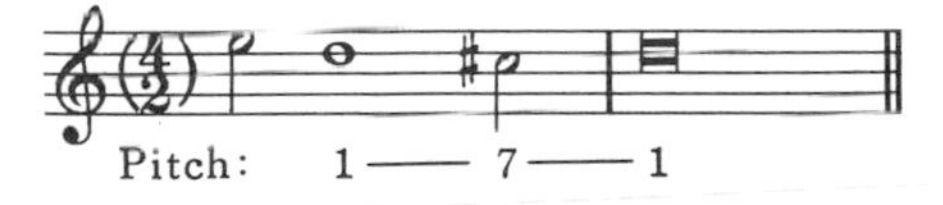

Ex. 4–8b. Palestrina: *Missa In dominicus quadragesima.*

Ex. 4–8c. Lassus: *Cantiones*, No. 1.

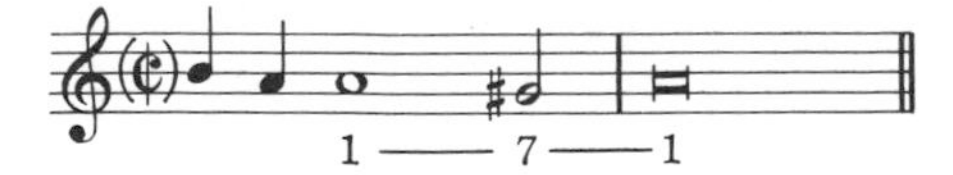

The use of these established signals of cadence goes somewhat beyond the mere rhythmic pause of the cadential effect as we discussed it earlier; their repeated use in music established them as the powerful "road signs" of musical form. The appearance of a conventionalized pitch-rhythm pattern reinforces the mere durational and tonal ingredients in differentiating the parts of melodic form.

Bach, Handel, Haydn, Mozart, and Beethoven shared as common property the perfect terminal cadence of 7–1, the leading tone resolving to tonic, in a weak-to-strong metric pattern. It is the power of this simple pitch-rhythm pattern to confirm tonality that makes it a significant cadential formula in the entire history of music. Aside from its frequent appearances in music written by composers of the classic and baroque eras, this cadence pattern can be found in the bulk of popular and community music whose most conspicuous features are simplicity of tonality and phrase organization.

One special adaptation of the 7–1 figure became a cadential trademark in the music of Haydn, Mozart, and Beethoven. In this pattern the usual weak-strong rhythmic placement of the two parts of the 7–1 pitch pattern was changed into a strong-weak relation of syncopation. The leading tone of such a cadence is suspended from a preceding weak position, thus delaying resolution to the tonic pitch.[3]

Ex. 4–9a. Haydn: Sonata in E-flat Major, II.

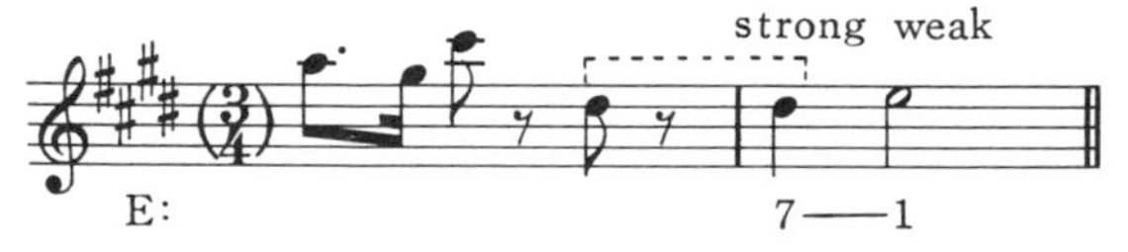

Ex. 4–9b. Mozart: Sonata in F Major, K. 533, I.

In our own day, some composers have used certain cadential patterns frequently enough to justify their identification with the composer's

[3] This delay is further enhanced, as we shall see later in Chapter 13, by the underlying chords.

personal style. Since harmony plays a crucial role in determining the character of most recent music, its is increasingly difficult to identify cadential patterns as melodic formulas alone. However, composers whose music emphasizes melody as a dominant ingredient use melodic cadences of some uniformity.

Ex. 4–10a. Hindemith: *Theme and Four Variations.* © 1947 by B. Schott's Soehne, Mainz. Reprinted by permission.

Ex. 4–10b. Hindemith: *When Lilacs Last in the Dooryard Bloomed.* © 1948 by Schott & Co., Ltd., London. Reprinted by permission.

It seems clear, then, that in addition to its role as a determinant of form, the cadence can assume a position of significance and individuality, contributing to the "personality" of a particular work, the works of a single composer, or even the compositions from an entire era of music making. In this latter role the cadence is a prime element that suggests, perhaps in a more direct way than other musical elements, the peculiar flavor that makes one melody utterly different from another.

Exercises

See Chapter 4 of the *Materials and Structure of Music I, Workbook* for more detailed work.

1. Write several melodies, each of which fits one of the following schemes:

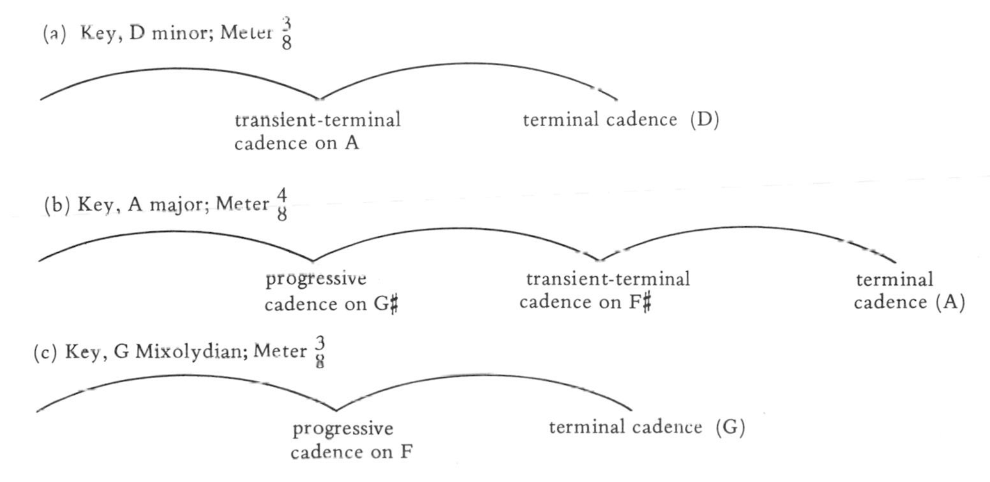

Compose other melodies with similar characteristics.

2. Copy several complete chorale tunes from a collection such as the 371 Bach Chorales. Using only the melody as a basis for determination, name the cadence types.
3. Write one- or two-measure fragments which illustrate each kind of cadence type. Use a variety of keys, major, minor, and modal.

   Example: [musical example] transient-terminal cadence in *D major.*
4. Analyze for scales the melodies of any chosen composition. Having determined the tonic pitch for a passage, arrange the pitch materials in an ascending scale that begins with the lowest note and extends to the highest. From this determine the basic scale.

Chapter Five

Formal Characteristics of Melody: The Motive and Phrase

In Chapter 4 we saw how cadences punctuate the form of tonal ideas by setting off melodic units from one another. In this sense cadences provide still another kind of structural frame. As a melody unfolds, this structural frame is filled in by various related or contrasted melodic patterns. Even in the most complex melody, these patterns are joined to create recognizable units between the cadential boundaries.

Since music takes place in time, we hear musical patterns in succession. A pattern may be repeated immediately; it may be restated after a contrasting unit or units; or it may be varied slightly or a great deal. It is this process of succession that produces form in music.

The Phrase Unit

Such a description of musical form is very general; however, a close look at several melodies will show what is meant by musical form. The terminal cadence in measure 6 of Ex. 5–1 divides the whole melody into two smaller sections. These two sections complement one another tonally and rhythmically, even though they are not of equal length.

Ex. 5–1. *America.*

Each of these two melodic sections is a *phrase.* As Ex. 5–1 illustrates, the phrases need not be of equal length; however, it is not until we count the measures that we become aware of unequal phrase lengths.

Both phrases of Ex. 5–1 are formed from successive statements of smaller patterns, each of which is two measures long. Thus, just as this melody is made up of two phrases, so each of its phrases is made up of smaller units. These subphrase units are simple pitch and rhythm patterns such as those seen in measures 1 and 2. When subphrase units recur consistently in a musical context they are called *motives.*

In many melodies a short pattern is the basis for the unfolding of the initial musical phrase and subsequent phrases as well. In some melodies this is not as easily observed as in the tune "America." In still others no short unit or section is repeated (see Ex. 5–2). However, some characteristic pattern often appears as a formal binder.

Ex. 5–2. Beethoven: Sonata in C Minor, Op. 13, II.

The Motive Unit

A motive is a short and distinctive pattern, usually of simple rhythm and pitch design. Because of its brevity, the motive is easily recognized and frequently plays an important role in melodic organization.

Ex. 5–3. Africa: Ganda play song.

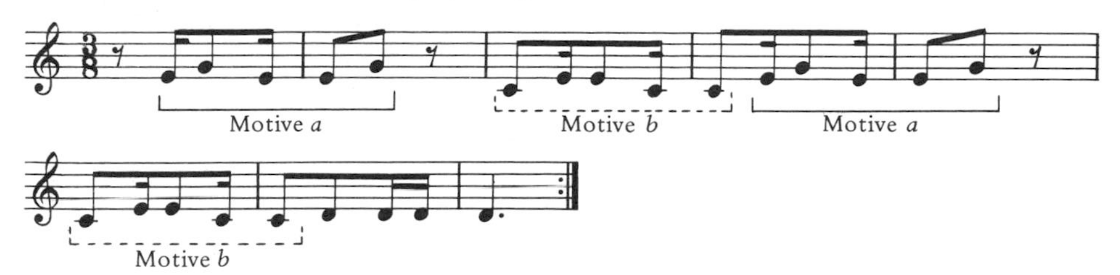

Both pitch and rhythm produce the distinct qualities that characterize a particular motive. Either the pitch or the rhythmic structure can be the dominating factor, or both can be combined and equally important. The motive illustrated in Ex. 5–4 does not have a noteworthy rhythm, yet its pitch outline forms a striking pattern of great melodic potentiality.

Ex. 5–4. Mozart: Symphony in C Major, K. 551 (*Jupiter*), IV.

On the other hand, rhythm may be the dominant feature of a motive. In Ex. 5–5, repetition of the rhythmic motive (|) dominates the whole phrase until the change at the cadence. As is frequently the case, this motive has an upbeat beginning, its first stress falling on the relatively longer duration of the first measure. The restatement of the pitch pattern at different levels, as well as at the same level, counterbalances the persistence of the rhythm.

Ex. 5–5. J. S. Bach: Brandenburg Concerto No. 3, I.

In many melodies the motive's pitch pattern is varied when it is repeated. The repetition of the rhythmic motive in Ex. 5–6 is an *inversion* (e.g., measures 2 and 4) of the initial pitch pattern. Chopin not only repeats the motive of measure 1 as a unit but also repeats the subphrase (measures 1 and 2) unit as measures 3 and 4. Measure 5 begins as a variant of measure 1, but with the upward leap a new dimension is introduced: repetition of the one-measure motive at a different pitch level.

Ex. 5–6. Chopin: Valse brillante, Op. 34, No. 2.

When a motive is repeated, both pitch and rhythm changes may occur. Ex. 5–7 shows some changes a motive might undergo when it is repeated. Notice that the characteristic rhythm of the first part of the motive () is retained. In addition, the varied repetition is shorter, three beats instead of four.

Ex. 5–7. Piston: Symphony No. 4, I. © 1953 by Associated Music Publishers, Inc., New York. Reprinted by permission.

Piacevole

Successive repetitions of a motive often occur in the same metric position. Such periodic statements are typical of musical phrases that contain few contrasting motives. In Ex. 5–8 the chordal motive unifies the melodic phrase and provides the harmonic direction for the phrase.

Ex. 5–8. Schubert: Symphony No. 5, I.

Subsequent statements of a motive may appear in a different metric position, as in Ex. 5–9. The repetition of the five-beat motive is an interesting example of variety created by metric relocation; the repetition of the motive begins on the second (instead of the first) beat in measure 2.

Ex. 5–9. Prokofiev: Violin Concerto No. 2, I. By permission of the International Music Company, New York.

Rhythm of the Phrase

At a larger level of structure, the phrase is a distinctive delineator of musical form. One common type of phrase structure is seen in Ex. 5–10. Each of the four phrases is marked off by a rhythmic cadence (♩. ♪ 𝄾). Therefore, by measure 5 we recognize, in retrospect, a complete rhythmic structure, a phrase. A succession of shorter rhythmic figures shapes the entire phrase. In this melody the shortest durations occur in the first measure of each phrase, and the second longest duration occurs in the second measure. Even if the phrases are performed without the assigned pitches, we recognize them as a complete rhythmic structure; nothing else is needed to complete them as a balanced rhythmic design.

Ex. 5–10. German folk song: *Die Lorelei.*

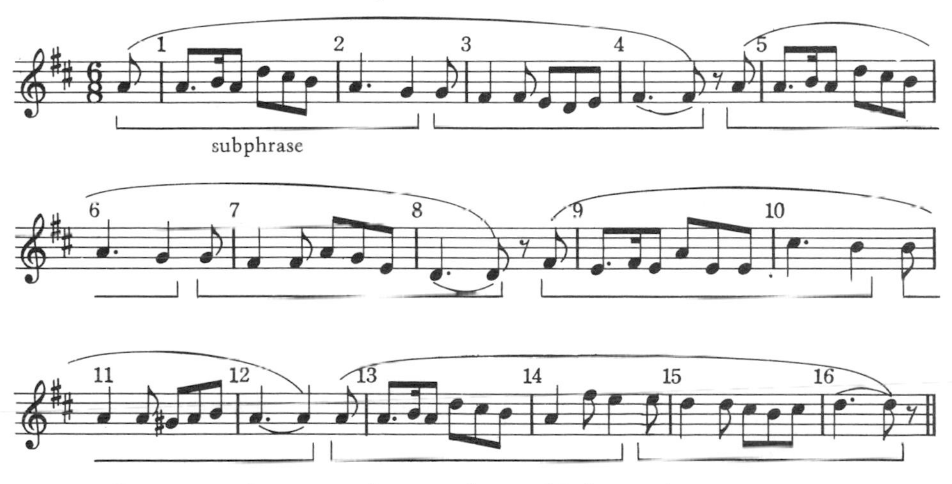

Cessation of activity does not by itself shape phrases. In Ex. 5–10 the first part of each measure always contains a longer duration, and an upbeat precedes it. This upbeat-to-accent pattern also occurs from measure to measure. Considered in this light, each phrase consists of two subphrases that complement each other but are not rhythmically identical. The subphrases are restated in each of the phrases with the exception of the slight pattern change in measure 14. The result is a rhythmically unified melody.

Phrases formed from two rhythmic subphrases occur frequently. Ex. 5–11 illustrates other possibilities. Here the first phrase consists of two subphrases, each of which is a complete statement of a motive. In both statements of the motive the rhythm is identical, but the pitch level changes, forming a sequence. The second phrase is formed in a similar fashion, with two repetitions of a one-measure rhythmic motive and closing with a contrasting rhythmic figure in measure 8.

Ex. 5–11. Beethoven: Quartet in C Minor, Op. 18, No. 4, I.

Although the rhythmic shaping processes are similar in the first two phrases of Ex. 5–11, their effect is quite different. The two-bar motive of the first phrase gives the impression of being able to stand alone rhythmically, whereas the one-bar motive of the second phrase does not. The rhythmic dependence of the secondary motive results principally from its syncopated structure, which leads us to expect a continuation to an accented beat.

Phrases produced by motivic or other subphrase repetitions occur frequently in some musical styles. Quite often these repetitions of subphrase divisions are by twos or by multiples thereof. On the other hand, in some styles such rhythmic groupings or divisions are not common.

Rhythmic repetition and restatement are not characteristic features of some of the following melodies; neither are their phrase lengths always predictable. Rhythm does not stand alone, however; other factors, such as pitch, also enter into the shaping processes. Pitch factors are discussed in the next section.

Ex. 5–12a. Schumann: Symphony No. 1, II.

Ex. 5–12b. Trouvére song: Virelais, *Or la truix.*

Pitch Structure of the Phrase

Pitch also influences phrase structure. We often speak of a *melodic line,* in analogy to something that might be seen. For example, if we perform only the rhythms of any of the preceding melodies (without a change of pitch), their pitch contours would be analogous to a horizontal line. A complete rhythmic structure still remains; yet most of us would agree that such phrases are comparatively dull, that they are not really melodies. When changes of pitch are added to our performance, a different kind of line results. Such a line usually corresponds to a wavy pattern, with the high points, low points, final note, etc. delineating the contour.

Melodic Contour

In the first phrase of Ex. 5–13 the pitch apex is in measure 4. After this highest point the primary pitch motion is down to tonic. The phrase forms one broad arch that includes several smaller waves.

Ex. 5–13. Trouvére song: *C'est la fin.*

An inverted arch is the contour of the second and third phrases. These phrases also contrast mildly with the first phrase because of their lengths and ranges. The rising inflection suggests a question, much in the same way that the pitch of a spoken word rises when we ask a question. And thus ascending contour, enhanced by a progressive cadence, makes us expect continuation of the melody.

In Ex. 5–14 the highest pitch appears at the beginning of each phrase. (The last pitch of each phrase is higher, but it is a duplication of the preceding pitch.)

Ex. 5–14. Madagascar: flute melody.

The five-tone melody in Ex. 5–15 forms another type of contour, a wave pattern that is characterized by descending motion until the rise to the metrically stressed *B* (measure 5). This ascent to the basic pitch (*B*) coincides with a change of tonal emphasis. The opening of the phrase outlines a *D* tonality (the filled-in perfect fifth, *A–D*). However, the tonality of the excerpt is *E*, created by using *B*, the dominant degree, as the apex of the phrase and *E* as the final pitch.

Ex. 5–15. Bartók: "Playsong" (*Mikrokosmos,* Vol. IV). Copyright 1940 by Hawkes & Son (London) Ltd., Renewed 1967. Reprinted by permission of Boosey & Hawkes Inc.

The arch formed by the phrase in Ex. 5–16 is common. In it the highest pitch is reached around the middle of the phrase. In tonal melodies this apical pitch is often (as here) the dominant scale degree.

Ex. 5–16. Brahms: *Salamander.*

The possibilities for different types of phrase contour are numerous. **Ex. 5–17** illustrates other types.

Ex. 5–17a. J. S. Bach: *St. John Passion,* "Ruht wohl, ihr heiligen Gebeine."

Ex. 5–17b. Bloch: Concerto Grosso for String Orchestra with Piano Obbligato, IV. Copyright by Universal Editions. Used by permission.

Ex. 5–17c. China: southern opera.

Ex. 5–17d. Maschera: Canzona.

Ex. 5–17c. Mozart: Concerto for Two Pianos, K. 365, III.

The apex of a line usually will be a pitch that is basic to the tonality frame: the dominant, the tonic, or the mediant scale degree. Other degrees also appear as highest points, but they frequently have a clearly decorative relationship to pitches that are basic to the tonality.

Pitch climax is also associated with the contour of phrases. As a phrase unfolds, motion to the highest pitch directs our attention to that pitch. In a manner of speaking, the "energy" of the directional pattern is concentrated in the pitch apex or in its opposite, the low point. Since a build-up of energy is usually followed by release, we expect the same to happen in a phrase of music. The pitch apex and the low point, then, outline the contour of a phrase or section of music.

A description of melodic contour is the beginning of the study of phrase structure and interphrase relations. Detailed study of pitch organization takes place in subsequent chapters. Here we continue with some of the pitch aspects that describe phrases as parts of melodic structure.

The Cadence Pitch

Cadence pitches signal the ends of phrases and serve as connecting links to phrases that follow. The two phrases given in Ex. 5–18 both have the tonic for cadence pitch, but their musical effects are not the same. At the end of the first phrase the cadence ascends and ends in a weak metric position. The second phrase has a stronger impression of closure because the overall pitch motion of the phrase leads to the tonic, which now occurs in a stronger metric position.

Ex. 5–18. Beethoven: Piano Concerto No. 3, Op. 37, III.

Combining Phrases

The cadential activity of the two preceding phrases (in Ex. 5–18) enhances their *antecedent-consequent* effect. This question-answer relationship is complemented by shared melodic material.

When adjacent phrases share the same material, the phrase relation is called *parallel phrase construction.* In such a phrase relation the sharing of material often occurs at the beginning of the phrases. The cadences are different, for if they were identical they would merely be *repeated phrases.*

Ex. 5–19 is another illustration of parallel phrases. In this instance only the last measure of the second phrase differs. The first raises the question by remaining tonally and rhythmically open, whereas the second phrase answers by closing on the tonic in a stronger metric position.

Ex. 5–19. Mozart: Sonata in A Major, K. 331, I.

Interphrase sharing of melodic material does not always occur. When adjacent phrases do not share material the relation is called *contrasting phrase construction,* as Ex. 5–20 illustrates.

Ex. 5–20. Dufay: *Craindre vous vueil.*

The Dufay excerpt is a balanced two-phrase structure, as are those in Ex. 5–18 and Ex. 5–19. In one respect, however, the balanced structure of Ex. 5–20 differs: the phrase lengths are unequal, 4 + 3, instead of 4 + 4.

When adjacent phrases are the same length they are said to form a *symmetric* structure; when the adjacent phrases are of unequal length, the result is *asymmetric*. In Ex. 5–21 the phrases also vary in length. Nevertheless, the melody is highly coherent because of its motivic and figural unity.

Ex. 5–21. Hovhaness: *Prayer of Saint Gregory,* for Trumpet and String Orchestra. Copyright 1952 by Peer International Corporation. Reprinted with permission of the copyright owner.

Melodies containing phrases of equal length are common, for they create an easily understood musical form. In Ex. 5–22 both phrases are four measures long. Moreover, each phrase is a complete rhythmic unit. However, the parallel phrases are dependent upon one another tonally; a terminal cadence does not appear until the end of the second phrase.

Ex. 5–22. Beethoven: Piano Sonata, Op. 31, No. 3, II.

The two phrases in Ex. 5–22 form a musical *period.* In a period, two or more phrases are joined by avoiding finality at the close of the interior phrase or phrases. In Ex. 5–22 this is accomplished by the progressive cadence in measure 4. The two-phrase formal unit, then, is understood when the terminal cadence appears at the end of the excerpt.

Many melodic periods consist of only two phrases, but, this is not always the case. In Ex. 5–23 three phrases combine to form a period. Each of the phrases contains similar elements. Since the second phrase does not have a strong rhythmic close, there is no suggestion of finality until the end of the third phrase.

Ex. 5–23. Beethoven: Symphony No. 8, I.

Melodies of four or more dependent phrases occur frequently. In Ex. 5–24 a larger formal unit does not end until all four phrases have been stated. Not only are the first and third and the second and fourth phrases rhythmically similar, but they are also alike in contour. Notice the slight pitch changes in the last phrase which provide variety and delay the arrival of tonic. The second cadence (measure 8) binds the first phrase pair to the last by closing on supertonic. Each of the phrase pairs forms a period. In this example, however, the two periods are dependent upon one another both tonally and rhythmically. Such joining of phrase pairs is often called a *double period.*

Ex. 5–24. Haydn: Symphony No. 93, I.

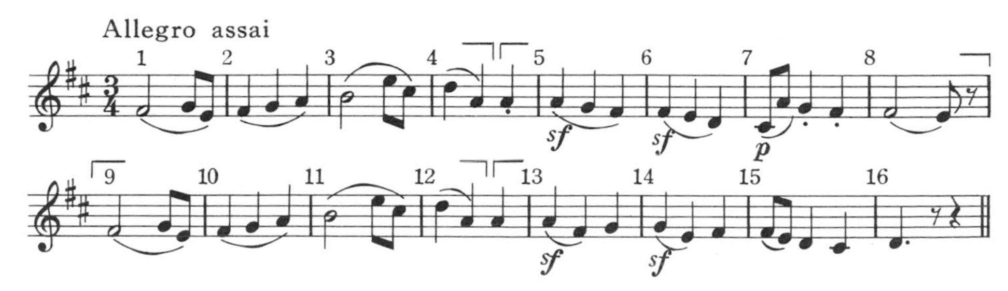

It is impossible to exhaust all the possibilities for constructing phrases; every composition presents new solutions. However, certain principles are present in all compositions.

1. A phrase is a rhythmic pitch unit marked off by a cadence. The accents produced by rhythm and pitch generally reinforce the meter of a phrase as indicated by the meter signature.
2. The length of phrases, considering only the number of measures, is variable. In part, the length is determined by tempo; more precisely, it is influenced by our phychological span of attention. Certain phrase lengths predominate (e.g., in a slow tempo, two-measure phrases; in a faster tempo, four or more). Other phrase lengths, such as three, five, etc., are also possible.
3. The shape or contour of a phrase is the result of the placement of high and low pitches. The apex and the lowest pitch of a phrase are usually either the tonic, mediant, or dominant.

Exercises

For more detailed assignments see *Materials and Structure of Music I, Workbook,* Chapter 5.

1. Perform each of the examples in this chapter. Listen for the larger formal sections. Isolate the motive, or motives, and describe the rhythmic structure and pitch structure of each motive.
2. Use several of the motives contained in examples cited in this chapter as the principal unifying factor in two-phrase melodies that you compose.
3. Devise three or four original motives. Then use these motives to organize original three-phrase melodies.
4. Listen to and analyze the phrase structure of songs by Schubert, Schumann, and Brahms. Describe phrase lengths, pitch structure, and rhythmic structure of the melodies selected.
5. Find melodies in the literature for your voice or instrument that contain parallel phrase construction, contrasting phrase construction, and period construction.
6. Listen to the first movement of Mozart's Symphony No. 40 in G Minor,

K. 550. Compare the prominence given to the initial motive with the use of the motive in the first movement of Beethoven's Symphony No. 5.

7. Find examples of melodies in a collection (such as the *Historical Anthology of Music*) in which motive repetition, phrase repetition, etc. play a small organizational role. Describe how unity is achieved.

Chapter Six

The Extended Melody

In a broad sense, a melody is the joining together of several phrases. One-phrase melodies are possible, but most of the melodies we hear are longer. Repetition and contrast form the organizational core of our musical experience in extended melody.

Repetition of a musical unit produces emphasis, but excessive repetition can be boring. For this reason, contrasting ideas usually mark off the various parts of a melody, thereby contributing to musical balance and variety.

Contrast and repetition are opposites. In between these two extremes changes can be wrought that combine features of both. In other words, rhythmic and tonal patterns can be *varied* to produce contrasts that are still within the bounds of similarity.

Repetition and Recurrence

A simple way of extending a melody is to repeat complete phrase units. The repetition of the initial phrase in Ex. 6–1 immediately focuses our attention on that phrase. In this excerpt the repetition is almost exact.

Ex. 6–1. Schumann: *Dichterliebe,* "Im Wunderschönen Monat Mai."

More frequently the repetition of a pattern will contain some change, usually at the cadence. In Ex. 6–2 two changes appear: the progressive cadence (measure 4) is replaced by a terminal cadence in measure 8, and the pitch contour of measure 7 is slightly altered from its prototype in measure 3. This relation is typical of a two-phrase period in parallel construction.

Ex. 6–2. Brahms: Symphony No. 1, IV.

In many melodies extension is achieved by the repetition of a phrase at a different pitch level. This type of varied repetition is called *sequence.* In Ex. 6–3 the intervals are not precisely the same in both phrases because the change of pitch level in the second phrase is not an exact transposition of the first. A sequence that is not an exact transposition of its model is called a *modified* or *tonal* sequence. The following illustrates such a sequence.

Ex. 6–3. Prokofiev: *Rigaudon,* Op. 12, No. 3. Reprinted with permission of Robert Forberg (Sole agents: C. F. Peters Corporation, New York).

Repetition of patterns, short or extensive, may persist throughout a melody, as in Ex. 6–4. Each of the four phrases of this tune has the same three-measure rhythm. The effect is a rhythmic *ostinato.* As is apparent, an ostinato is the persistent repetition of a pattern throughout a melody or a section of a composition.

Ex. 6–4. Hungary: folk melody.

Sequential repetition is an important procedure for extending a melody: it provides both continuity and variety, as well as simplicity and economy. In Ex. 6–5 both four-measure phrases use the same material but not in precisely the same manner. The first phrase consists of two subphrases, the second subphrase forming a tonal sequence of the first.

Ex. 6–5. Beethoven: Sonata in C Major, Op. 2, No. 3, I.

Ex. 6–6 illustrates another sequential section. Note that the melodic pattern remains identical because it is an exact transposition. Such sequences are called *exact* or *real* sequences.

Ex. 6–6. Elliott Carter: Piano Sonata, II. Used with the permission of the copyright owner, Mercury Music Corporation.

In Ex. 6–7 the motive that begins in measure 2 is treated sequentially, spinning out an extended contrasting phrase.

Ex. 6–7. Mozart: Quartet in D Major, K. 499, I.

In each of the preceding excerpts, the material used again is repeated immediately; this need not always be the case. Material presented at the beginning of a melody may recur after intervening material (often of a contrasting nature) has been presented. Such recurrence frequently is designated by *Da capo* (*D.C.*). Note how in Ex. 6–8 the first phrase is restated literally to close the melody.

Ex. 6–8. Anonymous: *L'homme armé.*

Recurrence need not be as obvious as in the previous examples. Some compositions repeat only the rhythm or motive of a phrase. In the melody of Ex. 6–9 none of the pitch patterns are exactly the same, but the phrases of the same rhythm contribute to the unity of the balanced design.

Ex. 6–9. Anonymous: *Sumer Is Icumen In.*

Just as melodies can be lengthened and unified by repetition and recurrence, so a phrase may be lengthened by adding material. One characteristic procedure is the repetition of a small melodic unit at the end of a phrase. The cadential *extension* in Ex. 6–10 lengthens the third phrase by reiterating the closing figure. The extended length of six measures better counterbalances the two preceding four-measure phrases and produces a more powerful effect of closure for the passage.

Ex. 6–10. Beethoven: Sonata in F Minor, Op. 2, No. 1, III.

Another type of cadential extension delays the appearance of the cadence pitch. We expect the cadence to occur at measure 8 in Ex. 6–11. But we are deceived, for the motion to tonic is temporarily halted by a *fermata*, followed by the repetition of measure 7 in a stretched-out version in measures 8 and 9 and measures 10 and 11. This delay intensifies our expectations and emphasizes the finality of this section.

Ex. 6–11. Beethoven: Sonata in C Major, Op. 53, I.

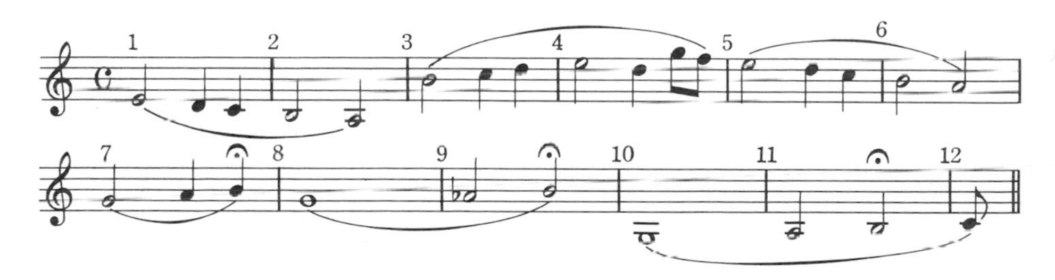

A phrase also may be lengthened by *internal extension*.[1] As in the

[1] Also referred to as a lengthening by *interpolation*.

cadential extension, the internal lengthening is accomplished by the repetition of some melodic unit, as in Ex. 6–12. Recognition of this type of phrase extension depends upon previously recognized phrase lengths.

Ex. 6–12. Brahms: Symphony No. 3, II.

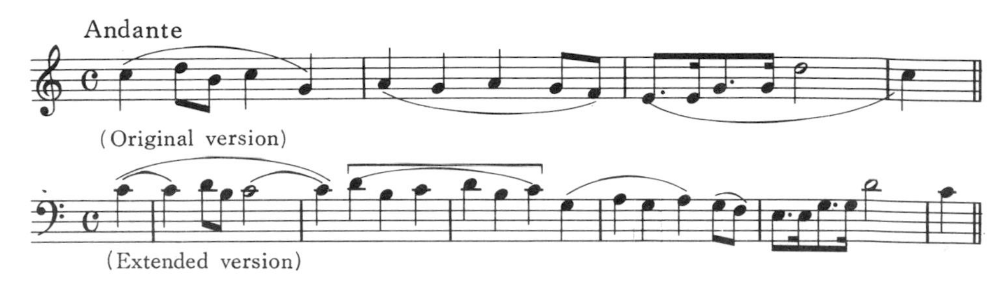

Succeeding phrases may also be shortened, as in Ex. 6–13. Again, an expectation of a four-measure phrase has been established; however, the second phrase is only three measures long. In this case the compression results from the omission of one measure in the second phrase. This type of compression is called *truncation*. Since truncated phrases result from shortening phrase duration, the effect of compression will be created only if the phrase lengths have been previously established, and if the truncated phrases are easily relatable to an earlier phrase.

Ex. 6–13. Schubert: Sonata in A Major, II.

Still another type of compression occurs when the close of one phrase is also the beginning of the next phrase, as in Ex. 6–14. Such phrase interlocking is called *elision*. When phrases elide, continuity is produced by avoiding a cadential "breathing point." Elision also creates a shorter total time span for the interlocked phrases than when a separation occurs between endings and beginnings.

Ex. 6–14. Bach: Sonata No. 3 for Flute and Harpsichord, II.

Contrast

Successive repetition of a single musical pattern provides rather limited possibilities for extending a melody. Generally, the repetition of a first phrase unit is "interrupted" by the introduction of a contrasting pattern, which makes later restatements of the initial pattern more interesting and welcome.

In Ex. 6–15 the second phrase forms a contrast to the first by a change of contour, by slight changes in rhythm, and by the transient-terminal cadence.

Ex. 6–15. Beethoven: Symphony No. 2, II.

The third and fourth phrases are repetitions of the first two. The two-part sequence of the fifth phrase contrasts with the preceding phrases, and the sixth phrase adds still further variety to the whole melody.

For convenience, a letter system of diagraming is used to designate the various parts of a melody. If we call the first phrase of the preceding melody *a*, the form representation of the total melody would be *ab ab cd cd′*.[2] There are four sections, each resulting from the combination of two phrases. Since each of these sections forms a larger unit, it is helpful to reduce the diagram to its lowest common denominator,

A A B B′
(ab ab cd cd′)

A change of tonality may coincide with other contrast-producing events, such as change of contour. Tonality change frequently is introduced at the end of a section, announcing that a new formal unit will follow. A return to the original tonality and a restatement of the opening material coincide in the following excerpt.

[2] The designation *d′* (*d*-prime) is used because the last phrase (*d′*) is not the same as its model. *Prime* denotes similar but slightly altered.

Ex. 6–16. Schubert: *Der Alpen Jäger.*

Variation

In their simplest forms, repetition, recurrence, and contrast are easily understood. Of greater interest are those melodic procedures which combine elements of both, that is, gradations of contrast and repetition brought about by varying the materials. The fourth phrase of Ex. 6–17 is obviously related to the second phrase. By inverting the perfect fifth in measure 3, the resulting perfect fourth produces a change of contour in measure 7. Note also that some of the pitches in measure 4 are eliminated in measure 8 to create a clearer cadential motion. As a whole, phrase 4 is a *variation* of phrase 2.

Ex. 6–17. Schubert: Impromptu, Op. 142, No. 3.

We already have observed that phrases in parallel construction share material but that the pitch structure frequently is changed. In Ex. 6–18 the second phrase begins like the first, but the subsequent pitch structure is a variant of the first phrase.

Ex. 6–18. Schubert: Trio in B-flat Major, Op. 99, II.

Each phrase is three measures long, containing a three-measure statement plus a one-measure extension. Both measures 4 and 8 are *variants* of measures 3 and 7, respectively.

Some forms of varying a melody normally occur when melodic units are restated in the later portions of a melody. In Ex. 6–19 both the pitch and rhythm patterns of the phrases are slightly ornamented by the addition of notes, producing a more active variation of the initial statement.

Ex. 6–19. Le Bégue: Bourrée.

Frequently only parts of a phrase are varied in a later appearance. In Ex. 6–20 the approach to the final cadence of the excerpt is the same rhythmically in both versions. However, the varied version contains figurations not hinted at in the original.

Ex. 6–20. Satie: Fifth Nocturne. © 1920 by Editions Max Eschig, Paris. Renewed 1948. Reprinted by permission.

In variation movements melodic embellishment sometimes is the principal procedure of melodic organization. Ex. 7–21 shows typical changes a phrase might undergo.

Ex. 6–21. Beethoven: Symphony No. 5, II.

These procedures of variation could be used in any composition, either forming the basis for an entire movement, or appearing less consistently as an extension procedure. In any event, the relation of a variation to the original is usually apparent. However, the embellishments could reach a state of complexity in which the original melody is no longer easily recognizable.

In some melodies rhythms are varied by changing the durational values of all or parts of a phrase. In Ex. 6–22 the pattern of measures 9–12 is an *augmented* (lengthened) version of the rhythm in measures 5–6 and 7–8.

Ex. 6–22. Beethoven: Quartet in G Major, Op. 18, No. 2, IV.

The pattern that begins in measure 11 of Ex. 6–23 is a *diminished* (shortened) version of the pattern that begins in measure 5. If the tempo remains the same, augmentation lengthens a phrase and diminution shortens a phrase.

Ex. 6–23. Beethoven: Quartet in G Major, Op. 18, No. 2, IV.

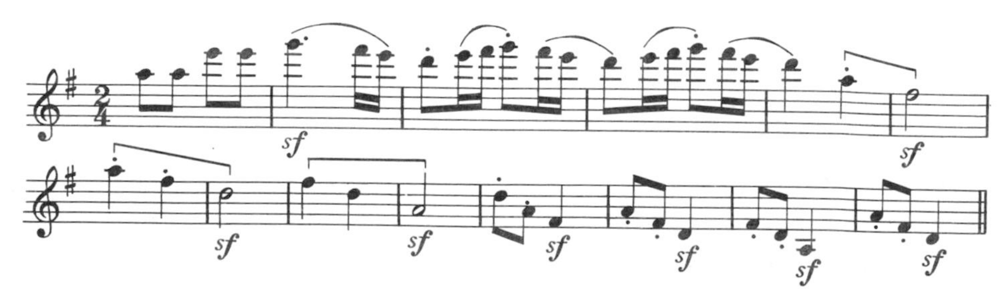

Sometimes a melody is extended by *inverting* the contour of the whole or a part of a phrase. The rhythm of the pattern that is *inverted* might remain the same, but its intervals are reversed, ascending motion duplicated by descent and vice versa, as in Ex. 6–24.

Ex. 6–24. Brahms: *Ein deutsches Requiem,* "Wie lieblich."

Variety of phrase structure frequently is produced by *mutation.* In Ex. 6–25a, the fourth phrase repeats the third phrase in the parallel minor key; the third phrase in Ex. 6–25b also is in the parallel minor. In the latter, mutation coincides with the beginning of a new section, while in Ex. 6–25a phrase repetition is involved.

Ex. 6–25a. Beethoven: Sonata in C Major, Op. 53, III.

Ex. 6–25b. Schumann: *Carnaval,* "Reconnaissance."

Varying all or part of a motive or phrase is one way of extending a melody. As a matter of fact, variation in some form is nearly always present in any musical composition.

Exercises

For more detailed assignments see *Materials and Structure of Music I, Workbook,* Chapter 6.

1. Extend Ex. 6–1 for four more measures. Use one of the procedures discussed in the chapter.
2. Find examples in music for your instrument or voice that contain sequence, variation, and change of tonality.
3. Write a melody that has as its basis the rhythmic structure of Ex. 6–7.
4. Listen to and analyze the phrase combinations of various works from Bartók's *Mikrokosmos,* Volume IV.
5. Use one of the motives invented for previous assignments as the basic unifying factor of a three-phrase melody. Create variety through the use of inversion.
6. Write a melody four phrases long that contains no repetition of pitch or rhythm patterns.
7. Listen to the first movement of Beethoven's Piano Sonata, Op. 2, No. 3. List and describe the ways in which Beethoven varies the motive and the phrase lengths.

Chapter Seven

Basic Melody

Thus far we have discussed a number of aspects—tonality, scale, cadence, phrase, and motive—that constitute the organizational features of melody. Now we shall study the full melody to understand better how its pitches interact, how some even perform more basic functions than others. Through this procedure many melodies can be seen as elaborations of simpler tonal plans. We shall call these fundamental outlines *basic melody*.

The pitches of a basic melody differ from less structural pitches because they receive special emphasis through their placement and function. In other words, the total pattern of tone is formed so that some individual parts are more important than others.

Strip an automobile of all its parts except its motor and drive mechanism, its chassis and wheel assembly, and, strictly speaking, an *automobile* still exists. The thousands of additional parts are in varying degrees elaborations or ornamentations of the core, the fundamental mechanism. No one would seriously advocate a return to such "fundamental autos," but clear knowledge of any object—car or melody—begins at the basic structure. And that is our immediate concern now.

The tonality frame discussed in Chapter 2 is one kind of drastic melodic pitch reduction. It represents the high-low tonal boundaries within which a melody is organized. In this sense, many melodies could have the same tonality frames; it is the varied elaborations of the frames that create the uniqueness and the charm of particular melodies.

The Mozart and Beethoven melodies in Ex. 7–1 not only share the same tonality frame types; they also resemble one another in the way this common pitch nucleus has been elaborated.

Ex. 7–1a. Beethoven: Sonata in F Minor, Op. 2, No. 1, I.

Ex. 7–1b. Mozart: Symphony in G Minor, K. 550, IV.

The tonality frame, then, is a basic level of pitch organization, serving as the tonal outline within which melodic activity takes place.

Moving on to a second higher level of organization, the pitches that determine overall melodic shape constitute *basic melody*. By shape is meant the general sweep of melody, its important high and low points, its beginning and ending, and the important junctional pitches in between.

Any analysis of melody for discovering "tones of greater importance" is to a certain degree subjective. See if you would not agree, however, with the reductions shown below.

Ex. 7–2a. Beethoven: Basic melody of Ex. 7–1a.

Ex. 7–2b. Mozart: Basic melody of Ex. 7–1b.

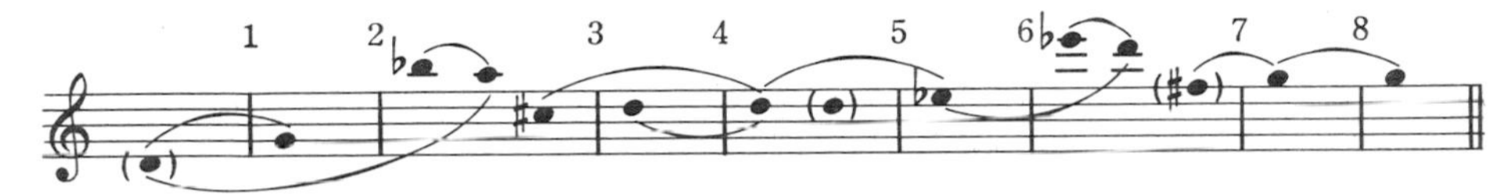

Perhaps we could be even more drastic in our reductions of these two melodies by further simplifying the above schemes to the more basic patterns shown next. This suggests that there can be more than one accurate basic melody for a single full melody, although any such representations should have a great deal in common.

Ex. 7–2c. Beethoven melody: a more drastic reduction to basic melody.

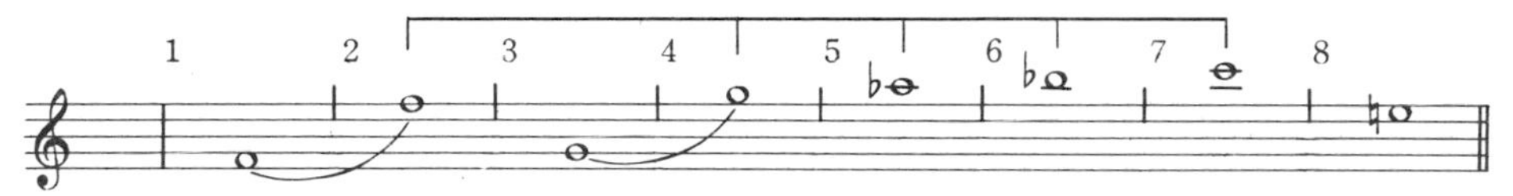

Ex. 7–2d. Mozart melody: a more drastic reduction to basic melody.

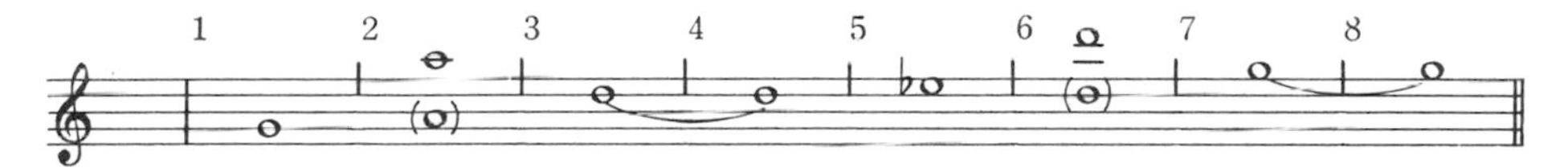

A third (and most complicated) level of melodic organization is the full-blown pattern, complete with the rhythmic life that creates the wonderful illusion of *moving tones,* the experience of music. In it the basic melody has been fleshed out with the patterns that link basic pitches and form the interesting relationships that make true melody. Look back to Ex. 7–1 and compare the whole melodic patterns there with the reduced forms of Ex. 7–2. These latter abstractions are mere skeletal outlines of their parent melodies.

For the present we shall view with greater interest the melodic skeleton, shifting our attention in Chapter 8 to the vital elaborations that are the final product, the full melody.

Terminal Pitches in Tonal Melody

From the standpoint of basic melody, the most important tones are the first and the last. As end-points of what is heard, these tones are the time boundaries of melody. The last pitch is particularly important because, as the last sound heard, it offers an ultimate point to which all preceding pitches can be referred. Thus the final pitch in most tonal melodies is the *tonic* (I). When it is not, the final pitch is usually a member of the tonic chord, the *dominant* (V), or the *mediant* (III).

The *first* pitch is the beginning of melodic pattern. As we observed in Chapter 2, it helps to lead the listener's attention into the rhythms and the pitch frames within which the whole melody operates. The first pitch of melodies beginning on a metric accent is generally tonic, with the dominant and the mediant as lesser possibilities. Whatever the first pitch of the downbeat beginning, it usually is linked immediately with another member of the tonality frame, thereby leaving no doubt as to pitch orientation. (If this does not occur, a tonally ambiguous melody may be the result.)

Tonic beginnings

Ex. 7–3a. Dufay: *Mon chier amy.*

Ex. 7–3b. Mozart: Sonata in C Major, K. 545, I.

Mediant beginnings

Ex. 7–3c. Schubert: Symphony in B Minor, I.

Ex. 7–3d. Hindemith: Third Piano Sonata, I. © 1936 by B. Schott's Soehne, Mainz. Renewed 1963.

Ex. 7–3e. Mozart: Sonata in A Major, K. 331, I.

Ex. 7–3f. Dvořák: Symphony in E Minor, II.

Dominant beginnings

Ex. 7–3g. de Lantins: *Puisque je voy.*

Ex. 7–3h. Schubert: Symphony in B Minor, I.

Melodies that begin with an upbeat pattern (*anacrusis*) do not often start with tonic. Their first pitch usually is the dominant, the mediant, or, in rare instances, the leading tone. The first pitch is then followed on the first strong beat by the tonic or another member of the tonality frame. The excerpts of Ex. 7–4 show various ways in which the anacrusis melody initiates its tonal pattern.

Ex. 7–4a. Liszt: Hungarian Rhapsody No. 9.

Ex. 7–4b. Telemann: Fantasia for Harpsichord No. 1.

Ex. 7–4c. Shostakovitch: Symphony No. 7, I. © Copyright by Leeds Music Corporation, New York, N.Y. Used by permission. All rights reserved.

Ex. 7–4d. Haydn: Sonata No. 6, II.

In still other melodies the first tone's relation to the tonality is not made clear immediately. In association with other parts of a texture the relation might be made clear by accompanying chords (as in Ex. 7–5a). But in terms of solely melodic pattern, the delayed appearance of the tonic pitch can create a degree of tonal suspense. This is particularly evident in melodies like 7–5c; here the tonic (*B*) occurs as early as measure 3. Its function in its early appearances is so decorative, however, that it seems to arrive *as tonic* only at the end.

Ex. 7–5a. Copland: Concerto for Clarinet, I. Copyright 1949, 1950, 1952 by Aaron Copland. Reprinted by permission of Aaron Copland, Copyright Owner, and Boosey & Hawkes Inc., Sole Licensees.

Ex. 7–5b. Chopin: Etude, Op. 25.

Ex. 7–5c. Bartók: Concerto for Orchestra, IV. Copyright 1946 by Hawkes & Son (London) Ltd. Reprinted by permission of Boosey & Hawkes Inc.

Interior Basic Pitches

Cadence pitches at phrase endings are also important links in the tonal chain. It is not an exaggeration to think of the cadence as a point of rest at which the listener can take stock of what has preceded, instantly forming an impression of the important tonal events that have led to this point in the melody. The role performed by cadence pitches is basic, then, to the total organization of the melody.

At this point we can make a rudimentary analysis of melody by abstracting the first and last pitches and all cadence pitches to reveal a good deal more than what is provided by the tonality frame.

Ex. 7–6a. Brahms: Intermezzo in E-flat Major, No. 1.

Ex. 7–6b. Barber: *School for Scandal,* Overture. Reprinted by permission of copyright owner, G. Schirmer, Inc.

Ex. 7–6c. Vivaldi: Violin Concerto in C Minor, III.

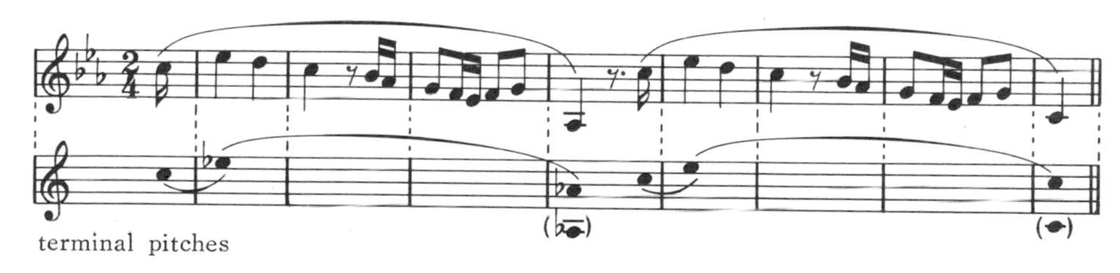

To make our search for basic pitches more penetrating we must look to units smaller than the phrase. In addition to the terminal pitches, others can be basic because of (1) their positions as parts of the overall melodic contour, (2) their relatively great duration, and (3) their favored metric position (as accented beat, for example).

Melodic Contour and Step Progression

If we regard a melody as a line that weaves through points on the musical staff, we see that the resultant wave usually possesses height and depth. Like the first and last pitches, the highs and lows of melodic motion are impressive parts of melodic shape.

The basic structure of Ex. 7–7 becomes clearer when these tops and bottoms of emphasis are incorporated into the reduction that was shown in Ex. 7–6b.

Ex. 7–7. Barber: *School for Scandal,* Overture. Reprinted by permission of copyright owner, G. Schirmer, Inc.

The *G* of measure 6 is not a low point of the immediate pattern, for the *E* that follows is still lower. The *G* is structurally important, however, because it is part of a *step progression* formed between the low pitch of measure 5 (*A*) and the final *F*. As one level in this brief descending stair step, its basic role in the melodic shape is established.

This does not mean that every step relation in a melody automatically forms a step progression. On the contrary, step progression refers to delayed ascending or descending steps *which outline the contour of the melody over the whole or a large segment of the phrase or several phrases.* To achieve this status such a pattern must create an obvious linking that controls the melodic progress from one melodic segment to another. Ex. 7–8 through 7–12 clarify the function of a step progression.

The circled notes of Ex. 7–8 establish a clear line of ascent by step for a sizable portion of the pattern. The successive steps in other parts are mere decorative motions, activities which lead from one basic pitch to another. Bach did not allow this rather strict and obvious ladder of steps to dominate his line altogether, for the *E* of measure 3 overshoots the end of the ascending pattern, thus avoiding monotony and stressing the pitch *D* as the beginning of the following part of the melodic shape.

Ex. 7–8. J. S. Bach: Fugue in G Major (*Well-tempered Clavier,* Book 1).

These tracings of pitch by separated steps sometimes form the backbone for whole melodies, sometimes for only isolated parts, and then in some melodies it is impossible to find a genuine step series that seems to provide this organizing function. When they do occur, they can lead the listener to expect melodic contours of a particular shape and to anticipate climactic points. In the latter case, the pitch of "arrival" usually will be a part of the tonality framework or a pitch that rhythmically "leans" on a member of this group.

In some melodies the step progression forms a periodic ascent or descent clearly allied with metric accent, as in the Bach melody of Ex. 7–8. In others its contour is more subtly imbedded in the pitch motion, as in Ex. 7–9b.

Ex. 7–9a. Lully: Overture to *Alceste.*

Ex. 7–9b. Palestrina: *Missa Vestiva i Colli,* Kyrie.

Ex. 7–9c. J. Strauss: *Emperor* Waltz.

Still other melodies display partial ascent or descent by delayed step relations without really forming a step progression. The patterns marked with brackets in Ex. 7–10 are fragmentary; none adds up to a pattern that controls the ascent or descent of the whole line.

Ex. 7–10. Glazunov: *Carnival* Overture.

The highest pitches of the smaller groupings in measures 2 and 4 do not lead in a *regular* way to the apex of the line, the *A* of measure 5. Even if *G* is heard as the most important high pitch (because of its repetition in measure 6), it too is not reached by delayed steps.

The ascending step progression is probably a structural feature in more melodies than the descending, but the same organization can be found as a falling pattern in enough melodies to justify recognition. In many cases the low pitch of a line will return after intervening patterns, creating a mild form of pedal or "drone." This kind of repetition serves as a structural ground over which the melodic motion freely unwinds, as in Ex. 7–11b.

Ex. 7–11a. J. S. Bach: Fugue in F Major (*Well-tempered Clavier,* Book I).

Ex. 7–11b. J. S. Bach: Three-voice Invention in B Minor.

Ex. 7–11c. Handel: Organ Concerto, Op. 4, No. 4.

The pitch basis of the melody in Ex. 7–11c is clearly a double step progression, the upper pattern moving in contrary motion to the lower. The combination of two such distinct step lines can create the illusion of two separate parts if the lines have a distinct separation of range. The

Bach melody in Ex. 7–12 is typical of such "one-line counterpoint." Its step progressions descend.

Ex. 7–12. J. S. Bach: Three-voice Invention in D Major.

Like two wires suspended in space, the delayed steps formed by these two lines frame the pitch activity sandwiched in between, which in this excerpt is negligible.

The pitches that form a clear step progression are significant parts of the melodic shape and are, therefore, parts of the *basic melody*. When no step progression is evident, only the peaks of melodic motion can be regarded as basic pitches, and then only when their metric location and duration favor them over their neighbors.

Duration and Metric Locations

If other elements are equal, a tone that sounds longer than those around it will attract more attention. Even when metric accent coincides with one pitch, another close by will be regarded as more important if its duration is considerably greater or if it acts as the cadence point for the phrase. This emphasis due to greater duration is known as *agogic accent*, as we defined it in Chapter 1.

Ex. 7–13. Tchaikovsky: Symphony No. 5, II.

When greater duration *and* metric accent are embodied in the same pitch, that pitch is thereby all the more impressive. Such couplings of organizational functions produce a simplicity of structure that reduces the listener's problem of understanding, because rhythmic stress coincides with metric stress. Note how agogic *and* metric accents coincide in the next excerpts.

Ex. 7–14a. J. S. Bach: Passacaglia in C Minor.

Ex. 7–14b. Brahms: Symphony No. 2, I.

The third measure of the Brahms melody of Ex. 7–14b shows how repetition within the measure can confirm a pitch's basic role. Obviously, repetition without intervening pitches is a simple extension of duration, for no other pitch competes for attention. But repetition within the immediate pattern (of approximately one measure), even after intervening tones, also emphasizes the returning pitch.

The Beethoven melody in Ex. 7–15 shows arabesques of eighth notes moving around the repetition of the pitches that fall on metrical accents in measures 1 and 2. Because of their subsequent return these pitches are confirmed as basic. Note the three step progressions formed by the sequence in the final three measures.

Ex. 7–15. Beethoven: Symphony No. 5, III.

In highly ornamented music, consisting of a broad range of rhythmic values, some pitches act as pivots around which others skitter as orbitings around a mother planet. Repeated returns to a single pitch as the rallying point substantiate it as basic for the pattern. The melodies in Ex. 7–16 contain some pitches that are basic because of their extended durations; others are fundamental because of this concentration of neighbors around the one pitch.

Ex. 7–16a. J. S. Bach: Prelude in E Minor (*Well-tempered Clavier,* Book I).

Ex. 7–16b. Corelli: Concerto Grosso.

The basic melody and the tonality frame reveal the underlying organization of pitches within a particular melody in barest forms. Just as a map shows only the main features of a geographical terrain, these reductions show only the main pitch features of a melodic terrain. As we have seen, the basic melody and the tonality frame are similar; the tonality frame itself is a maximum reduction of a melody to its tonality boundaries. The basic melody adds only those notes which flesh out the individual melody's shape in time.

Melodies that lack the kinds of pitch organization we have examined thus far still usually have some pitches that serve as basic reference points. So while some melodies don't have a tonality frame, few defy a reduction to what we are calling the basic melody.

In the following chapter we shall examine some of the ways basic pitches are linked to create the tonal flow that characterizes a successful melody. Naming these links *elaborations* or *decorative patterns* is no indication of lesser importance. Everything in a melody—decorative or basic—counts. Our distinction between these two kinds of functions is made for purposes of understanding rather than as a standard of musical judgment.

The pattern *a* in Ex. 7–17 by itself would interest no listener for long. But when used as the pitch basis for the pattern shown at *b*, it is transformed into a dynamic melodic statement that seizes a listener's attention and demands continuation.

Ex. 7–17. Beethoven: Quartet in F Major, Op. 18, No. 1, I.

Any melody is to a certain extent unique; it therefore draws attention to its features that are different from those of another melody. Because of its singularity, each melody demands recognition of its peculiar arrangement of tones. In discovering the basic pitches of any full melody, pay particular attention to the following aspects:

1. *Boundary notes,* both first and last (within phrases) and highest and lowest;
2. *stressed notes,* because of agogic, dynamic, or metric accent;
3. *repeated notes,* both immediate or delayed within short patterns; and
4. *step-progression notes.*

Exercises

For more detailed assignments see *Materials and Structure of Music I, Workbook,* Chapter 7.

1. Select a number of melodies six to eight measures long (from a collection of sight-singing melodies, violin sonatas, songs, etc.). Copy each melody on manuscript paper, leaving one blank staff beneath each line of melody. On the blank staff plot the basic pitches for the accompanying melody, using whole note heads for basic pitches and black note heads for any less basic pitches which seem too important to exclude. Keep in mind the four points made at the end of this chapter in determining which pitches are basic.
2. Make up several basic melodies, assigning one pitch to each measure of any meter. Using this framework as a basic guide, add other pitches in a variety of rhythms which make a full and logical melody that you can sing or play. Be sure that the basic pitches are preserved as the dominating elements in each measure.
3. Follow the same procedure as in 2, but improvise (by singing or playing) the patterns around the selected basic pitches. Be sure to keep a steady tempo in your performances.
4. Abstract basic pitches from any melody or use basic pitches from melodies shown in this chapter and create new melodies which use these as a basis.

5. Write a melody that corresponds to each of the following basic contours. Use any key, meter, and scale desired.

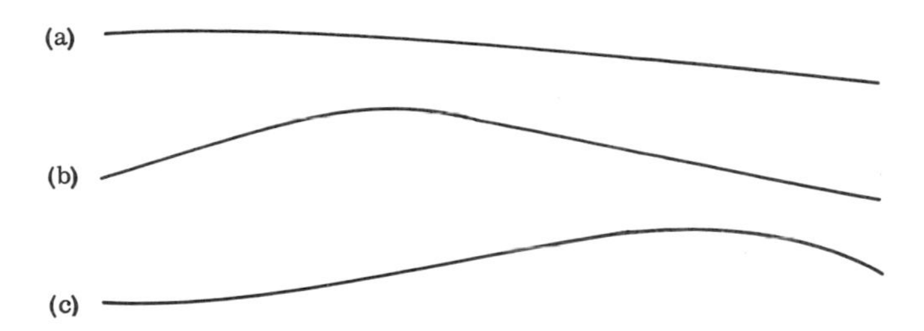

Make up other contour patterns to be used as guides for melodies, and analyze the contours of melodies found in literature.

6. Find several melodies which clearly incorporate a step progression (or step progressions) as a main feature of organization.
7. Have a friend play a melody for you. Measure off the number of bars contained in the melody and plot the basic pitches of the whole pattern. Don't try to get every pitch at first; begin with the first and the last pitches, proceed to the highest and lowest, and then fill in other pitches as they become known.

Chapter Eight

Melodic Elaboration

Reduction of a melody to its basic melody reveals pitch organization in its simplest form. Few melodies exist in such bare outline. In most melodies the skeletal structure is a support for the distinguishing pitch activity by which we recognize melodic individuality. The pitches that are the overlay of the melodic skeleton are elaborative; they decorate and link the basic pitches.

The simplest form of melodic elaboration is created by repeating a note. In Ex. 8–1 the repetition of *G-flat* emphasizes that note.

Ex. 8–1. Bartók: "Fourths" (*Mikrokosmos,* Vol. V). Copyright 1940 by Hawkes & Son (London) Ltd., Renewed 1967. Reprinted by permission of Boosey & Hawkes Inc.

Secondary Pitches

The basic pitches of melodies (particularly those of the classical period) often are elaborated by chord outlining. In Ex. 8–2 *E-flat* and *B-flat* are the basic pitches by virtue of their metric position and duration. Because of their unaccented positions and lesser durations, the notes marked * have a lesser structural significance.

Ex. 8–2. Beethoven: Symphony No. 3, I.

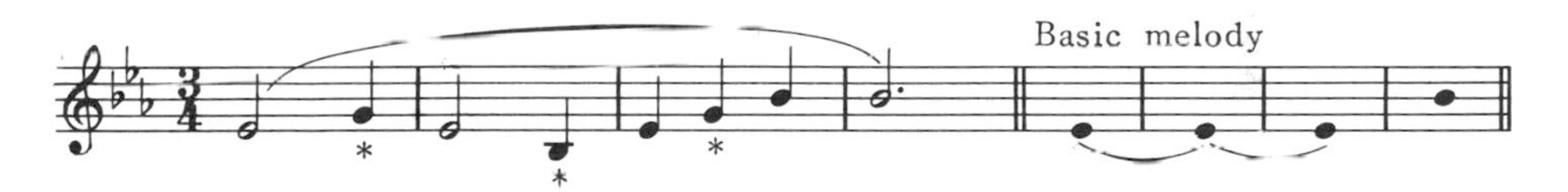

We shall call these less important pitches *secondary* pitches. Secondary pitches are joined to basic pitches by leap and generally occur in unaccented rhythmic positions. There are essentially two types of secondary pitches: (1) those with clear chordal associations (as in Ex. 8–2), and (2) those with only intervallic associations with adjacent basic pitches, as in Ex. 8–1 and measure 2 of Ex. 8–3.

Ex. 8–3. Schoenberg: Piano Piece, Op. 11, No. 2. Used by Permission of Belmont Music Publishers, Los Angeles, California.

The secondary and repeated pitches are important aspects of melodic organization, but they represent only two types of melodic elaboration. Other, less obvious decorative patterns are also significant.

The sequential phrase shown in Ex. 8–4 uses two different types of melodic elaboration.

Ex. 8–4. Stravinsky: Octet, Sinfonia.

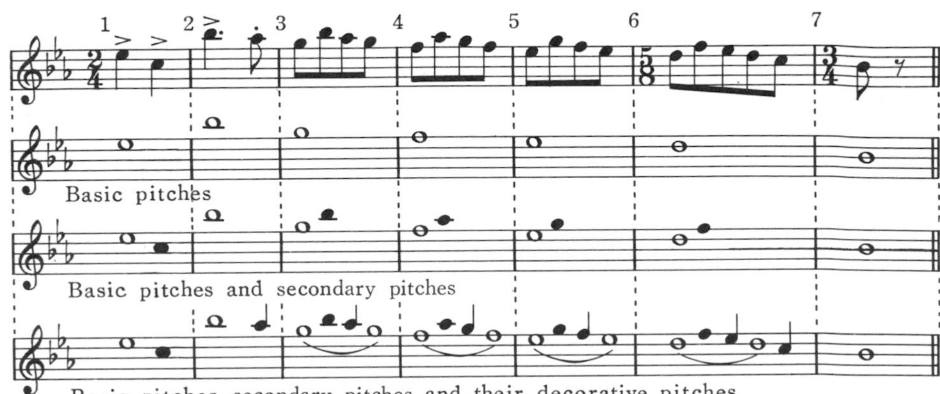

In measures 3–6 the first note of each measure is a basic pitch because of its metric position and its return within the measure. The predominant pitch activity is a sequence of thirds. The upper note of each third has a subsidiary structural significance; hence it is a secondary pitch. In the descending motion to the last note of each pattern the third is filled in. This filler tone smooths out the motion and at the same time embellishes each basic pitch.

Decorative Patterns

The decorative notes (shown as ♩ in the sketch of Ex. 8–4) participate in a step progression that links a secondary pitch to a basic pitch.

Decorative pitches can embellish a basic melody with either of two different types of tonal activity: (1) the decorative pitch *exceeds* the range of two basic pitches or a basic pitch and a secondary pitch (as in Ex. 8–5a and Ex. 8–5b); or (2) the decorative pitch remains *within* the range of two basic pitches or a basic pitch and a secondary pitch (as in Ex. 8–5c). In Ex. 8–5, and in all subsequent examples, the basic pitches are represented by o, the secondary pitches by •, and the decorative pitches by ♩. The tie, ‿, denotes that the same basic pitch is being decorated over a period of time.

Ex. 8–5.

a b c

Passing Tone

Decorative pitches have names that describe clearly the roles they play. For example, since most melodies use a preponderance of steps, decorative pitches called *passing tones* appear frequently. This is an apt description, because passing tones connect two different basic pitches (or a basic pitch and its secondary pitch), as in Ex. 8–6.

Ex. 8–6. Passing tones.

Passing tones are often shorter in duration than the pitches they connect, and they appear in both accented and unaccented positions. Since accented tones tend to impress us as more important than unaccented, the unaccented passing tone is more common.

Ex. 8–7a and Ex. 8–7b show both types. The *D-natural* in measure 4 of Ex. 8–7c is a chromatic passing tone. Note that the diatonic passing tones (notes belonging to one diatonic scale) link two notes a third apart; chromatic passing tones generally link two notes a major second apart.

Ex. 8–7a. Beethoven: Quartet in E-flat Major, Op. 74, IV.

Ex. 8–7b.

Ex. 8–7c. Beethoven: Sonata in A-flat Major, Op. 110, I.

In highly ornamental melodies several tones sometimes link structural pitches that are more than a third apart. These linking notes usually are of short duration, playing the same decorative role as a single passing tone. For this reason they also are referred to as passing tones (bracketed in Ex. 8–8).

Ex. 8–8. Bach: Gigue (*Little Notebook of Anna Magdalena Bach*).

Neighbor Tone

Another decorative pitch that appears frequently is the *neighbor tone.*[1] Like the passing tone, this type of embellishment can be found in both accented and unaccented positions. Step motion is again involved, the neighbor moving away (either up or down) from a basic pitch and returning to it. Neighbor tones also may be diatonic or chromatic. Since neighbor tones embellish a single pitch, delayed repetition is involved. This emphasizes the repeated tone, creating a more interesting pattern than simple repetition.

In Ex. 8–9 the neighbor tones are indicated by N.T. The neighbors in Ex. 8–9b are chromatic.

Ex. 8–9a. Mozart: Sonata in D Major, K. 576, III.

Ex. 8–9b. Beethoven: Sonata in E Minor, Op. 90, II.

[1] Sometimes called *auxiliary tone* or *returning note.*

Chromatic passing tones and neighbor tones do not alter tonality. Even if a note has the appearance of a new leading tone, duration determines the amount of influence it can exert and helps to distinguish a chromatic *decorative pitch* from a chromatic *structural pitch*.

The frequent use of passing tones and neighbor tones does not make them more significant than other kinds of decorative pitches. Thus, in those melodies containing structural pitches that are a third apart, passing tones smooth the line by filling in gaps, thereby bringing the structural pitches into closer relationship. Similarly, if repeated tones play an important part in a melody, the effect of such repetition is intensified by the incorporation of neighbor tones and secondary pitches.

Both the passing tone and the neighbor tone are approached and followed by step. Motion by step is a factor in most decorative patterns. Yet some types do not use step-step pitch configuration; at times a decorative tone is given greater emphasis because it is either approached or left by skip. This added emphasis directs attention to the decorative tone; consequently, decorative patterns containing skips appear infrequently. Two different decorative pitches can be classified in this way: the *appoggiatura* [2] and the *escape tone*.[3]

The Appoggiatura

Appoggiaturas are approached by skip and then step to a structural pitch. The appoggiatura directs attention to the note of arrival by delaying it momentarily. Furthermore, the motion by step to the embellished pitch creates the impression of leaning, which explains the use of this particular descriptive term.

Ex. 8–10.

[2] Literally, *leaning tone*, which some prefer to the Italian *appoggiatura*.

[3] Sometimes called an *échappée*.

Appoggiaturas occur in both accented and unaccented metric positions. They are usually shorter in duration than the notes they embellish, and the motion to the subsequent basic pitch is frequently in the opposite direction from the skip that begins the pattern. In all cases it follows the pattern of skip (either up or down)-step.

In Ex. 8–11 the appoggiatura in measure 1 is easily recognized because its relative importance is indicated by the notation. This literal representation of a leaning tone is common.

Ex. 8–11. Mozart: Sonata in D Major, K. 284, III (Variation 12).

If this type of notation is not used, the duration of the appoggiatura is designated the same way as the other notes. In Ex. 8–12 the appoggiaturas are not set apart by notation. In this example the basic pitches create a rising step progression.

Ex. 8–12. Beethoven: Sonata in C-sharp Minor, Op. 27, No. 2, III.

Sometimes the appoggiatura and the pitch it embellishes have the same duration. When this occurs it can be difficult to differentiate between decorative and basic notes. However, in Ex. 8–13 the appoggiatura is also the leading tone of the key, and it embellishes the tonic note.

Ex. 8–13. Mendelssohn: *A Midsummer Night's Dream,* Intermezzo.

In Ex. 8–14 the chromatic appoggiaturas emphasize the second and third scale steps, while the diatonic appoggiaturas emphasize the tonic and the subdominant. Notice that the duration of the structural pitches varies, and the half-step relations create a strong motion to the structural tones.

Ex. 8–14. Beethoven: Sonata in G Major, Op. 14, No. 2, I.

A more complex situation is illustrated in Ex. 8–15. Here the duration of the appoggiatura is greater than that of the embellished note. In measure 3, *A* is a secondary pitch to *F-sharp*; even though *G-sharp* lasts longer, its melodic role is decorative.

Ex. 8–15. Carter: Woodwind Quintet, I. © 1952 by Associated Music Publishers, Inc., New York. Reprinted by permission.

The Escape Tone

The melodic opposite of the appoggiatura, the *escape tone*, resolves to a basic or a secondary pitch by skip, while the motion preceding it is by step. Although it can be found in both accented and unaccented positions, it is usually an unaccented elaboration.

Ex. 8–16.

Like the appoggiatura, the motion away from an escape tone usually involves a change of direction, as shown next. In both examples the decorative note escapes from one important tone before moving to the next.

Ex. 8–17a. Chopin: Sonata in B Minor, Op. 58, I.

Ex. 8–17b. Bach: *St. John Passion,* "Wäre dieser nicht ein Übeltäter?"

Sometimes, however, the motion continues in the same direction, as in Ex. 8–18. We can still recognize this as a variation of the more common pattern, which changes direction.

Ex. 8–18. Beethoven: Sonata in A Major, Op. 101, I.

Whichever direction it moves, the escape tone is usually of shorter duration than the tones surrounding it. If not, it normally appears in a less prominent metric position.

The Neighbor Group

The decorative patterns discussed in the preceding sections involve only one embellishing tone, with the exception of a group of passing tones. The figure called a *neighbor group* (n.g.) always involves two decorative tones that embellish a single basic pitch. Both decorative notes are neighbors to the basic tone, one located a step above, the other a step below; a skip occurs between the two neighbor tones, the resulting pattern forming a step-skip-step sequence. Often one of these decorative tones is unaccented, the other accented.

The neighbor groups in Ex. 8–19 embellish the cadence pitch. Since the repeated cadence tone is in evidence for a relatively long period of time, the neighbor groups in this excerpt merely elaborate the cadential function.

Ex. 8–19. Haydn: Quartet in F Major, Op. 74, No. 2, I.

In Ex. 8–20 the neighbor groups extend the duration of basic pitches. Notice how closely the decorative activity of this figure resembles the neighbor tone figure.

Ex. 8–20. Mozart: Quartet in A Major, K. 464, I.

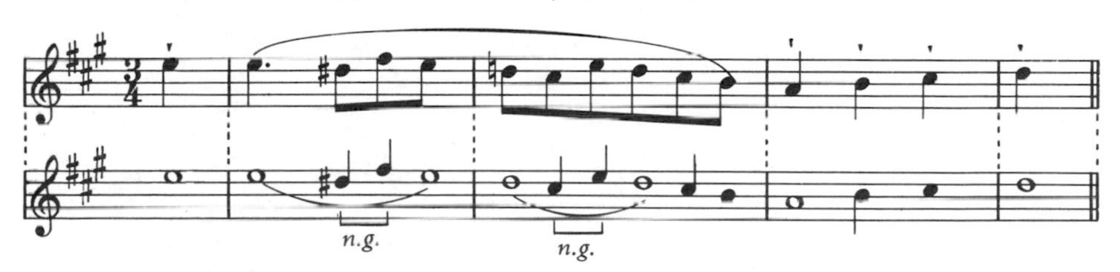

The Anticipation

Another type of decorative pitch, the *anticipation*, prepares for the appearance of a basic pitch. It is by nature an unaccented pattern, almost always of lesser duration than the pitches surrounding it. The pitch motion is generally step-rearticulation, as in Ex. 8–21.

Ex. 8–21. J. S. Bach: Two-voice Invention in C Minor.

Sometimes the motion preceding the anticipation is by skip, resulting in a skip-rearticulation pattern. When this variation of the more common pattern occurs, disjunct secondary pitches usually are also present. The anticipation thus announces one of the notes that is contained in the line, as can be seen in the opening of Ex. 8–22. As is apparent, the anticipation is primarily a rhythmic elaboration.

Ex. 8–22. Beethoven: Sonata in E-flat Major, Op. 31, No. 3, III.

The Suspension

Melodic suspension is another form of rhythmic elaboration. The suspension figure is characterized by the following: (1) a basic pitch is prolonged by means of a tie or rearticulation; (2) this basic pitch extends past a metric or rhythmic accent; and (3) this suspended basic pitch moves to an unaccented basic pitch or secondary pitch, usually by step downward.

Ex. 8–23. Suspensions with tie and rearticulation.

In Ex. 8–24 a suspension appears on the first beat of measure 3. Here the suspension is created by the tied basic *F*. The result is an elaboration of the phrase rhythm. In addition, the entire process emphasizes the basic pitch more than if the suspension had not occurred.

Ex. 8–24. Hindemith: *Mathis der Maler,* I. Copyright 1934 by B. Schott's Soehne-Mainz. Copyright renewed 1962 by B. Schotts Soehne-Mainz.

In Ex. 8–25 the duration of the basic *G* in measure 3 is extended by its rearticulation on the first beat of measure 4. This delays the anticipated appearance of a different pitch on an accented first beat.

Ex. 8–25. Tchaikovsky: Symphony No. 5, II.

Sometimes the motion of the suspended basic pitch to the second note of the pattern is "interrupted" by the interpolation of another decorative pitch, as in Ex. 8–26. Here the two tones of the suspension figure are themselves decorated, adding intensity to the melodic motion.

Ex. 8–26. Bach: *Art of the Fugue.*

If melody alone is considered, the distinction between basic pitches, secondary pitches, and decorative pitches may not always be readily apparent. Most melodies occur in association with other melodies or chords. When all factors are weighed, including tempo, the distinctions will become more apparent; similarly, some interpretations based purely on melodic premises may have to be changed according to the texture in which the melody occurs.

Outline of Decorative Pitches

Type *	*Pitch Motion*	*Rhythmic Characteristics*
Passing Tone (p.t.)	Step-step	Accented or unaccented
Neighbor Tone (n.t.)	Step-step	Accented or unaccented
Appoggiatura (app.)	Skip-step	Accented or unaccented
Escape Tone (e.t.)	Step-skip	Usually unaccented
Neighbor Group (n.g.)	Step-skip-step	Accented or unaccented
Anticipation (ant.)	Step-rearticulation; or skip-rearticulation	Unaccented
Suspension (sus.)	Step	Accented

* Abbreviations for each pitch appear in parentheses.

Exercises

For more detailed assignments see *Materials and Structure of Music I, Workbook,* Chapter 8.

1. Determine the basic pitches of familiar melodies. Then use these basic melodies as the pitch framework for melodies that you write.
2. Use the phrase patterns from any example as the rhythmic basis for melodies that you write. Before writing, sketch in a pitch framework.
3. Create "new" melodies by elaborating the basic melodies of any of the examples in this chapter.
4. Create an original basic melody. Then elaborate this framework, using the same basic melody for melodies in simple and compound meters.
5. Describe all of the decorative pitches not identified in the analyses given in this chapter.
6. Analyze melodies selected from the following: Bartók, *Mikrokosmos,* Volumes I and II; Bach, *English Suites;* Mozart, Piano Sonatas; Beethoven, Piano Sonatas; Stravinsky, Sonata for Two Pianos; etc. Reduce each of the melodies selected to its basic pitches; then identify the role of each of the decorative pitches.

Chapter Nine

Two-Voice Combinations

Although we usually associate melody with a single prominent voice or instrument, it is essential that we see how melody exists in one way or another in each voice or part of a composition, and how features of melodic organization are present in varying degrees in different styles, forms, and textures of music.

Texture

Texture is a word that has taken on several different meanings for musicians. In the broadest sense it refers to the whole fabric of music, resulting from the interweaving of its basic elements (melody, rhythm, harmony, and timbre). More specifically, it refers to the number of voices or parts in a composition and the relationships of those parts to each other.

In this latter sense of texture we can talk about four basic kinds: *monophonic,* comprising a single voice; *homophonic,* in which a predominant melody is supported by an essentially chordal accompaniment; *polyphonic,* which literally means "many voices"[1] ; and *heterophonic,* in which two or more parts are individual embellishments of a single basic melody.

Rhythmic Association

The possibilities of rhythmically combining two or more voices are enormous, but several basic observations can be made. A study of the examples in this section will reveal several different kinds of rhythmic combinations, each of which represents a common treatment of two relatively independent parts.

Ex. 9–1. Leonin: Organum.

Ex. 9–1 contains two voices of different rhythms. The upper part clearly dominates because of its greater activity. Both parts are unified through the use of recurrent patterns. This is a rudimentary kind of rhythmic association.

A rhythmic relationship of 2 to 1 ( ) is established in Ex. 9–2.

Ex. 9–2. Handel: Suite No. 7, Allegro.

[1] *Polyphonic,* in the commonly used sense, refers to contrapuntal music consisting of rhythmically independent voices.

A more active and more interesting upper line is accompanied by a slower, lower voice, which by itself is somewhat dull, since it consists mainly of continuous eighth notes outlining chords. However, it is a logical foil for the more active part, providing a solid tonal-rhythmic basis for it. (In the second measure the lower voice momentarily assumes a leading role.)

A different kind of supporting part is seen in Ex. 9–3. Here the two voices are completely independent, and each makes a perfectly acceptable melody.

Ex. 9–3. Marini: Sonata for Violin and Organ (two outer parts).

More equality of movement occurs in Ex. 9–4, and the distinction between main voice and accompaniment is less obvious than in Ex. 9–1 and Ex. 9–2.

Ex. 9–4. Haydn: Sonata in E-flat Major, III.

Both phrases are begun by the upper part alone, and its rhythmic diversity establishes it as the more interesting. In the second phrase, however, the voices enter imitatively, the lower part matching the upper for two measures. The close of the second phrase restores the original relationship.

Two parts compete for attention in Ex. 9–5. Such competition is not infrequent in two-voice textures and we tend to shift attention from one voice to another rather than hear two truly equal parts at one time.

Ex. 9–5. Ockeghem: *Missa Mi-mi, Agnus Dei.*

In contrast to Ex. 9–5, a clear rhythmic distinction between voices can be noted in Ex. 9–6. Both parts reveal individual contours and remain rhythmically independent. Although the lower (piano) voice clearly provides a strong tonal framework (*A* minor) for the upper, its rhythm makes it equally important.

Ex. 9–6. Piston: Sonata for Violin and Piano, III. © 1940 by Associated Music Publishers, Inc., New York. Reprinted by permission.

In Ex. 9–6 the rhythmic separation of parts 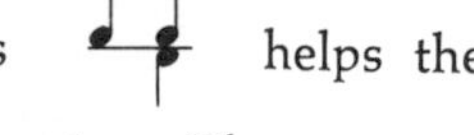 helps the listener to grasp more readily the activity of both voices. The recognition of equally important, simultaneously heard melodies is easier when the voices have contrasting rhythms. When identical rhythms occur simultaneously, independence is minimized, although other factors (pitch association, timbre, loudness, and contour) can produce independence of parts.

Ex. 9–7 contains the same kinds of activity in both parts. The listener is drawn from voice to voice, so to speak, by the give-and-take relationship that establishes the lower part as "borrower" from the upper. The lower voice systematically echoes the opening motive of the top voice and punctuates the movement of the upper voice with its octave leaps followed by rests.

Ex. 9–7. Bach: Two-voice Invention in E Minor.

The opening of Béla Bartók's First String Quartet, shown in Ex. 9–8, contains a rhythmic association similar to the Bach excerpt discussed previously. It affords an excellent study of two-voice association in contemporary music and illustrates several of the basic principles noted in this chapter.

Ex. 9–8. Bartók: String Quartet No. 1 (opening). Reprinted by permission of Boosey & Hawkes Inc. Sole agents for "Kultura" (Hungarian Trading Company) in the U.S.A.

We have surveyed three basic kinds of rhythmic associations thus far: (1) a predominant melody supported by a less engaging associate; (2) a combination of two independent parts, each of which makes an acceptable melody, yet one understood as a leading voice; and (3), two equally active parts which successively share patterns. When two voices have identical rhythms (note-against-note style), the upper part usually prevails. If there is independence it results from melodic direction, registration, or other aspects of pitch organization or instrumentation.

Pitch Association

Vocal Ranges and Spacing

In our beginning two-voice studies we shall be concerned only with the human voice, later expanding our study to include instrumental combinations. The necessity of performing all musical exercises and illustrations cannot be overstressed.

Consistent with most vocal compositions, we shall employ the following as practical voice ranges:

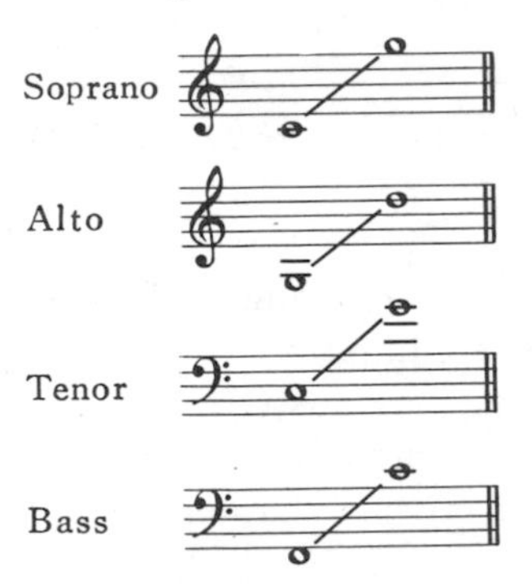

Each voice is granted a potential range of a twelfth. Needless to say, considerable care should be taken in approaching the extremities of any voice range. The effectiveness of the high or low areas is lost when overused, and singers are uncomfortable with melodies that remain in extreme lows or highs for long periods. Low tones in the bass, like high notes in the soprano, are often thin and lack definition.

The distances between two parts will depend partially on the particular voices used. For example, the widest gap that might occur between alto and soprano (in two-voice writing) would be two octaves, considering the given ranges of both voices. Although effective in isolated cases, such a wide space between two adjacent, unsupported voices would be rare. On the other hand, unisons represent the closest distance (or relationship) between voices and are quite common at cadences. The usual limit for two adjacent voices is the octave.

Two-voice combinations such as tenor with soprano, or alto with bass, may exploit wider spacings because of the natural separation of the individual registers. In these cases the interval of a twelfth should be regarded as normal, with two octaves as the usual limit of separation. Common two-voice spacings are shown in the following excerpts.

Ex. 9–9. Palestrina: *Sicut cervus.*

Ex. 9–10. Josquin des Près: *Tu pauperum refugium.*

Ex. 9–11. J. S. Bach: B Minor Mass, "Cum sancto spiritu."

The principles we have outlined for two-voice spacing can be summarized as follows: adjacent voices seldom exceed the octave, while non-adjacent pairs (such as soprano and tenor, or alto and bass) may move as far apart as two octaves. These principles apply even when more than two parts are present; they will be modified later when applied to instrumental textures.

Harmonic Considerations; Consonance and Dissonance

We have been concerned up to now with horizontal aspects of pitch. But if we are to combine melodies, there must exist a basis for the selection of the harmonic intervals that they will create. A glance at any two-voice composition will show a variety of vertical combinations, and further study will reveal that composers employ systematic techniques for organizing harmonic intervals and successions of interval roots.

We discussed interval roots in Chapter 2. Intervals that are most stable (octaves, fifths, and thirds) occur most often as the beginning and cadential harmonic intervals in two-voice textures. Because of the roles that they have played in music they are described as cadential, or basic, consonances. It is only in recent times that composers have chosen to begin or close on less stable inervals.

The perfect fourth and major and minor sixths seldom occur as cadential intervals in two voices. These intervals are regarded as decorative consonances.[2] The perfect fourth, in particular, is generally afforded a special kind of preparation and resolution in two-part music.

You should note in Ex. 9–12 that most on-the-beat intervals are consonances; all phrase beginnings and endings involve stable intervals. Dissonances arise from passing melodic activity as seen in measure 2, beat 4; measure 4, beat 2; measure 5, beat 4; and elsewhere in the piece.

Ex. 9–12. Bach: Overture in F Major for Harpsichord, Bourrée.

Motion Between Parts and Approaches to Structural Intervals

An important consideration in counterpoint is the directional relationship formed by the combined voices. When the parts proceed in opposite directions they produce *contrary motion.* Contrary motion is an important feature of cadences in two-voice textures, and it is often found in the interior of a phrase as well. Any two-voice work will reveal a variety of motion types: *similar, parallel,* and *oblique.* Those are illustrated in the examples below.

[2] This applies, of course, only to tonal music.

Ex. 9–13a. Contrary motion.

Similar motion results from movements in the same direction but which involve changing interval combinations.

Ex. 9–13b. Similar motion.

Parallel motion occurs when both voices move in the same direction while maintaining the same generic intervallic distance.

Ex. 9–13c. Parallel motion.

Oblique motion is produced by movement in one voice with a stationary second voice, whether in sustained or repeated tone, or one repeated with intervening rests.

Ex. 9–13d. Oblique motion.

Perform Ex. 9–14, then study its counterpoint, especially the types of motion that are employed.

Ex. 9–14. J. C. Bach: In dich hab ich gehoffet, Herr.

A further consideration of contrapuntal motion involves the approach to cadential consonances, particularly the octave, fifth, and unison. Since these intervals produce stability, it is logical that they have been used consistently as the basis for achieving musical repose. However, when these intervals are used in uninterrupted successions they produce an effect of mutual dependence that opposes the very nature of counterpoint, which is melodic independence.

For these reasons, and to avoid monotonous repetition, composers have generally avoided consecutive fifths, octaves, and unisons in contrapuntal writing. Furthermore, the movement to these intervals is often by contrary motion, with at least one voice (or both) moving by step. Movement in contrary motion to basic intervals is more often found where these intervals fall on strong beats, or strong parts of the beat, as in Ex. 9–15.

Ex. 9–15. Zachau: *Vom Himmel hoch da komm ich her.*

In Ex. 9–15 the composer has used a wide variety of consonances as basic intervals. Unstable intervals are the result of decorative patterns. The choice of intervals used and, to a large degree, the way in which they are used, differ somewhat between individual musical styles. However, the proportion of thirds and sixths usually exceeds that of fifths, octaves, unisons, and fourths.

A comparison of Ex. 9–16 with Ex. 9–17 will suggest the intervallic variety possible in two-voice writing of different historical periods.

Ex. 9–16. Bach: Two-voice Invention in D Minor.

Ex. 9–17. Hindemith: *Das Marienleben.* © 1924 by B. Schott's Soehne-Mainz, Renewed 1951. Reprinted by permission.

In Ex. 9–16 Bach has relied primarily upon thirds and sixths, as on-the-beat sonorities. Not until the cadence to *A* is a prominent octave heard. It is approached by contrary motion. The excerpt by Hindemith (Ex. 9–17) reveals considerably greater intervallic variety, but it shows a kinship to the Bach example in the way fifths and octaves are approached by contrary motion.

Rhythm also affects vertical relationships. Fifths and octaves that fall on strong beats naturally attract more attention than those falling on weak beats, and so the approach to these cadential intervals is controlled more carefully. Fifths, octaves, or unisons on strong beats are usually approached by contrary or oblique motion, yet similar motion is not uncommon at cadences to the octave. In such cases the upper voice most often moves by step, while the lower voice skips up or down, as in Ex. 9—18a and Ex. 9–18b. Final cadences to a perfect fifth (which are rare after the 16th century) are almost never approached by similar motion.

Ex. 9–18a. Bach: Two-voice Invention in G Major.

Ex. 9–18b. Bach: Two-voice Invention in D Minor.

In two-voice textures perfect fourths seldom are used as cadential intervals or between basic pitches that approach a cadence. Rather, fourths usually occur within the interior of a phrase. Typical appearances of the interval of the fourth in two-voice writing occur in the next excerpt.

Ex. 9–19. Bach: Suite in B Minor, Allemande.

The fourths found in this example involve either a step approach, step resolution, or both. Like fifths, most accented fourths in two-voice textures are reached by contrary motion, seldom by parallel or similar motion. Examples of both voices moving in similar motion by skips to a fourth are rare. As we shall see, fourths usually resolve to thirds. When parallel fourths do occur, they generally involve duration of less than the prevailing basic duration. Thirds occur cadentially, while sixths seldom do. Unlike other consonances, these intervals are often approached by similar and parallel motion, as well as by contrary and oblique motion. As a rule, composers avoid more than three parallel thirds or sixths consecutively. When these do occur, they are generally mixtures of major and minor rather than three consecutive major or three consecutive minor thirds or sixths. Parallel motion can destroy melodic independence and undermine tonality.

The degree to which intervallic variety and treatment contribute to interesting counterpoint is apparent in the following Mozart illustration.

Ex. 9–20. Mozart: Quartet in D Major, K. 575, IV.

While subject to exceptions, the following principles of intervallic succession and melodic movement are maintained in most two-voice counterpoint and should be adopted and applied in written assignments.

Summation of Melodic Movement
and Intervallic Succession of Two-voice Combinations in Tonal Music

1. Any succession of parallel thirds or sixths should include a mixture of both major and minor thirds or sixths. For example, a major third will most often be followed by a minor third, or a minor sixth will generally follow a major sixth. (See 1 of Ex. 9–20.)
2. Simultaneous leaps in both voices are rare; when they occur, they usually will be in contrary motion. (See 2 of Ex. 9–20.)
3. Open consonances (octaves, fifths, fourths, and unisons) on strong beats are usually approached in contrary motion. (See 3 of Ex. 9–20.)
4. A skip in one voice is usually balanced by a step or no motion in the other. (See 4 of Ex. 9–20.)
5. Melodic or harmonic tritones, like most augmented or diminished intervals, usually resolve by step. (See 5 of Ex. 9–20.)
6. Parallel and consecutive fifths, octaves, fourths, and unisons are generally avoided. (See Ex. 9–21 a–d below.)

Ex. 9–21a. Parallel fifths (avoid).

Ex. 9–21b. Parallel octaves (avoid).

Ex. 9–21c. Consecutive fifths (avoid).

Ex. 9–21d. Consecutive octaves (avoid).

Contrapuntal Treatment of Unstable Intervals

The unstable and ambiguous quality of the melodic tritone gives it a special quality of expressiveness that many composers have favored, as in Ex. 9–22.

Ex. 9–22. Wagner: *Tritsan und Isolde,* Act II.

The tritone is perhaps most prominent where it occurs between the subdominant and the leading tone (4–7) of the major or minor scale.

Ex. 9–23. Tritones in major-minor scales.

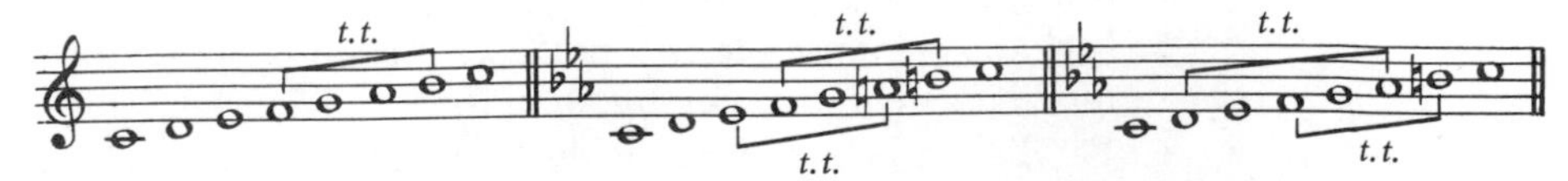

This relationship occurs both melodically and harmonically in two-voice counterpoint, and is quite effective in developing melodic or harmonic tension and in building strong "resolution tendencies." We shall see in subsequent study that the tritone figures significantly in two-voice cadences.

There are predictable treatments of melodic and harmonic tritones. Some of the more common treatments are shown in Ex. 9–24.

1. Skips up or down an augmented fourth are usually followed by stepwise motion in the same direction as the skip. This is generally true with *all* augmented intervals.
2. Like skips of an augmented fourth, skips of an ascending or descending diminished fifth are normally succeeded by stepwise motion, but generally in the *opposite* direction from the skip. This is usually true with all diminished intervals.
3. Tritone leaps, like most leaps, are most often approached by step, generally in the opposite direction from the leap.
4. Leaps that follow melodic tritones occur in the opposite direction. They frequently resolve to pitches that form a step progression with one member of the tritone.
5. Harmonic tritones formed by two voices usually resolve by stepwise movement common to melodic tritones. (Augmented fourths expand by step, while diminished fifths contract.)

Relate all melodic and harmonic tritones in Ex. 9–24a and Ex. 9–24b with the principles described above.

Ex. 9–24a. Bach: Suite in A Major, Courante.

Ex. 9–24b. Haydn: Sonata in E-flat Major, Minuet.

Ex. 9–24c. Bach: Minuet (*Little Notebook of Anna Magdalena Bach*).

Most of the tritones in these excerpts are the result of decorative patterns. Rarely are both members of a harmonic tritone basic pitches. Furthermore, the tritone illustrated in Ex. 9–24a and 9–24b involves the 4–7 scale degree relationship, while the tritones in Ex. 9–24c occur in a chromatic passage leading to the dominant.

Organization of Two-voice Phrases

The contour relationship of both voices is a basic consideration in organizing a two-voice phrase. If one voice is a mere follower, reaching high and low peaks simultaneously with the other, its interest is diminished in the same way that rhythmic duplication minimizes the independence of parts.

In Ex. 9–25 the lower voice is essentially accompanimental. Its contour, like the upper part, is primarily descending, so its independence is created mainly by rhythm.

Ex. 9–25. Haydn: Sonata in D Major, II.

In contrast to Ex. 9–25, the voices in Ex. 9–26 have more independent melodic curves. Here the voices *take turns* as predominant parts, but even so, they outline basic pitches in essentially contrary motion, and the high and low points of succeeding motives occur one after the other rather than simultaneously.

Ex. 9–26. Bach: Two-voice Invention in D Major.

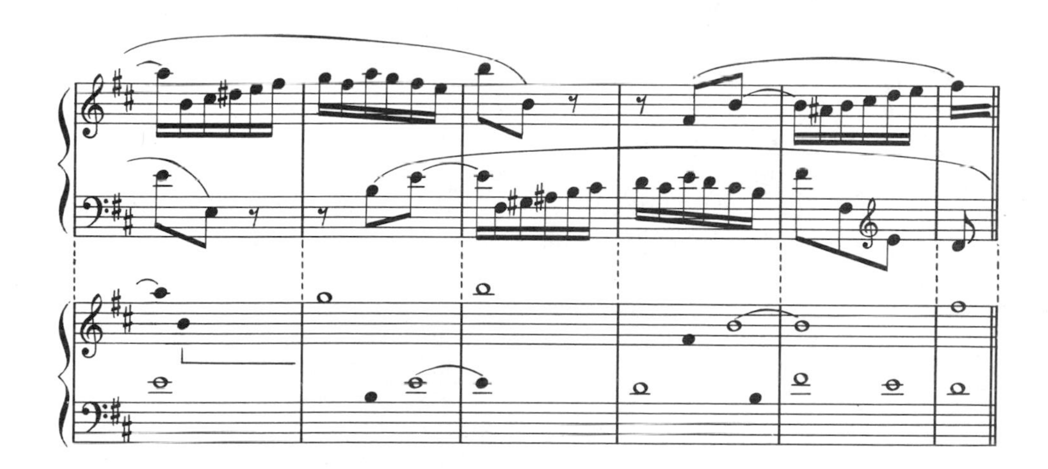

Two equal voices compete imitatively in Ex. 9–27. Although they use identical melodic materials, successively, the two voices are delineated effectively by two simple processes. Each successive basic interval is approached through contrary motion. The highest note of the upper line occurs with the lowest note of the bottom line. Furthermore, each basic pitch, as shown in the reduction, is approached in contrary motion. The effectiveness of the example illustrates the degree to which contrasting contours can contribute to melodic interest and independence, even when other factors are virtually equal.

Ex. 9–27. C.P.E. Bach: Keyboard Sonata.

Pitch Material in Tonal Music

A glance at any of the preceding musical examples will confirm the fact that both voices in most two-voice textures employ the same key or mode. We also have seen that the addition of a second part often clarifies the tonic in a melody whose tonality is ambiguous. Comparing Ex. 9–28 and Ex. 9–29, we find that the tonic (*A-flat*) is strongly asserted by both voices in Ex. 9–28, but only by the lower part in Ex. 9–29. The upper voice of the latter example is apparently in *E-flat* (considered as a separate line), while the lower clearly establishes *A-flat* (the actual tonic of the combined parts).

Ex. 9–28. Bach: Fugue in A-flat Major (*Well-tempered Clavier,* Book I).

Ex. 9–29. J.S. Bach: Prelude in A-flat Major (*Well-tempered Clavier,* Book I).

Although *both* parts must be considered in any discussion of tonality, the lower voice, because it is the tonal foundation, often exerts more *tonal force* than the upper. This is well illustrated in Ex. 9–29, which is heard in *A-flat* primarily because of the pull toward *A-flat* created by the lower voice.

Considerable variety of pitch resources has been used in the two parts of Ex. 9–30. The tonality is *D,* but it incorporates all twelve notes of a chromatic scale.

Ex. 9–30. Hindemith: *Ludus Tonalis,* Fugue in F © 1943 by Schott & Co., Ltd., London. Reprinted by permission.

Cross Relation

Cross relation (sometimes called *false relation*) results when chromatic variants of the same note occur in close succession between *different* voices. In Ex. 9–31, for instance, *G-sharp* in the lower part is followed by *G-natural* in the lower. A cross relation results, although the melodic effect of each voice is perfectly satisfactory.

Ex. 9–31. Cross relation in two voices.

Several generalizations about cross relations can be made:

1. Ascending movement in one part with descending movement in the other frequently creates acceptable cross relations, as in Ex. 9–31, which involves the ascending and descending forms of the melodic minor scale.
2. Cross relations occur naturally from combinations of basic diatonic notes in one part with embellishing chromatic alterations in another.

Chromatic alterations, such as those in Ex. 9–32, are essentially decorative.

Ex. 9–32. Cross relation.

3. Mutation, as found in Ex. 9–33 with exchanges of modes from minor to major, frequently results in cross relation.

Ex. 9–33. Cross relation.

Some composers of the twentieth century have created further independence of lines by employing two keys simultaneously, thus increasing the probability of cross relations.

Ex. 9–34. Bitonality.

Exercises

For more detailed assignments see *Materials and Structure of Music I, Workbook,* Chapter 9.

1. Invent two-voice rhythmic phrases of eight measures, choosing rhythms from examples in the beginning of the chapter as a basis for repetition.
2. Identify the kinds of rhythmic associations of several examples in this chapter.
3. Write out the normal ranges of soprano, alto, tenor, and bass voices.
4. Construct all of the diatonic intervals within an octave span and label their precise sizes; then identify each as a basic or decorative consonance or dissonance.
5. Discuss Ex. 9–12 from the standpoint of types of motion, rhythmic association, treatments of consonant and dissonant intervals, and dual contours. What factors tend most to unify the composition?
6. Transpose the upper voice of Ex. 9–12 down a perfect fifth and add a new bass, employing an accompanimental rhythmic association and emphasizing basic and decorative consonances.
7. Invent three phrases, each illustrating a different rhythmic association. Use any pitch materials and vertical combinations that interest you. Vary the length, tempo, meter, and mood of each phrase.

Chapter Ten

Continuation of Two-Voice Combinations

The Basic Framework

Recall that most melodies have an underlying structure whose pitches constitute a basic melody. The basic melodies of two parts form a basic framework. All of the factors that determine the basic pitches of a single line—duration, contour, step progression, metric accent, cadence pitches, etc.—contribute to the content of the basic framework. It is merely two basic melodies combined in their appropriate vertical relationships.

The next example shows three things: (1) a musical passage of two voices, (2) a reduction of the two lines to a basic framework, and (3) a synopsis of implied chords.

Ex. 10–1. Bach: Overture in F for Harpsichord, Bourée.

In Ex. 10–2 the harmonic progression is far simpler, although the cross relations between *B-natural* and *B-flat* in measures 2 and 4 make the excerpt sound more complicated. The first four measures are the elaboration of a single chord, as shown in the harmonic reduction of the excerpt.

Ex. 10–2. Bartók: *Mikrokosmos.*

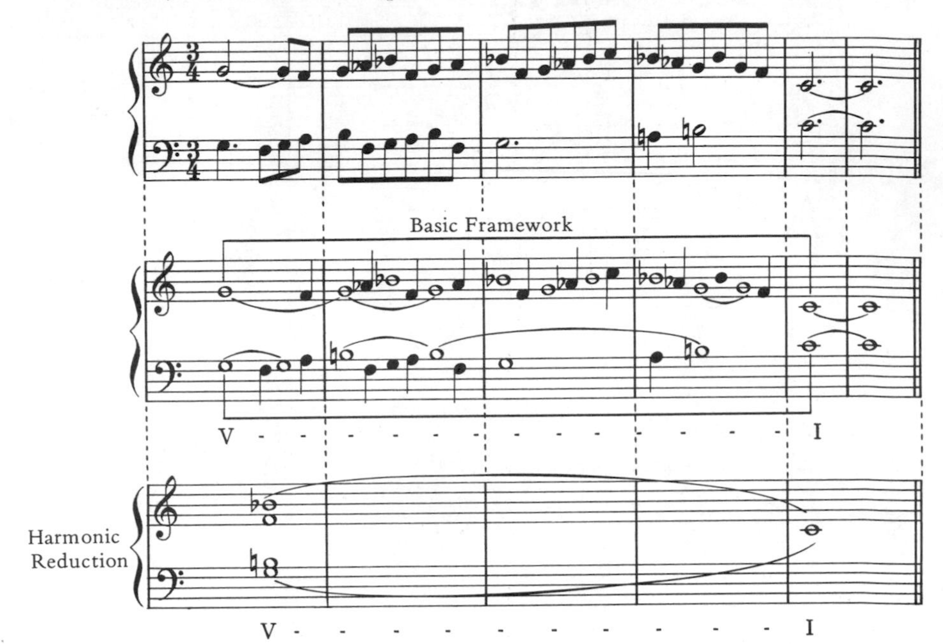

Cadences in Two-voice Textures

Cadences are significant events in any composition, regardless of the music's harmonic or melodic style, its texture, or its overall form. It is at cadences that both tonal and rhythmic elements must be drawn to a convincing and satisfying conclusion, whether temporary or permanent.

Three major events usually occur when a cadence takes place: (1) there is a slackening of motion, usually produced by longer durations; (2) a tonal center is in some way confirmed; and (3) consonant intervals occur between the two parts. Compare the cadence patterns found in the previous example by Bartók and those found in Exs. 10–3 and 10–4. Although these three composers lived in three different centuries (twentieth, sixteenth, and eighteenth), each confirms our statement of cadential principles.

Ex. 10–3. Josquin des Près: Chanson.

Ex. 10–4. Bach: Two-voice Invention in D Minor.

In each of these three passages the cadence occurs on a strong beat. Cadences that fall on weak beats or weak parts of the beat (sometimes called "feminine endings") are exceptions. Prominence is assured cadential tones because of their duration (usually more than one beat), their strong metric location, and their obvious importance as the last tone of a melodic pattern. Furthermore, this prominence is often signaled by slowing the melodic pace with longer note values introduced in the approach to the cadence. Such is the case in the next-to-last measure of Example 10–4.

Composers sometimes prolong activity in one voice after the cadential tone has been reached. Through such an extension, each voice maintains its individuality and independence into the cadence proper. In Ex. 10–5, the lower voice asserts cadence pitch *A*, while the upper voice, having touched upon a^1, continues down by a series of leaps to the lower *a*.

Ex. 10–5. Bach: Two-voice Invention in A Minor.

Any basic consonance (unison, octave, fifth, third) may occur as the cadential sonority of a two-voice work so long as it confirms the prevailing tonality. Regardless of the interval, the tonic pitch is always the lower tone at a final cadence. (It may also be in the upper part if the cadential interval is an octave or unison.) Final cadences to intervals other than basic or cadential consonances are exceptional.

The particular choice of cadential interval is determined by the prevailing tonality, the kind of melodic activity that reaches its fulfillment in the cadence, and the composer's choice of sonority. The octave is common as a closing sonority, and it and the unison are the strongest in terms of tonal stability. The perfect fifth, though embodying a strong tonal relationship, is not found as often in two-voice cadences as octaves, unisons, or thirds. Both major and minor thirds, the choice of which is determined primarily by the mode of the work, occur frequently.

The cadential interval is often called the *ultimate interval,* and the interval that immediately precedes it is called the *penultimate,* or *approach, interval.* Cadence patterns are formed by the movement from an approach interval to an ultimate interval. Some of the most common two-voice cadence patterns are shown in Ex. 10–6.

Ex. 10–6. Basic cadences in two voices (approach and ultimate intervals).

(a) Stepwise contrary motion.

Tonic: C

(b) Contrary motion, one voice moving by step.

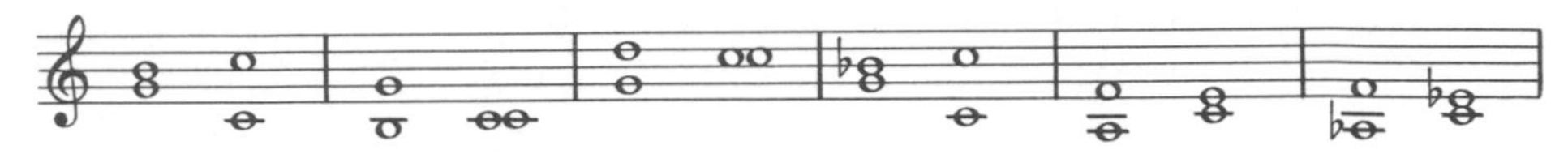

Tonic: C

(c) Similar or parallel motion.

Tonic: C

(d) Skips in contrary motion.

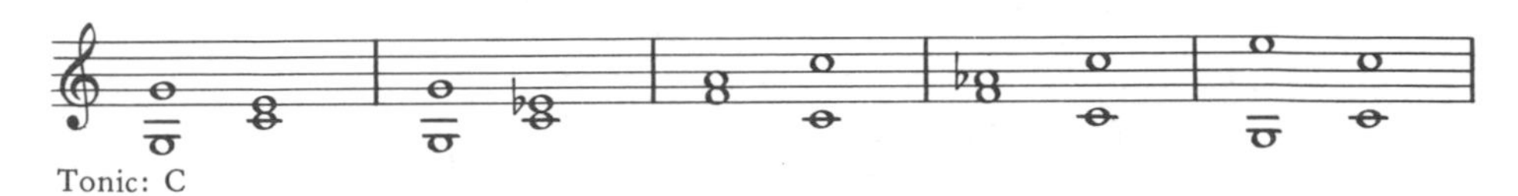

Tonic: C

Various forms of scales are implicit in the different cadential patterns, and the cadence pattern is sometimes described according to the scale degree contained in each voice. For instance, the first pattern in Ex. 10–6a might be indicated as 7–8/2–1 and the first pattern in Ex. 10–6b as 7–8/5–1.

The numbers 7–8 indicate movement from leading tone (or subtonic) to tonic, whereas 2–1 indicates a descent from supertonic to tonic. Each pattern constitutes an intervallic framework that results from melodic movement at the cadence. Moreover, any of the basic pitches of each could be decorated with passing tones, neighbors, or other elaborative pitches and retain the basic pattern.

Two voices moving in similar motion to a perfect fifth or octave produce the *direct fifth* or *direct octave*. This has been generally avoided in two-voice cadences, except when the upper voice moves by step.

It is significant that all of the approach intervals of the patterns shown in Ex. 10–6 contain cadential and decorative consonances. Perfect fourths or tritones do not occur frequently as approach intervals in two-voice writing.

Modal Cadences in Two Voices

Earlier we discussed some of the characteristics associated with modal melodies, and the group of scales known as modes. Just as modal melodies exploit certain characteristic interval relationships, so two-voice combinations often adhere to a group of basic cadence patterns that incorporate modal patterns. Many of these patterns are not limited in use to modal melodies but are also found in compositions oriented around major-minor scales, and more chromatic forms. The cadences illustrated in Ex. 10–7 involve the basic pattern $\begin{matrix}7-8\\2-1\end{matrix}$ or its inversion, $\begin{matrix}2-1\\7-8\end{matrix}$.

Ex. 10–7a. Willaert (Aeolian mode).

Ex. 10–7b. Giovanni de Florentia (Phrygian mode).

Ex. 10–7c. Josquin des Près (Dorian mode).

Aeolian and Dorian compositions, as shown in Ex. 10–7a and 10–7c, usually employ terminal cadences that approach tonic from the whole step below and the whole step above, while Phrygian cadences approach tonic from the whole step below and the half step above.

Cadences in the Lydian mode, as in major and minor, involve a leading tone to tonic ascent while the other voice (usually the lower) moves by a descending whole step from 2–1.

Mixolydian cadences, like Dorian and Aeolian, contain no half step; tonic is approached by whole step below and above tonic. All of these are cadences to the octave or unison, reached by contrary motion. Other patterns can be found in two-voice textures employing modal melodies, but the octave or unison as ultimate intervals being most common.

Two-voice Cadences in Major and Minor Keys

Major or minor scales are akin to altered Dorian, Phrygian, Mixolydian, and Aeolian modes in which the seventh degree has been raised a semitone.

In Ex. 10–8 a cadential *F-sharp* has been introduced in two cadences to create a leading tone, thereby emphasizing *G* as a tonic. The scale structure of the whole example is a mixture of *G* Mixolydian and *G* major.

Ex. 10–8. Obrecht: *Missa Sine Nomine,* Agnus Dei.

Terminal Cadences

The most common final cadence pattern of music written during the past five hundred years is the V-I cadence. It is comprised, usually, of the following: (1) melodic movement in the lower part up a perfect fourth or down a perfect fifth, and (2) motion in the upper voice from leading tone to tonic. The roots of the intervals that form the V-I pattern correspond to the dominant and tonic degrees of the prevailing tonality, as illustrated in Ex. 10–9.

Ex. 10–9. Handel.

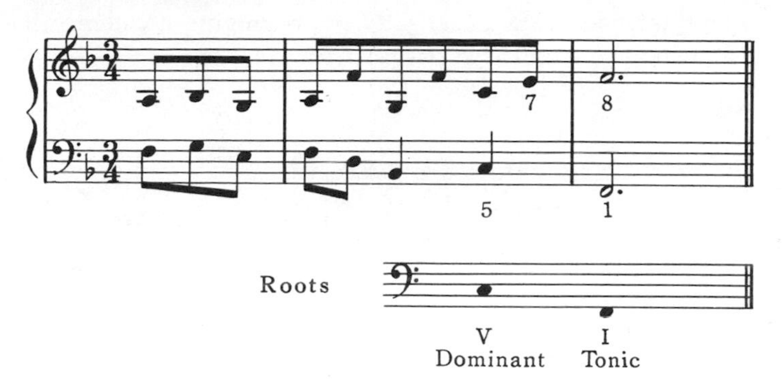

A summary of principles governing two-voice cadences will provide you with some guidance in composing examples of your own.

1. Contrary motion prevails, although direct octaves may be found when the upper voice moves by step.

Ex. 10–10.

2. Ascending movement to tonic is most often by semitone (leading tone to tonic), but movement by a whole step (subtonic to tonic) also may be found.

Ex. 10–11.

3. The cadential interval frequently occurs on a strong beat.

Ex. 10–12.

Cadences often are embellished by decorative pitches. *Codettas,* extensions of musical activity prolonging a cadence, frequently occur as extensions of these basic patterns.

Ex. 10–13.

Progressive Cadences

Composers have employed a great variety of patterns to terminate interior sections of two-voice compositions. The types fall into two principal groups: progressive and transient-terminal cadences.

While the possibilities for creating progressive cadences are enormous, several basic observations can be made about them: (1) Tonic usually will not be the *root* of the cadential interval (although some progressive cadences do include tonic); (2) active pitches such as the leading tone or subdominant usually will be members of the cadential interval; (3) decorative consonances as well as cadential consonances (and even dissonances) may occur as cadential intervals; (4) rhythmic activity may be maintained in one or even both voices, thus lessening the cadential effect.

In Ex. 10–14 a progressive cadence in the key of *b* minor occurs in measure 6.

Ex. 10–14. Handel: Fughetta.

The cadential major third is formed by the leading tone *A-sharp* and *F-sharp*. The root of this interval, *F-sharp,* is the dominant of *b* minor; "more to follow" is strongly implied. A progressive cadence to an interval whose root is the dominant of a key is traditionally called a *half cadence.*

Another form of progressive cadence involves root movement from the dominant to the submediant (V to VI). The resulting progression is deceptive because anticipated movement from the dominant to the tonic root is evaded. This pattern, commonly called a *deceptive cadence,* is exemplified in measure 4 of Ex. 10–15.

Ex. 10–15. Bach: Two-voice Invention in D Major.

Anticipated movement to *D* in the lower part is replaced by movement to *B,* the submediant, in a root progression up a second. The root of the approach interval in the deceptive cadence is usually the dominant (V), which in moving to the submediant creates the root progression V–VI. (Deceptive cadences involving other root progressions occur, as we shall see later.)

In closing this discussion it should be noted that the tritone, although not used often as a basic harmonic interval in final cadences, can be found as the approach interval in progressive (and transient-terminal) cadences. Cadential tritones are usually the product of decorative activity in one or both voices.

Cadence Patterns and Change of Tonal Center

Cadences that confirm or imply changes of tonal center are an important means of creating tonal variety and delineating melodic form. Such cadences, occurring at phrase or sectional closes, are often of the V–I group, although one may find $\begin{smallmatrix}7-8\\2-1\end{smallmatrix}$ cadences and other cadences which are terminal in effect. As in final cadences, the root of the cadential interval is generally in the lower voice.

The opening eleven measures of Ex. 10–16 contain a terminal cadence to *G,* a transient-terminal cadence to *B-flat,* and a modulation to *D* minor. All of the cadences are elaborations of the basic V–I pattern. Each marks the close of a phrase signaled by longer durations in one of the voices. Melodic activity continues in the other voice, however, thus diminishing the rhythmic effect of caesura.

Ex. 10–16. Bach: Two-Part Invention in G Minor.

Measures 5 and 6 contain a modulatory sequence, which represents a patterned means of effecting a change of key from *G* minor to *D* minor through *B-flat* major. Two shifts of tonality, each up a third and each punctuated by a cadence, bring about the change.

Root Relations in the Two-voice Frame

The melodic and harmonic action of the cadence has been described in terms of root relations such as V-I, V-VI, I-V, and so forth. Similarly, any interval pattern can be described with roman numerals representing the roots of basic intervals. In other words, having discovered the basic harmonic intervals and their roots, one can represent their relationship to *tonic* by using a roman numeral for each scale degree.

The passage of Ex. 10–17 consists of the *basic* harmonic movement I-VI-II-V-I, as a study of the accompanying reduction will show.

Ex. 10–17.

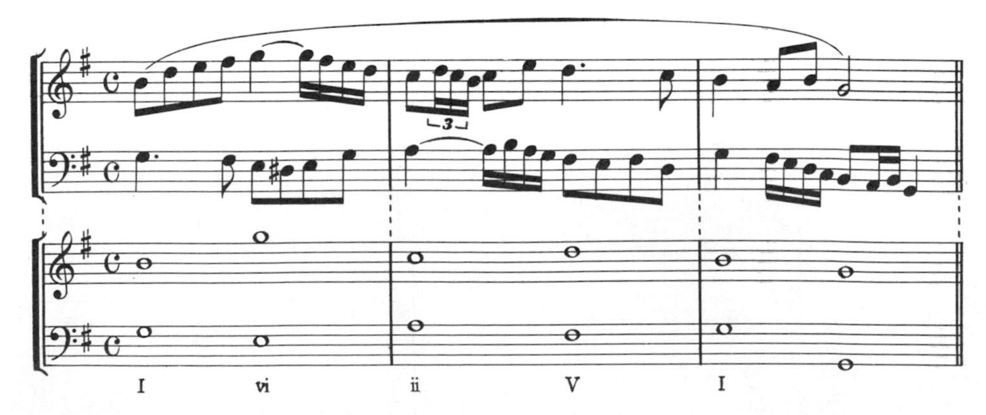

When a change of tonality occurs, the same procedure can be used, as shown in Ex. 10–18. The application of these analytical symbols will be discussed extensively in subsequent chapters. They present a convenient way for both planning and analyzing the basis of two-voice writing.

Ex. 10–18. Handel: Suite, Allemande.

Implied Triads

The harmonic intervals that occur in two-voice music often imply harmonic units more complex than the intervals themselves, namely chords. The most common chordal unit in tonal music is the *triad,* which is a chord of three different pitch classes, often arranged in stacked thirds. Two voices often *imply* triadic chords and chord progressions, even though they alone cannot produce vertical arrangements of three different pitches.

The basic and secondary pitches in one voice often will correspond to those in the accompanying voice. In some instances these basic and secondary pitches will complement each other, so that together they form a complete harmonic unit. Many two-voice textures from the classic and romantic periods of music history consist of arpeggiations of simple chords, as the excerpt in Ex. 10–19 illustrates. The resultant harmonic progression—created solely from combined melodic play—is shown on the staff below the music.

Ex. 10–19. Mozart: Sonata for Piano in C Major, I, K. 545.

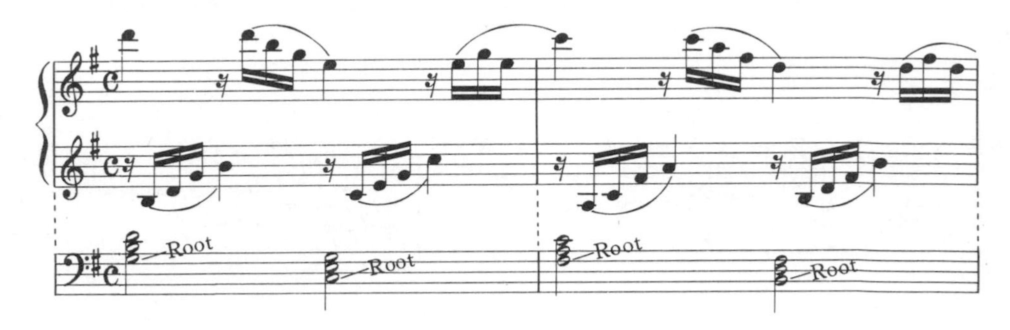

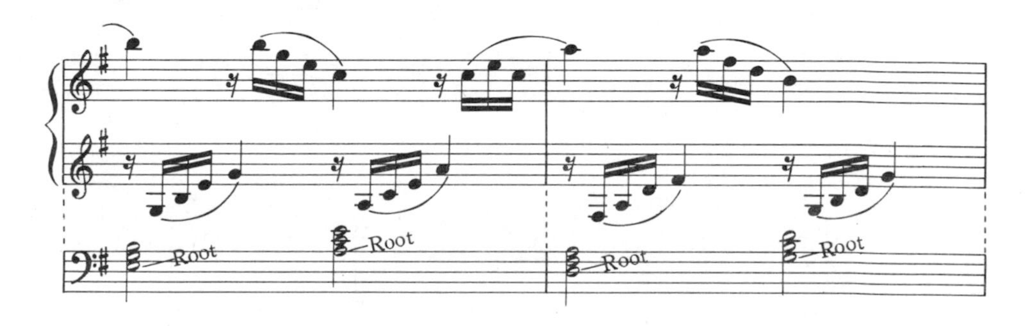

In the next excerpt two voices project a different yet equally clear harmonic progression complete with some decorative patterns, such as the suspensions denoted by *sus.*

Ex. 10–20a. Bach: *Twelve Little Preludes,* Prelude No. 1.

Counterpoint in this passage is minimal, being achieved primarily by rhythm. Directional contrasts and suspension figures produce further independence of parts.

Example 10–20b shows the chordal basis of 10–20a distributed among four voices. Examples such as this show clearly how chords may form the basis for melodic combinations. While our concern in this unit is primarily with linear matters, a study of tonal counterpoint must take into account the interrelationship between melody and harmony. Although melody and harmony always interact to some degree in effecting a contrapuntal texture, it is emphasis on linear independence that creates counterpoint.

Ex. 10–20b. Chordal realization of Ex. 10–20a.

Exercises

For more detailed assignments see *Materials and Structure of Music I, Workbook,* Chapter 10.

1. Invent ten two-voice cadences to the note *D*, using a variety of directional patterns. Then elaborate several of them by interpolating passing and neighboring tones.
2. Use the succession of roots shown in Ex. 10–17 as the basis for eight measures of two-voice counterpoint in $\frac{6}{8}$ meter. Adapt the root relations of the example to the key of *E-flat* major. Employ a texture similar to that of Ex. 10–17.
3. Extract an analysis of the implied triads in Ex. 10–18.
4. Make up two-measure phrases in each of the following modes: Dorian, Phrygian, Mixolydian, and Aeolian. Employ cadences typical of such modal compositions.
5. Compose a singable melody in $\frac{5}{4}$ meter, *c* minor, that outlines the harmonic pattern: I–VI–IV–V IV–II–V–I. Then add a supporting voice.
6. Treat the notes *F, A-flat, E, C-sharp,* and *D* as root, third, and fifth of major and minor triads, writing these on manuscript paper.
7. Use the harmonic pattern given in No. 5 as the basis for improvising a two-voice phrase at the keyboard.
8. Write out a modal popular tune and make a sketch of its implied harmonic basis; add a simple accompanying lower part.

Chapter Eleven

Continuation of Two-Voice Combinations

Decorative Patterns

Passing Tones

When one voice is added to another, a new dimension is created in the form of harmonic intervals. Thus our perception of basic and decorative pitches in two-voice combinations is affected by both melodic and harmonic relationships.

The roles of decorative and basic pitches in a single melody usually will be confirmed by the accompanying melody. This is illustrated in Example 11–1, where the decorative pitches of the melody are heard as nonchord tones in association with the lower voice.

Ex. 11–1.

Typical passing tones are shown next in Ex. 11–2. They occur in both voices, and in some instances they occur simultaneously. Both diatonic and chromatic forms occur, filling in melodic spans as small as the major second and as large as the perfect fourth. Dissonance between voices is a common byproduct of these motions.

Ex. 11–2. Illustrations of passing tones.

Play Ex. 11–3 and observe the effect of all passing tones.

Ex. 11–3. Frescobaldi: *Canzona dopo l'Epistola.*

In identifying decorative tones it is important to relate them to basic pitches. For example, the e^1 (top voice) after the first beat of measure 3 is a passing tone, although it forms a consonance (fifth) with the lower voice (a^1). However, the e^1 connects two basic pitches, f^1 and d^1 (as does the e^1 on the third beat of the same measure), so it is a passing tone. The f^1 is a basic pitch both because of its duration, its metric position, and because it forms a step progression with the preceding g^1 and the e^1 of the next measure.

Neighbor Tones

Neighbor tones are embellishing notes above or below more basic pitches. For example, the e^2 in figure *a* is a dissonant lower neighbor to the basic pitch f,^{2} while the g^2 in *b*

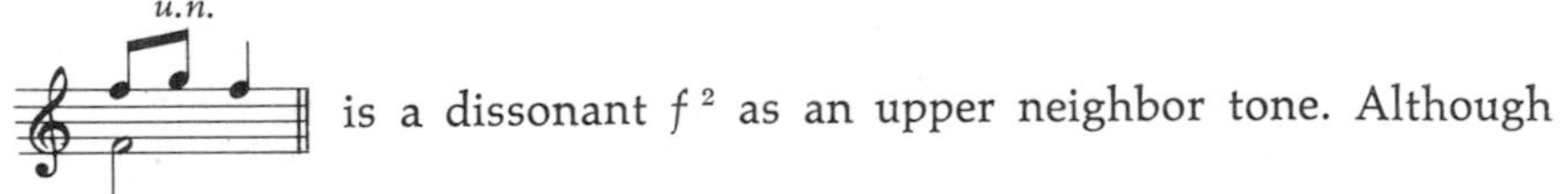

is a dissonant f^2 as an upper neighbor tone. Although neighbor tones appear most often as rhythmically unaccented, they may occur in an accented position, as in *c*.

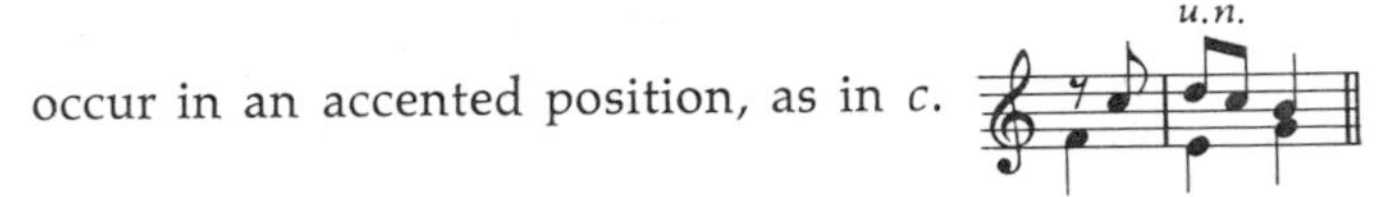

Like the passing tone, upper or lower neighbor tones may occur without creating harmonic dissonance. For example, in figure *d* the c^2 is a melodic neighbor tone to b^1, but it does not form a dissonance with the e^1 of the lower voice.

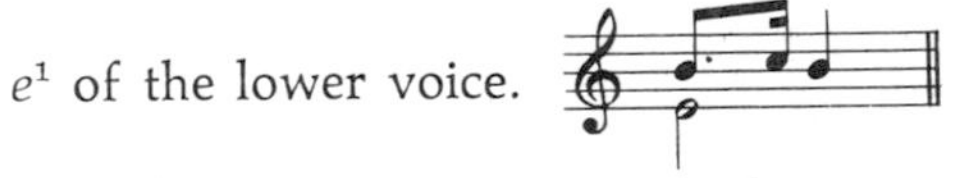

The neighbor tone, which may occur as a chromatic or diatonic embellishment, is a useful figure for developing rhythmic activity while focusing attention on one pitch. This pattern frequently forms two successive dissonances with an accompanying voice, as in *e*.

Both neighbor and passing tones occur in Ex. 11–4. Identify them and relate them to the structural pitches they embellish.

Ex. 11–4. Bach: Two-Voice Invention in F Minor.

Suspension

In Chapter 8 we described the suspension as a kind of melodic delaying action, in which a basic or secondary pitch is sustained through a subsequent rhythmic accent, then resolved by step on the following weak beat to another basic pitch. The three elements that form the suspension figure are shown:

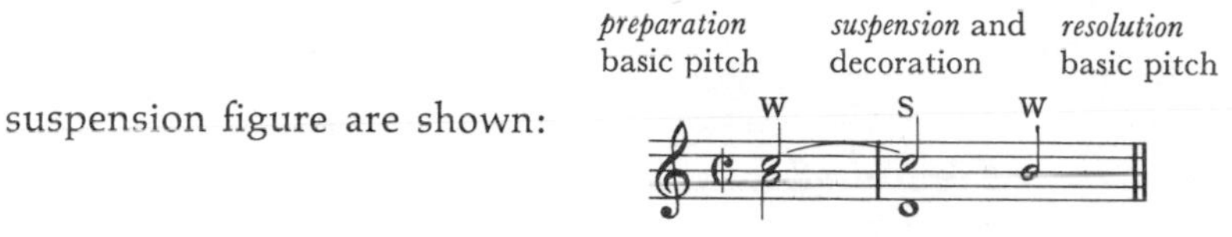

With the addition of a second voice, a dissonance usually is created at the midpoint of the pattern, which completes a process of stability-instability-stability. We shall study first the suspension figure as a cadential embellishment, although its use is by no means limited to cadences.

Consider two versions of a $\begin{matrix}7\text{–}8\\2\text{–}1\end{matrix}$ cadence to *g*, the second being the elaboration of the first through the use of a suspension figure.

Ex. 11–5a. Cadence to *G*.

Ex. 11–5b. Elaborated with suspension.

In the second version the drop from g^1 to f^1 *sharp*, in the upper part, has been delayed, or suspended. Several observations pertinent to the approach to and resolution of the suspended g^1 may be made:

1. g^1 was *prepared* as a consonance (upper member of a minor third), on the last beat of measure 1.

2. g^1 was sustained into the next strong beat so that it created a dissonance (minor seventh) with the lower voice.
3. g^1 resolved by descending step to f^1*-sharp*—a consonance (major sixth)—on the subsequent weak beat.

As mentioned earlier the suspension is a figure of three parts: *preparation, suspension,* and *resolution.*

Preparation, then, refers to the point at which the suspended pitch (g^1) is introduced. The preparation is usually as long as the suspension (dissonance) itself. In Ex. 11–6, the preparations are of differing lengths.

Ex. 11–6. Suspensions.

In *a* through *c* of Ex. 11–6 the preparations are at least as long as the basic duration and they are no shorter than the dissonance itself. A less typical pattern is shown in Ex. 11–6d, where the preparation is shorter than the suspended tone.

Suspension patterns usually are described by the interval formed between the two voices at the point of suspension (or dissonance) and the interval of resolution. For instance, in Ex. 11–7 a seventh is formed by suspending f^2, which becomes a sixth when it resolves to e^2. Make certain that you don't confuse these *harmonic* denotations with the *melodic* denotations (scale degrees) we used earlier in Chapter 10.

Ex. 11–7. Suspensions.

The resulting pattern is a 7–6 suspension. There are five basic types of suspensions: 7–6, 4–3, 6–5, 9–8, and 2–3. Except for the 2–3 suspension, all of these patterns have one important common feature: the suspension pitch is in the *upper voice*. Ex. 11–8 shows 4–3 suspensions.

Ex. 11–8. 4–3 suspensions.

The 6–5 suspension involves a decorative consonance resolving to a cadential consonance, and it occurs frequently in the approach to a V-I cadence, as in Ex. 11–9 (*a*).

Ex. 11–9. 6–5 suspensions.

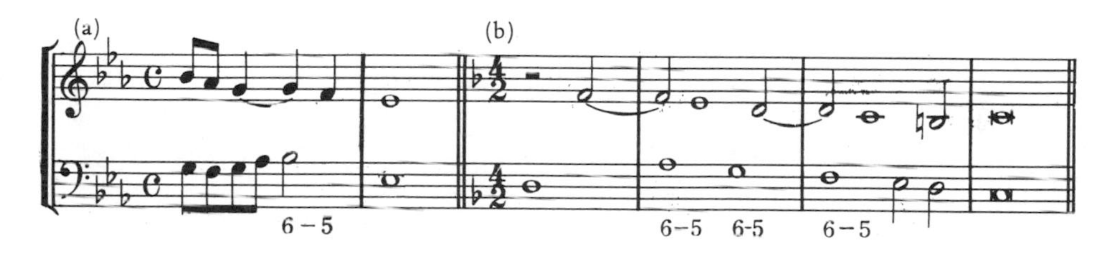

While common in three- and four-voice music, the 9–8 suspension is rare in two-voice writing. One instance occurs in the next example, measure 2.

Ex. 11–10. 9–8 suspensions.

In two-voice music the 2–3 (or 9–10) suspension figure occurs in the *lower* part. This pattern is not often found in *final* cadences, however, but more often in sectional or phrase endings.

Ex. 11–11. 2–3 suspensions.

Ornamental Resolutions of Suspensions

When one or more pitches occur between the suspension and its note of resolution, the resolution is called *ornamental.* In most instances decorations of the suspension involve step movement. However, movement to secondary pitches may also occur as an embellishment of the suspended tone.

In measure 3 of Ex. 11–12 the basic pitches of the upper voice are ornamented by neighboring and passing tones. The resolution of the suspension then occurs on the fourth beat of the measure.

Ex. 11–12.

The note of resolution of a suspension may be more pronounced because it forms part of a step progression. In Ex. 11–13 the g^2 of measure 4 is the resolution of the suspended a^2 first heard on the downbeat of measure 3. Five ascending passing notes intervene between the suspension and its ultimate resolution.

Ex. 11–13. Bach: Two-voice Invention in D Major.

A summary of the foregoing study of the suspension should recall the following principles:

1. The suspension figure in a two-voice texture usually involves a dissonance or unstable tone, most often in the form of a syncopated pattern.
2. The three steps that comprise the figure are: preparation (weak), suspension (strong), and resolution (weak).
3. Suspensions are usually, but not always, of the same duration as the prevailing basic duration.
4. The duration of the preparation is usually equal to or greater than the suspended tone. The duration of the resolution may be equal to or less than the suspended note.
5. Suspensions are denoted according to the vertical intervals formed at the suspension and its resolution; they include the 7–6, 4–3, 9–8 (rare in two parts) and 6–5 and 2–3.
6. Suspensions that resolve by ascending step motion are sometimes called *retardations*.
7. Series of suspensions that form a sequence are called *chain suspensions*.
8. Ornamental resolutions result from the interpolation of one or more pitches between the suspension and its resolution. Such interpolated pitches, usually no more than two, are often called *changing tones*.
9. The resolution of the suspension may coincide with the introduction into the other voice of a new tone. The change of bass generally occurs in contrary motion with the upper voice and forms a consonance with the tone of resolution.

The anticipation almost always forms a dissonance with its accompanying voice. Example 11–14 shows a cadential pattern in which the anticipation creates a fourth with the bass.

Ex. 11–14. Bach: Chorale, *Christ lag in Todesbanden* (outer voices).

When anticipations occur at the beginning of or within a phrase, they generally form segments of characteristic motives, often treated sequentially.

Ex. 11–15. Haydn: Sonata in E-flat, I.

Tied anticipations create syncopations that appear to be similar to those found in suspensions. In the example by Stravinsky (Ex. 11–16), *F-sharp* in measures 2–3 is an anticipation tied to the basic pitch that follows.

Ex. 11–16. Stravinsky: Octet for Winds, III. Copyright 1924 by Edition Russe de Musique; Renewed 1952. Copyright & renewal assigned to Boosey & Hawkes, Inc. Revised version Copyright 1952 by Boosey & Hawkes, Inc. Reprinted by permission.

An interesting form of the anticipation often occurs in traditional Japanese music, which although essentially monophonic, combines slightly modified versions of the same melody (*heterophonic texture*). In

Example 11–17 note that within brackets *a* and *b* the Koto part anticipates that of the Shamisen by one beat. The remainder of the excerpt consists, generally, of a single melody duplicated by tones an octave apart.

Ex. 11–17. Japanese: Shin Ukifune.

Appoggiatura (Leaning Tone)

Appoggiaturas in two-voice writing usually occur in the upper part, as illustrated in Ex. 11–18. The appoggiatura pattern is always one of skip-step, that is, skip to dissonance and step resolution to consonance.

Ex. 11–18. C.P.E. Bach: Prussian Sonata.

The appoggiatura is a particularly expressive melodic element, and its appearance is a predictable feature of many works of the eighteenth and nineteenth centuries. Most appoggiaturas create harmonic interval patterns similar to those of suspensions: 4–3, 7–6, 6–5, 9–8, and 7–8. When the pattern creates augmented or diminished intervals, it usually resolves in a way consistent with the resolutions of those intervals.

Like most other decorative patterns, appoggiaturas may be accented or unaccented, the latter of which appears in the next example.

Ex. 11–19. Bach: Prelude in D Major (*Well-tempered Clavier*, Book I).

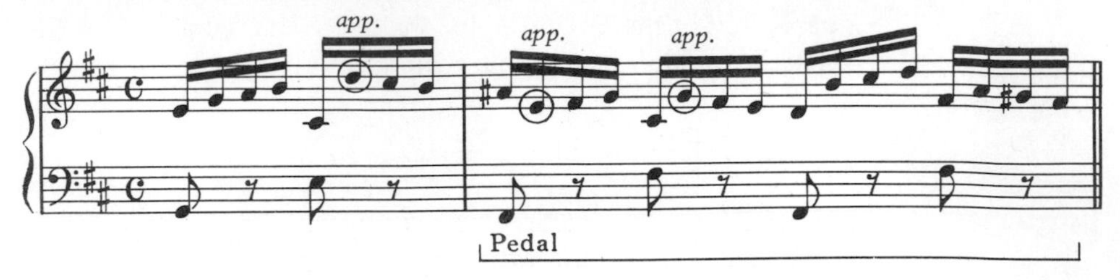

Escape Tones

Escape tones, which are approached by step and left by leap, are usually unaccented and occur most often within the phrase rather than at cadences. Like appoggiaturas, escape tones are usually found in the upper of two voices, as seen in the next example.

Ex. 11–20. Bach: Two-voice Invention in E Minor.

Pedal Point

We have seen how decorative pitches connect and embellish basic pitches of a melodic line. Let us now consider another type of pattern, the pedal point, which in fact is not decorative but is structural within any passage where it occurs. A pedal point is a sustained (or it can be re-articulated) pitch against which other melodic-harmonic activity takes place. In the next example a dissonance is formed by pitches that are related to a recurrent basic pitch, the *E-flat* of the left-hand part.

Ex. 11–21a. Haydn: Sonata in E-flat, Minuet.

Except in measures 7 and 8, the note *E-flat* occurs throughout the passage as the lowest accompanying pitch. In the second measure it creates a persistent dissonance with *D* in the upper line, a conflict continuing through measure 3 but finally resolved in measure 4. There is nothing *decorative* about the continued *E-flat*, for it is established as a pitch of structural importance. Its role is that of strong tonal reference for the melodic activity that occurs above it. Two voices are implicit in the accompanimental pattern, as the harmonic analysis of Ex. 11–21b reveals.

Ex. 11–21b. Harmonic basis of Ex. 11–21a.

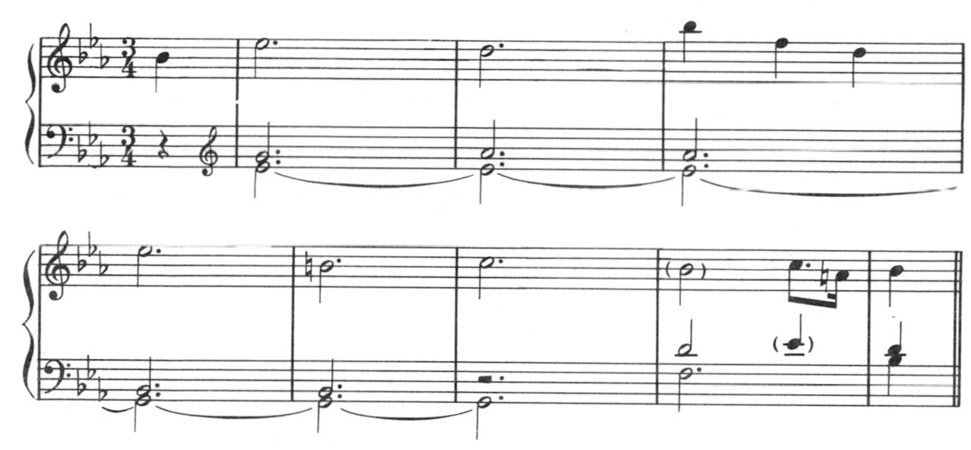

Continuity and Recurrence

Repetition

We earlier discussed several processes such as rhythmic repetition, motive repetition, and sequence. These same processes and others are equally fundamental to phrase and sectional organization in two-voice textures. For example, both voices in Ex. 11–22 employ repetitions of a short motive.

Ex. 11–22. Haydn: String Quartet in E-flat Major, Op. 76, No. 6, I.

The activity fluctuates between the two parts, creating continuous motion to the cadence. Both voices are punctuated by rests, and the different rhythms make it easy for the listener to shift attention from one voice to the other. This kind of counterpoint occurs frequently in two-voice music.

In many such textures rhythmic continuity is provided by one voice (upper or lower) of steady, recurring patterns. This is the case in Ex. 11–23.

Ex. 11–23. Handel: Sonata No. 6 for Flute and Continuo.

In other instances continuity may be achieved by motivic repetitions. An example is shown in Ex. 11–24, which contains two rhythmically repetitive yet independent voices, each unfolding through reiterations of its own motive.

Ex. 11–24. Beethoven: Fugue, Sonata, Op. 110.

Sequence

Sequential activity in one voice usually is matched by a corresponding sequence in the other. Ex. 11–25 shows three statements of a one-measure pattern in the upper part accompanied by a sequential lower part. The sequence is broken, however, in the third measure of the lower voice.

Ex. 11–25. J.S. Bach: Two-voice Invention in D Major.

Imitation

Imitation results from the statement of a melodic pattern by one voice, followed by the restatement of the same pattern (exact or modified) by another voice. Compositions of two are more voices that systematically employ strict imitation are called *canons.*

Shostakovitch uses canonic imitation at the octave in Ex. 11–26. The time lapse between statements is quite close—one beat.

Ex. 11–26. Shostakovitch: Symphony No. 5, Op. 47, I.

Although an imitating voice may enter at any pitch interval above or below the initial statement of a pattern, it usually occurs at the unison (beginning the imitative answer on the same pitch), octave, fifth, or fourth. Furthermore, the imitation of a melodic unit may be strict—the answer duplicating the first statement in rhythm and interval—or it may be modified in rhythm or pitch.

Points of imitation—that is, imitative phrase beginnings or sectional beginnings—often occur to signal the mutual sharing between voices of similar thematic material. Recurrence in such situations is a product of polyphonic restatement, while devices such as sequence, motivic repetition, or rhythmic repetition, are produced by a single voice.

Imitation at the fifth above occurs in the opening measures of the passage in Ex. 11–27a. The imitation is sustained in the top part for only two measures, while it continues for five measures in Ex. 11–27b.

Ex. 11–27a. Josquin des Près: *Homo quidan fecit coenam magnam.*

Ex. 11–27b. *Ibid.*

As mentioned earlier, the systematic employment of imitation for an entire composition or section is called *canon.* In the passage that follows, a two-voice canonic relationship is maintained throughout. Note that the composer consistently reinforces the two-voice texture by coupling the violins and viola and cello in octaves. Since the upper parts form a composite voice, as do the two lower strings, the result is of two, not four, parts.

Ex. 11–28. Haydn: String Quartet in D Minor, Op. 76, No. 2, III.

The next excerpt, from a two-voice composition by Lassus, presents a good opportunity to see how motivic and rhythmic recurrence, sequence, and imitative processes can be integrated into a larger segment of a work for two voices. Sing it, then study the details of the work, considering such factors as melodic motion and directional patterns, treatment of consonance and dissonance, and root relations.

Ex. 11–29. Lassus: *Sequentur Cantiones* (first part).

The texture of this passage is imitative counterpoint. Both voices are developed by rhythmic variations from two motives heard first in the lower voice (indicated as *1* and *2*). Note that the second motive is a modified repetition of the first.

These motives are transformed rhythmically through syncopation, augmentation, and diminution to produce continuous motion between two equal parts. Despite the similar melodic content of the two parts, contrapuntal independence is maintained by staggering the entrances and avoiding the simultaneous use of identical rhythms. Not until the final cadence of the excerpt do the two voices converge rhythmically.

Exercises

For more detailed assignments see *Materials and Structure of Music I, Workbook,* Chapter 11.

1. Continue Ex. 11–3, by Frescobaldi, for eight or more measures in such a manner that several suspensions are introduced.
2. Identify all decorative pitches in Ex. 11–4 as to type.
3. Invent an extended version of Ex. 11–12, using passing and neighboring tones.
4. Use the harmonic basis of Ex. 11–21a, shown in Ex. 11–21b, as the basis for a two-part composition utilizing a pedal point similar to that of the original. Transpose the harmonic sketch to E major before proceeding. Introduce all forms of decorative activity dealt with in this chapter as a basis for creating an elaborate upper part.
5. Use the opening motive of Ex. 11–22 as the basis of a section of two-voice imitative counterpoint for violin and viola. Write in a different key from the example.
6. Write a short canon of sixteen measures or more based on the upper voice in Ex. 11–24.

Chapter Twelve

Chord Structure

By adding another part to a two-voice texture a new unit of structure emerges: the chord. This does not represent a drastic shift of perspective for us, for chords are collections of intervals. The sound and the function of any chord in music are determined by the intervals it contains and by the relation it bears to other chords linked with it.

Harmonic Sonance

In Chapter 2 we discussed the relative *consonance* and *dissonance* of intervals. As a general rule, a consonant chord is one that contains only consonant intervals, while a dissonant chord contains one or more dissonant intervals.

Ex. 12–1 shows four different chords, the last three of which are considerably more dissonant than the first. Note that each of these last three contains at least one unstable interval.

Ex. 12–1. Chords.

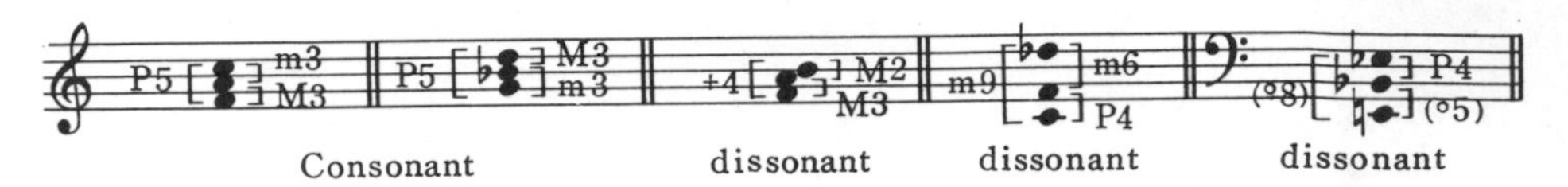

The more complicated the interval structure within a chord, the greater that chord's dissonance. Thus we could make a scaling of harmonic sonority that would extend from the most consonant sound combination to the most dissonant, in which all twelve pitches of the chromatic scale might sound together in a biting combination.

Ex. 12–2. Chords of different sonance.

Not only is chord *b* more dissonant than chord *a,* its many different pitch classes (and thus many different intervals) also impart to it a high degree of *harmonic density* that a chord of fewer pitch classes would not have.

Between these two chords of Example 12–2 lie the chord types that are found in most music. The bulk of our musical heritage contains a restricted harmonic palette that lies closer to the sonority of Ex. 12–2a than to Ex. 12–2b, but since the beginning of our century composers have considerably broadened harmonic color toward the dissonant side of the scale. One of the trademarks of any composer is the kinds of chords found in his music and the ways these are linked together in harmonic successions. Many of our subsequent discussions will be concerned with the recognition and classification of chord types.

The Triad

Any chord that can be reduced to no more nor less than three different pitch classes is called a *triad*. That is, even a chord made up of five different pitches may still be reducible to a triad if two of its five pitches are octave replicas of two others.

Ex. 12–3. Triads.

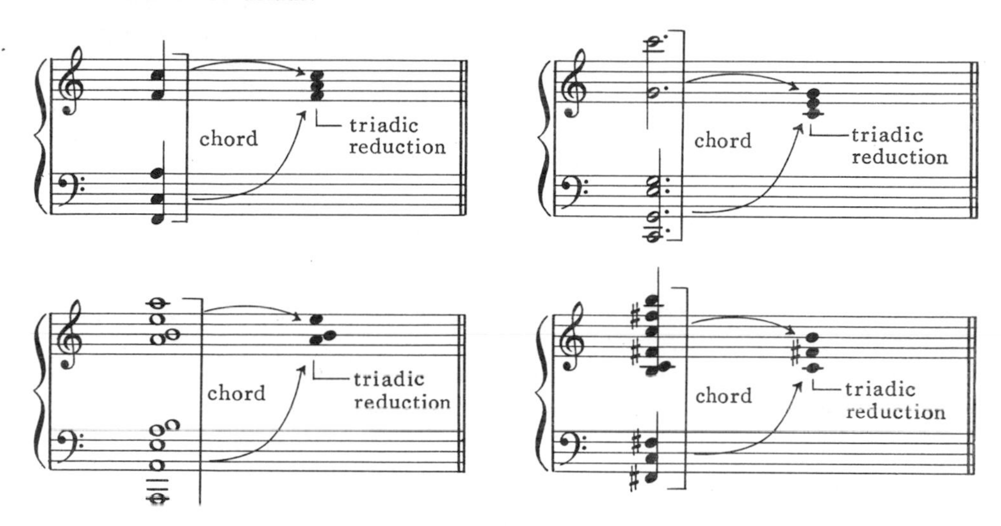

The simplest triads are relatively consonant. They consist of intervals no less stable than major and minor thirds, so they are among the most stable chords. These are the *major* and *minor triads,* each of which consists of a perfect fifth divided by a major and a minor third.

Ex. 12–4. Major and minor triads.

It is the location of these thirds that determines major or minor quality. When the third above the root is major, a major triad results; when the third above the root is minor, a minor triad results.

Two other simple triad types are known as *diminished* and *augmented.* These names are derived from the intervals that encompass their outer tones, the diminished and the augmented fifths, respectively.

Ex. 12–5. Diminished and augmented triads.

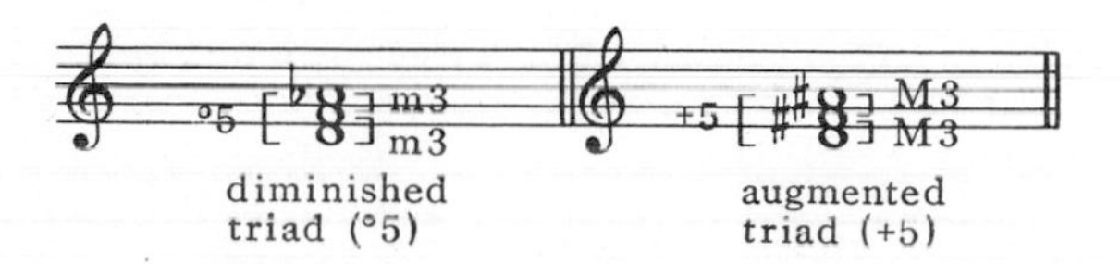

Both of these triads are relatively unstable. Neither contains a perfect fifth or fourth, and the diminished triad contains the unstable tritone. Since both the augmented and diminished triads involve two equal-sized intervals (minor thirds in the diminished triad, major thirds in the augmented), they lack the clarity of tonal focus that creates a root effect.[1]

Major and minor triads are stable, and so they are more important to our present discussion. Furthermore, they form the basis of many other chords that will be discussed later. Note for the present that major and minor scales yield more major and minor triads than diminished and augmented triads.

Ex. 12–6. Triad types derived from major and minor scales.

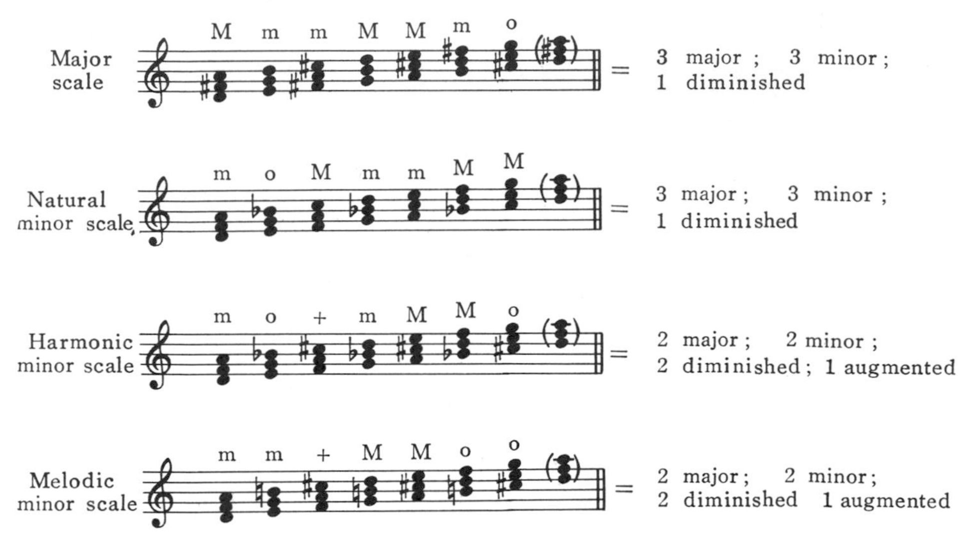

Each of the chords of Ex. 12–6 is a *diatonic* chord for the particular scale it is built within.[2] Thus the triad *G–B–D* is diatonic to *D* major, but it is nondiatonic (or *chromatic*) for *D* natural minor; and the triad *B-flat–D–F* is a diatonic chord of *F* major, nondiatonic for *C* major.

Chord Function

In addition to its sonority type—major, minor, diminished, or augmented—another vital bit of information about any chord is its relation to other chords. That is, like people, chords "behave," or reflect their own identities, only in relation to others, and these relationships are a necessary aspect of chordal description.

[1] We use the term *prime* for the fundamental pitch of chords that do not have roots.

[2] Since only pitches of the respective scale are contained within each chord.

In tonal music an individual chord's position (or *function*) is denoted by the roman numeral that represents its scale position. If we build a triad on each degree of the major or minor scale, we can identify the resultant chords according to their relationships to the tonic degree of that scale.

Ex. 12–7. Chord nomenclature of diatonic chords.

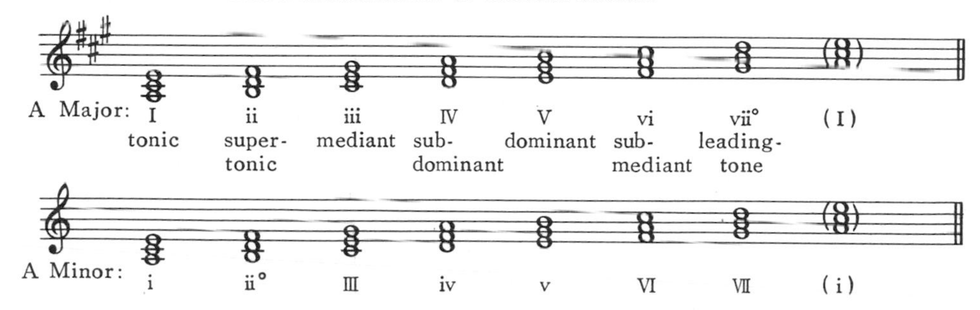

And thus the two essential facts about a particular triad within a tonality are its *sonority type* and its *tonal function.* And so it is important that a distinction be made between upper and lower case roman numerals; these, in conjunction with the ° sign for diminished and the + sign for augmented, are concise ways for indicating these two basic facts about any diatonic chord.
For clarification of this statement, consider the following:

Numeral type (upper or lower case, *plus* ° or + when applicable) shows the basic sonority. Thus

V or IV denotes major triad
vi or ii denotes minor triad
ii° or iv° denotes diminished triad
III+ or II+ denotes augmented triad

Numeral value shows scalar degree relationship to tonic pitch. Thus V (or v) denotes a root tone that is the fifth scale degree. I (or i) indicates the triad built on the tonic scale degree.

Chord Position

The structural names for the individual pitches within any major or minor triad are derived from the intervals they form together. Thus the three parts are called *root,*[3] *third,* and *fifth.* These terms are meaningful only when they are derived from the simple position of the triad. In a triad's simple (or *fundamental*) position its members are in their closest relationships, as illustrated in Ex. 12–8.

[3] With the exception of diminished and augmented triads and other rootless chords, which we shall discuss presently.

Ex. **12–8.** Structural names of chord members.

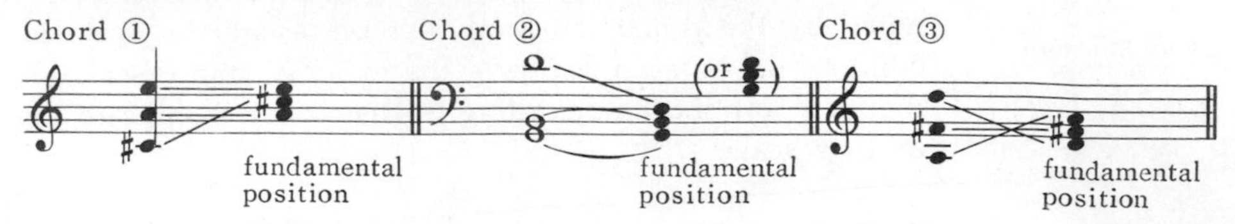

Even when the position of a chord changes, the individual parts are still named according to their unexpanded relations, as illustrated in the fundamental triad above. That is to say that each of the chords in Ex. 12–9 consists of the same root (*E-flat*), the same third (*G*), and the same fifth (*B-flat*), even though vastly different note distributions are present.

Ex. 12–9. *E-flat* major triads.

Even when more than three pitches make up the chord, if all are duplications of triad notes, then the basic harmonic structure is still the fundamental triad. Chord type remains the same although voicing and texture change.

Ex. 12–10. Chord reductions.

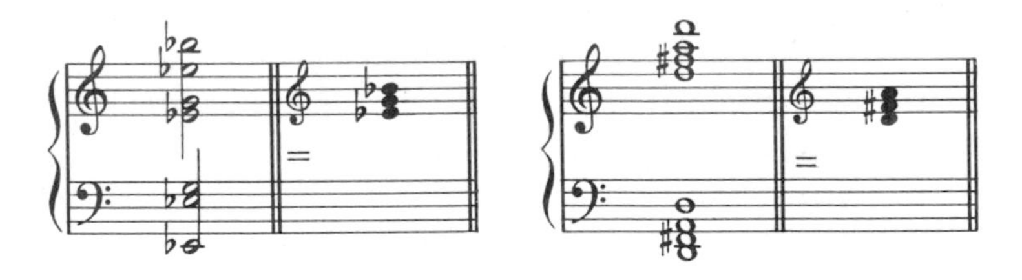

Simple chords can be turned upside down and internally reordered without changing their basic structure. This is so because these topsy-turvy arrangements do not alter root effects in any appreciable way. Note that the same harmonic root is retained in any distribution of the pitches of a major triad.

Ex. 12–11. Chord inversion.

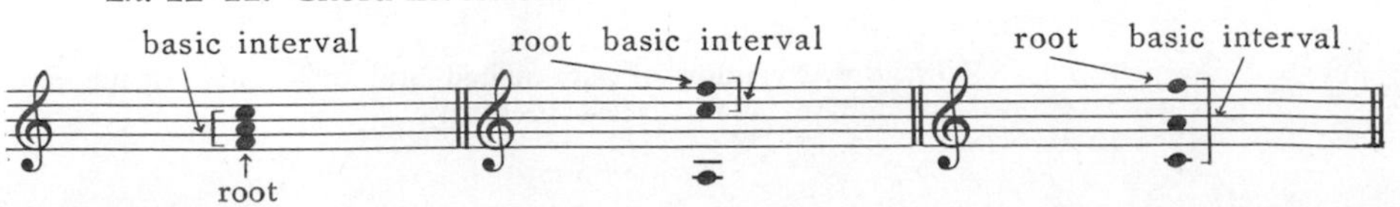

For the reasons illustrated in the foregoing example, any distribution of tones is known by the name of its fundamental or reduced form. And thus both chords in Example 12–12 are *F major triads,* even though *F* is not the bass pitch in either.

Ex. 12–12. Inverted chords.

Chord *a* is in first inversion, while chord *b* is in second inversion. These denotations refer to the number of note shufflings away from the *root position* that are required to achieve the particular chord form. That is, beginning with the root position, the first inversion requires one shuffling of the bass note; the second inversion requires two.

Ex. 12–13. Inverted chords.

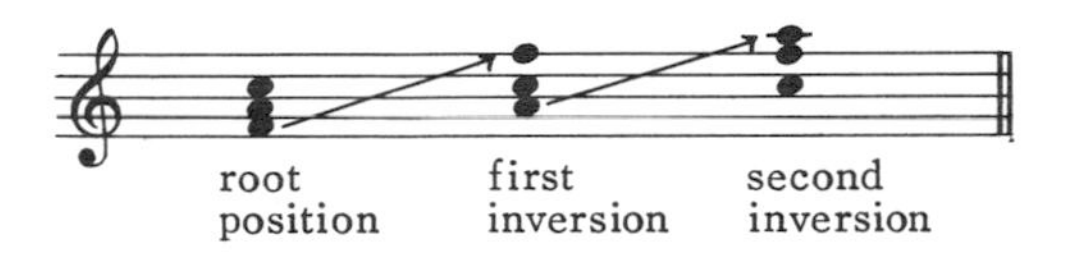

Another explanation for the three possible triad positions is that the root note is the lowest member in a root-position chord; the third is the lowest member in a first inversion; and the fifth is the lowest member in a second inversion.

Figured Bass

Musicians have a shorthand way of representing the distribution of chord members. Called *figured bass,* this system employs arabic numerals along with the roman numeral that represents the root tone. The arabic numerals denote intervals above the bass note. A complete representation for triads is as follows:

Ex. 12–14. Figured bass notation for triad positions.

It is important to note that these numerical designations are derived from the intervals above the bass *as if the chord members all were contained within a single octave.*

This system of chord symbols usually is abbreviated. When no arabic numeral accompanies a chord it is understood that the chord is in its root position (or ${}^{5}_{3}$ in structure). And the designation ${}^{6}_{3}$ normally is simplified into just 6, which can be taken to mean first-inversion triad. The full designation ${}^{6}_{4}$ is necessary for the second-inversion triad, of course, in order to distinguish it from the first inversion.

As we mentioned earlier, diminished and augmented triads lack the perfect fifth (or fourth) and the unequal thirds that produce the root effect of major and minor triads. In other words, a chord is in root (or prime) position when all of its members can be stacked one above the other in successive thirds. Therefore chords 1a, 2a, and 3a in Example 12–15 are not in fundamental position; their rearrangement in 1b, 2b, and 3b reveals their noninverted forms.

Ex. 12–15. Inverted and noninverted chords.

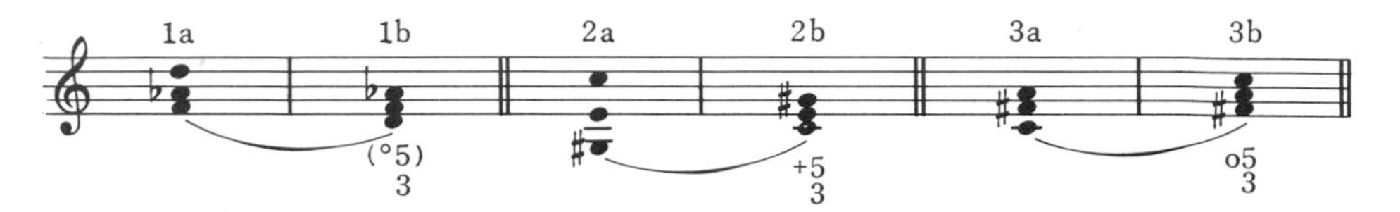

We shall study other principles of chord structure later, when our harmonic material includes more than the simple triad. For the present, the principle of inversion is helpful in that it simplifies the problem of chord classification.

To describe a chord, one must first locate the root of its combined intervals. With major and minor chords this can be simplified by a search for a perfect fifth or fourth. The root pitch of either of these combinations will be the root for the whole chord. Lacking any of the above evidence (as in diminished and augmented triads), the principle of stacked thirds produces a workable answer. The process is illlustrated in our next example.

Ex. 12–16. Locating roots of chords.

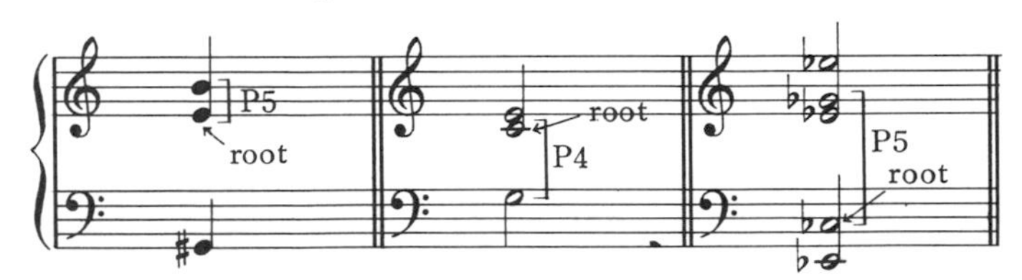

When a triad does not contain a fifth or fourth, the next simplest interval, the major or minor third (or sixth) determines the root. Many three-voice textures contain these nontriadic kinds of chords. Notice that

Ex. 12–17 ends with a two-note chord (or *diad*) because the composer demanded certain resolutions of the melodic lines.

Ex. 12–17. Chorale: *Wer weiss, wie nahe mir.*

Chord Succession

Within a tonality the most important chord is the tonic (I or i, depending upon whether it is a major or minor sonority). It is the most stable chord within the diatonic set of chords. Just as almost all tonal melodies end with their tonic pitch, so almost all chordal music ends with a tonic chord. It is the sonority that best produces the release of tension normally associated with musical termination.

The next most important chord within a tonality is the dominant (V or v). In the traditional key schemes of major and minor (and in some modes) this triad contains the important dominant and leading tone scale degrees. The combination of the two in the same chord makes the dominant chord secondary only to the tonic (I or i) chord. In conjunction with a tonic chord, the dominant chord most clearly defines an intended tonality. When the V chord precedes I in a weak-strong metric relationship, there can be little doubt about which chord is tonic.

The V-I relationship serves as the basis for much of the harmony in the music of our Western tradition. This basic two-chord association has been used to accompany every conceivable kind of melody, from children's songs to art works of considerable complexity. Two simple examples from quite different pieces follow.

Ex. 12–18a. Folk song: *Have You Ever Seen a Lassie?*

Ex. 12–18b. Beethoven: *Dance.*

Strictly speaking, any shift away from the tonic chord weakens tonality. However, the root of the dominant chord lends emphasis to the tonic pitch, so the movement from I to V weakens tonality least. This can be illustrated if we note in Ex. 12–18 that the interval formed between the roots of I and V is a fifth (or a fourth); the root of both of these intervals is the same pitch: the root of the tonic chord.

Ex. 12–19. V to I chord progressions.

If the harmony of a composition remained solidly entrenched in only the tonic chord, no harmonic tension would result, and the important feeling of completion that comes from departure and eventual return to a tonic would be missing. The total effect would be dull and static if significant rhythmic, melodic, or textural contrasts did not compensate for this harmonic sameness.[4] Viewed as melodies, bugle calls suffer from this severe harmonic sameness. They are the mere spinning out of a single chord pattern that is based on the instrument's harmonic series.

[4] Listen to Richard Wagner's prelude to the opera *Das Rheingold* for an example of a complete musical section that is based on a single chord, in this case an *E-flat* major triad.

Ex. 12–20. Bugle call: *Reveille.*

Static harmony might be desired for some musical functions. One way a composer can heighten the sense of motion in one section of a piece is to precede that section by music that lacks harmonic change. The excerpt of Ex. 12–21 illustrates the avoidance of forward propulsion in an introductory passage. A static fanfare sound is the result.

Ex. 12–21. Monteverdi: *L'Orfeo,* Toccata.

Most music incorporates chord successions of one kind or another. In some textures chords are simple vertical blocks, each of which moves to another, thereby achieving direct harmonic change, as in Ex. 12–22.

Ex. 12–22. J. S. Bach: *Alle Menschen müssen sterben.*

In other textures, however, the chords might result from melodic outlines, these patterns adding up to particular chords, as in the next example.

Ex. 12–23. Schubert: *Der Müller und der Bach.*

In order to understand better the harmonic content of a piece of music, it is customary to analyze its chords and to plot these in graphic form. The roman numerals mentioned earlier are most useful for denoting chord types and root relations within a key. Ex. 12–24 shows a simple analysis of a musical phrase.

Ex. 12–24. Haydn: Sonata No. 18, I.

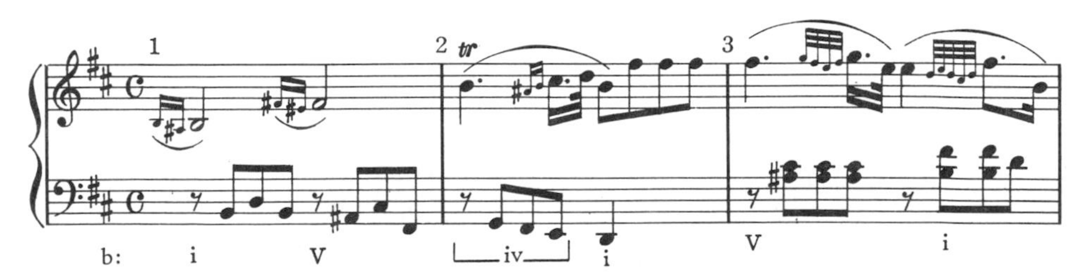

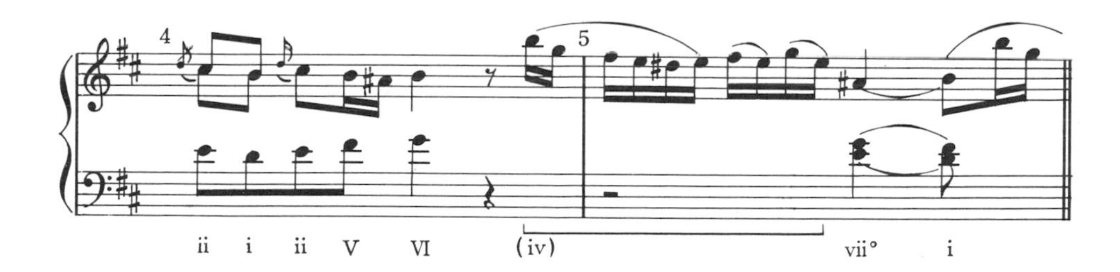

In some passages, as in the previous example, it is impossible to assign chord names with any assurance to every vertical alignment of tones. There often will be more than one possible chordal interpretation. Measure 5, for instance, is subject to more than one interpretation; the first two beats of its highly mobile top line *might* be heard as a *ii* chord in *b* minor rather than as a iv chord. If we rely on our guide of basic melody analysis, the pitch *E* appears to be the most important pitch in the passage, so the iv chord is a more likely interpretation of the *implied* harmony. (In ways such as this, basic melody analysis and harmonic analysis are mutually complementary paths to musical insight.)

Melodic-Harmonic Synthesis

Few compositions of any scope contain only the simple chords and voice movement seen in Ex. 12–17 (the chorale *Wer weiss, wie nahe mir*). In listening to most music, our awareness of chords is so affected by melodic play that melody and chords form an inseparable synthesis; each reinforces the other. Study the following passage carefully, listening to it several times.

Ex. 12–25. Beethoven: *Quartet in F Major, Op. 18, No. 1, I.*

If we attend only to the chords found *on each beat,* we have to acknowledge that some of these (such as on the first beats of measures 2, 3, and 4) do not accurately represent the harmony we hear. Secondly, in trying to make sense of both the *B-naturals* and the *B-flats* that sound together in measures 1, 3, and 4, we could produce an implausible representation of that passage's harmony.

Actually, this whole passage is the melodic animation of just one chord.

The top voice (Violin I) unfolds the upper three notes of the chord *E, G, B-flat* over a range of two octaves. The viola part is coupled with the top part; it reiterates the three lower notes of the chord (*C, E,* and *G*) in pairs. The technique used in these two parts is, of course, arpeggiation, the melodic spinning out of a single four-note chord.

The second violin and cello parts are organized in a different way. They are more melodic. They imitate each other in contrary motion, each spanning an octave that is filled by pitches within this boundary. The *B-naturals* are simply passing tones that embellish Cs as they occur. They are brief leading tones that, because of their short duration, do not conflict with the more basic (the more *harmonic*) *B-flats* sounding above. It is not difficult to see here that the continued reemphasis of *C* in these two parts produces a harmonic function of V (dominant) in the key of *F.*

We might conclude, then, that the chord in this passage can best be described as the frame that channels the passage; it is through essentially melodic means, however, that this frame comes about.

Our next example appears to involve a change of harmony on each successive eighth note.

Ex. 12–26. Beethoven: *Missa Solemnis.*

But again, harmony is better understood by noting how melodies project a single chord over a span of time, in this case a V chord over two measures.

Note that the upper voice in Ex. 12–26 spans an octave (leading tone to leading tone), while the alto repeats the pitch *B* before passing upward by step. The two lower parts are coupled, moving by steps in parallel thirds. Each voice forms an approach to the closing tonic chord, and each voice displays a fundamentally melodic character: movement by step prevails.

The listener to this brief passage is swept forward by the movement of separate parts, the momentary chords formed by their motion adding to an overall sense of momentum. The passage is an elaboration of the V chord moving to I. Its structure is a product of passing motion over a pedal tone on the dominant scale degree. The "chords" that occur, as each voice carries out its elaboration of the basic chord, must be understood as *passing chords*. They are the projection of a single underlying chord.

Melodic elements do not always dominate a texture as they do in the two examples we have just cited. Yet any chordal analysis of music must nonetheless acknowledge the coordinate relationship between melody and harmony in creating musical structure.

Exercises

See Chapter 12 of *Materials and Structure of Music I*, Workbook, for more detailed exercises.

1. Practice spelling (orally and in notation) various major, minor, diminished, and augmented triads from a given note as root or prime. Think through the component intervals of each chord before spelling with notes. For example:
   B-flat augmented triad:
   Augmented triad = augmented fifth, major third and major third
   B-*flat–F-sharp* = augmented fifth
   B-flat–D = major third
   D–F-sharp = major third
   Spelling: *B-flat–D–F-sharp*
2. Analyze a passage of relatively simple harmonic content by denoting each chord with its proper symbol.
3. In a group or with one other person, listen to major, minor, diminished, and augmented triads played randomly at the piano or organ. Identify each as to type. If possible, identify what chord member (root, third, or fifth) is in the soprano and bass voices.
4. Using a three-voice texture, write a passage that is based on the following series of chords. Write the outer two parts first, add the middle voice, then elaborate each basic melody to create an effective musical passage.
   G major: I I_6 V vi V_6 I V I
5. Plot a simple chord progression about four measures long, one chord per measure in any meter. Using an instrument or your voice, improvise a melody that corresponds to the selected chords. Use an uncomplicated rhythm for your melody, perhaps a single motif.

Example:

Progression: |I |vi |v |I ||

Rhythm: ♩. ♪♩

Result:

Chapter Thirteen

Three-Voice Combinations; Homophonic Textures

Our study of two-voice textures actually dealt with principles of organization that can be applied to any number of parts, thereby revealing the importance of a two-voice framework for any multipart texture. Adding more voices creates new problems of spacing, part clarity, and harmonic logic, but the basis for effective three-part combinations—coherent melodic structure—is not different from that of two parts. Except for the introduction of the chord as a unit of harmonic reference, the vertical alignment of three voices poses no drastically new problems.

Three-voice Combinations

Rhythmic Association

The degree of individuality displayed by the separate parts of a three-voice texture can vary from total dependence to total independence. The term *homophony* is usually applied to combinations in which a single part is clearly the principal melody, the remaining parts accompanimental.

Homophony will be the subject of discussion later in this chapter. Let us turn now to consideration of three-voice combinations, keeping in mind that in much music the differences between homophony and counterpoint are not always distinct, for composers often combine elements of both within a single formal section.

To fit the description *contrapuntal* a three-voice combination must contain parts that have some degree of individuality and yet still combine into a unified association. In fulfilling these basic requirements the parts may be combined in one of the three following types:

Type 1: One voice dominates, the remaining voices serving as accompanying parts that vary one from the other, only to the extent that their separate identities are preserved.

Ex. 13–1. Hindemith: *Ludus Tonalis,* Fugue in E. © 1943 by Schott & Co., Ltd., London. Reprinted by permission.

Even in this example of the one basic type of counterpoint, some linear interest is displayed by the subordinate parts. For example, the upper parts move in shorter note values than the bass and move in contrary motion to it.

Type 2: Two voices of about equal interest are pitted against a third voice that is decidedly subordinate.

Ex. 13–2. Franck: Symphony in D Minor, I.

In Ex. 13–2, the two outer parts dominate because of greater rhythmic interest and imitation (the bass imitates the soprano, measures 1 and 2).

In somewhat the same manner, the outer voices in Ex. 13–3 dominate the three-part texture. The texture is heterophonic; Koto and Shamisen parts are based on the pitches of the voice's melody.

Ex. 13–3. Japanese: *Shin ukifune.* (Matsuura Kengyò, Yaezaki Kengyò).

Type 3: Three voices of approximately equal interest combine, each vying for the listener's attention in a "give-and-take" succession. An imitative relationship often prevails.

Ex. 13–4. Handel: Suite in D Minor, Fugue.

In Ex. 13–4 the bass line imitates the top (beginning in the last half of measure 2), and the top imitates the bass (beginning in measure 3). The middle voice weaves its own separate and quite individual thread through this imitative texture.

While almost any contrapuntal texture of three parts can be fitted into one of these three categories, music does not normally remain fixed in a single type for long. For the sake of achieving variety, the composer often changes or varies textural relationships, and consequently, it is often futile to attempt to describe an entire composition or large section by any single one of these three basic types.

Rhythmic Unity and Variety

The rhythms of the three separate voices normally are related. The voices usually share the same rhythmic divisions, although these divisions often are not articulated simultaneously. For instance, in Ex. 13–5 the basic duration (𝅗𝅥) is divided into a continuous stream of quarters among the combined parts. The result is consistency and continuity of flow throughout the texture.

Ex. 13–5. Beethoven: Quartet in C-sharp Minor, Op. 131, I.

Although the basic duration is not so consistently divided in contrapuntal textures, the separate voices often use the same (or closely related) rhythmic patterns. Ex. 13–6 shows a less constant division of the basic duration resulting in less propulsion than in Ex. 13–5.

Ex. 13–6. Handel: Clavier Suite in E Minor, Sarabande.

The rhythmic individuality of voices is most commonly achieved by contrasting note durations, that is, parts composed of mixed long and short values. Combinations of three equally active voices usually incorporate a broad diversity of motion, in this way accentuating further the individuality of each part.

One finds that extended passages of three-voice textures often are comprised of parts which move in different divisions of the basic duration. In Ex. 13–7 the basic duration (the quarter note) is divided into eighths (bass voice) and sixteenths (middle voice) in a continuous relationship, while the basic duration is articulated above (top voice).

Ex. 13–7. J. S. Bach: Fugue in E Major (*Well-tempered Clavier*, Book I).

While the uniformity of such patterns—most typical of music written during the late Baroque period—creates a rhythmic thrust that is absent in music whose lines are formed by a greater variety of note durations, each line is less interesting *rhythmically* as a result.

Aside from diversity of rhythms, individuality of parts can also be achieved by combining contradictory divisions of the basic duration. Duplet patterns combined with triplet patterns (example) create more individuality of parts than do two combined versions of a single metric division. (It should be noted that when such contrast is prolonged, it is difficult for the listener to determine the fundamental metric division unless a third part reinforces one of the patterns.

In addition to contrasting or contradictory beat divisions, the displacement of accents in one part (syncopation) forcibly differentiates that part from its associates. The ties across bars Ex. 13–9 contribute to rhythmic definition of each of the parts, as well as to harmonic interest.

Ex. 13–8. J. S. Bach: *Art of the Fugue*, Contrapunctus IX.

The degree of variety (or unity) of voices in a three-voice texture is also determined by the coincidence or noncoincidence of cadences in the separate lines. Contrapuntal textures generally avoid unanimity of cadence, the individual parts sometimes being of dissimilar phrase lengths and thus cadencing separately. This condition avoids rhythmic stagnation by allowing continued motion in at least one voice while another pauses at its own cadence. The phrase structure of each part of Ex. 13–9 is indicated by brackets, a study of which will reveal the variety of cadence locations that create this constantly mobile texture. The imitation between the three voices enhances this high degree of motion, motion that ceases only in measure 6, where all voices combine momentarily in a move toward closure.

Ex. 13–9. Lassus: Penitential Psalm No. 3.

Pitch Association of Three Parts

It may prove helpful to view a three-voice texture as a two-voice framework to which a third part has been added, the added part forming two-voice counterpoint with *each* of the original voices.

Since the outer voices of a three-part texture form the structural pitch limits, they constitute the vertical outer limits (framework) of the pitch combinations. For this reason, the effectiveness of a three-part union depends largely upon the compatibility of its outer voices, the two-voice framework.

This basic framework follows the same organizing principles developed in earlier sections devoted to two-voice textures. The cadence formulas are generally identical, as are the intervallic relations between the two outer lines, which are cadential consonances except when decorative patterns form dissonances.

The middle part in some combinations often serves as a rhythmic and harmonic supplement where other parts pause momentarily or where they alone fail to complete the desired sonority.

Ex. 13–10. Handel: Clavier Suite in E Minor, Courante.

The octave, fifth, thirds, and sixths are the intervals most frequently used on strong beats, with the fourth often appearing as a basic interval between the two upper parts. Ex. 13–11 illustrates three-part combinations which, when reduced to their basic outlines, reveal typical uses of basic intervals and decorative patterns. (The arabic numerals used herein are not to be confused with figured bass, in which all intervals are calculated from bass pitches.)

Ex. 13–11. Handel: Suite in E Minor, Gigue.

All other interval combinations (including seconds, sevenths, fourths, and tritones) usually arise from a decorative pattern of some kind. We shall discuss these subsequently.

Spatial Distribution of Parts

The distances maintained by the voice pairs of a three-voice texture and the overall pitch range enclosed by these combinations are determined by the particular sound desired by the composer and the relative contours of the individual lines. Two outer parts that move in predominantly contrary motion inevitably will lead to fluctuating texture that varies from narrower to wider. Similarly, lines of highly different melodic contours render uniformity of spacing impossible, although relatively uniform spacing is maintained in order to unify the texture. Consider the following basic types of spatial distribution.

Type 1: Generally, parts are spaced equidistantly with no consistent couplings of any two of the three. Such dispositions usually reveal considerable individuality of pitch contour and rhythm within each voice.

Ex. 13–12. J. S. Bach: Three-voice Invention in A Major.

In this example, each of the three parts remains within a clearly delineated range, maintaining its unique patterns of activity.

Type 2: Two parts are coupled in close range, the third part separated from them by approximately an octave or more. (The coupling can occur between the two upper or the two lower voices.)

Ex. 13–13a. Schumann: Fugue on B.A.C.H. (upper voices coupled).

Ex. 13–13b. J. S. Bach: Fugue in D Minor (*Well-tempered Clavier,* Book I) (lower voices coupled).

The two previous excerpts show the registral coupling possibilities of three parts. In the Schumann sample the upper parts are combined closely together, while the bottom part winds through a range approximately two octaves below the middle voice. In the Bach excerpt the upper part is separated from the coupled pair of lower parts. In both instances, the separate part is more conspicuous because of its highly contrasted octave placement.

Spatial distributions in a texture depend upon the instrument or instruments that play them, in addition to the musical effect desired by the composer. For example, a distribution such as in Ex. 13–14 is impractical for piano because of wide spacings for the right hand. Such a passage would be easily playable by a combination of instruments whose individual articulations and timbres would readily differentiate the separate lines.

Ex. 13–14. Copland: *Appalachian Spring*, Bride's Dance. Copyright 1945 by Aaron Copland. Reprinted by permission of Aaron Copland, copyright owner, and Boosey & Hawkes, Inc., Sole Licensees.

In general, unequal spacing *between* voices occurs more in contrapuntal textures in which individuality of lines is paramount. In homophonic textures a more equal (homogeneous) spatial distribution is usual.

Let us now turn to more specific guides for the distribution of voices, first considering the overtone series as a useful point of reference:

The similarity between the intervallic arrangement of the series (widest intervals at the bottom) and the most common arrangement of vocal parts (widest intervals between lower voices) suggests a relationship between musical practice and the inherent properties of musical sound.

In the madrigal shown in Ex. 13–15 we find a typical spacing of parts. The upper voices lie generally within an octave of each other, the two lower parts are occasionally as far apart as two octaves, and the outer voices seldom are farther apart than two octaves and a fifth.

Ex. 13–15. Marenzio: Madrigal.

Exceptional spacings sometimes occur as the result of decorative pitches. These unusual separations occur most often in weak metric positions, and they do not attract the same attention or create the sense of imbalance that would result from their use in accented positions or longer durations. Several examples of exceptional spacings that result from melodic decorative activity are illustrated in Ex. 13–16.

Ex. 13–16. Exceptional three-voice distribution.

The principles of spacing three voices should not be taken as absolute rules but rather as guides for achieving clarity and balance of pitch relationships.

1. The upper voices usually lie within an octave or less.
2. Comparatively larger intervals occur more often between lower parts, smaller intervals between upper.
3. A variety of spacings may be employed (prolonged parallel movement being avoided) if melodic independence of parts is desired.
4. Abnormally wide or narrow spacing may result momentarily from decorative activity.
5. Outer voices are seldom more than two octaves apart.

Crossing Voices

An interesting contrapuntal effect is achieved in both instrumental and vocal textures by *crossing* voices. If the alto moves above the soprano or below the tenor, for example, the voices involved are said to have crossed. Crossing most often occurs between adjacent parts, and it is usually the result of the completion of a particular melodic pattern, as exemplified in Ex. 13–17.

Ex. 13–17. Byrd: Madrigal.

The possibilities for organizing three voices are, as we have seen, almost unlimited. No two works are identical, nor do any two derive their musical interest from identically developed compositional techniques, no matter how similar they may appear. Nonetheless, just as the most complex counterpoint may adhere to certain harmonic formations, so even the most simply developed homophony will rely on rudimentary principles of counterpoint.

Homophonic Textures

Thus far our emphasis has been on combinations of individual voices related contrapuntally. Further, we have seen how linear patterns may be combined and how, in three voice writing, these produce chords.

All music is not conceived as combinations of independent melodic lines. In fact, in much music one line is prominent, while subordinate lines (often in corresponding rhythms) produce an accompanying harmony. The following example is homophonic: There is one dominating melody and the remaining texture forms a chordal background that complements the important top voice. Notice that the basic framework is still a revealing outline for the total texture.

Ex. 13–18. Schubert: "Ständchen" (*Schwanengesang*).

Basic framework

Even when one voice is of decided prominence, the other lines certainly may be "melodic," in the sense that they contain some rhythmic or contoural independence. In textures such as the following the overall effect is not exclusively that of counterpoint or of pure homophony; the result is rather that of a succession of block harmonies interwoven with some isolated rhythmic activity and lines of simple melodic distinctiveness.

Ex. 13–19. Palestrina: *Adoramus te Christe.*

Basic framework

Example 13–20 shows still another kind of homophonic texture, this one achieved through only two lines that are rhythmically differentiated. The lower part outlines simple chords, while the melody unfolds simple decorative patterns (upper neighbors) around a basic pitch line that belongs to the chords of the lower part.[1]

Ex. 13–20. Beethoven: Sonata in G Major, Op. 79, III.

[1] The accompanimental figuration of this passage is typical of classic-period works, both as piano and string patterns. It is called an *Alberti bass,* after the composer Domenico Alberti, who apparently pioneered its use.

It is clear, then, that homophonic textures vary from clear-cut combinations of a melody with block-chord accompaniment to less obvious examples in which contrapuntal elements are present in one or more of the subordinate voices. The common element of all is a singularity of melodic interest and, frequently, a common bond of rhythmic motion.

Part Designations and Notation

In earlier chapters we discussed principles that govern contrapuntal associations. For the present we shall be concerned with tones related as blocks of harmony rather than as combined horizontal lines. It will be apparent that many of the principles related to the connection of chords have their basis in principles discussed earlier in terms of counterpoint. We shall begin with principles of a generalized nature.

It is customary to designate the four parts of a texture according to the voice names of choral music, even when human voices are not involved. Thus four parts are named, from top to bottom, *Soprano, Alto, Tenor,* and *Bass.* (See Chapter 9 for the usual ranges of these voice parts in the chorus.) In notating parts for four voices, choral or instrumental, the score can be "closed," in that it consists of all parts written together on two staves, soprano and alto combined in the treble clef, tenor and bass combined in the bass clef, as shown in Ex. 13–21.

Ex. 13–21. Closed score.

Observe that the stems of individual parts indicate to which voice the particular note belongs, even when parts cross.

Doubling of Pitches

If we limit our harmonic resources to triads for the present, a four-voice texture necessitates the duplication of one member of each triad, and in some instances (because of linear factors or the desire for a particular sonority) one member might even be tripled or quadrupled. This doubling can be accomplished at the octave, double octave, etc., as well as at the unison.

Ex. 13–22. Doubling in triads.

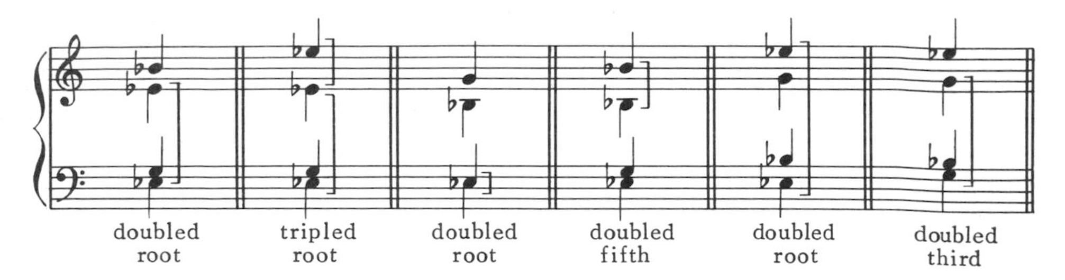

At best, rules of doubling represent the practice of a particular composer, the "norm" of an era of composition, or merely the unique sonority desired by the composer at a particular moment. Furthermore, individual voice motion frequently determines how chord members are used in a particular sonority. However, when sonority alone is the determining factor, the following can be regarded as a general guide:

Triads in Root Position

(a) Major	root doubled
(b) Minor	root doubled (or third)
(c) Diminished	third doubled ($°{}^{5}_{3}$ seldom occurs)
(d) Augmented	third doubled (seldom occurs in any form)

Triads in First Inversion

(a) Major	root doubled
(b) Minor	third doubled (or root)
(c) Diminished	third doubled (or fifth)
(d) Augmented	third doubled (seldom occurs)

Triads in Second Inversion

(a) Major	fifth doubled (bass pitch)
(b) Minor	fifth doubled
(c) Diminished	third doubled (or fifth)
(d) Augmented	fifth doubled (or third)

Doubling the root of a major or minor triad emphasizes that chord's stability. In the case of tonic, subdominant, and dominant triads, this doubling also reinforces important scale degrees, 1, 4, or 5. Since these tones remain constant (do not vary with change of mode), they act as the fixed tonal elements of any key. As a consequence, they are often doubled within a four-pitch chord.

As you can deduce from the chart above, certain duplications are generally avoided. For example, we expect the leading tone of a key to resolve by step upward. To double this tone in a chord would exaggerate this expectation. And in chords containing a tritone (ii° in minor, vii° in major and in melodic and harmonic minor) the member that is *not* a part of the tritone, the third, is usually doubled.

Ex. 13–23. Doubling in tritone chords.

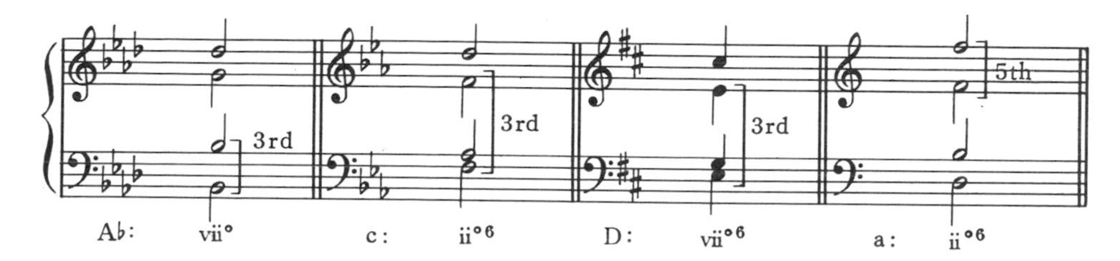

In homophonic textures the principles of doubling just cited are often violated if the linear progression of a particular voice would be hampered. In Ex. 13–24 chord number six (*E* major triad) contains a doubled third, even though this third also is the leading tone of the key. The extenuating factors are the melody's dip to *E* in the subsequent chord (thus not resolving its *G-sharp* leading tone) and the more graceful line created in the tenor voice by the step upward of *F-sharp–G-sharp–A*. Note that the root, *A*, of the cadential tonic chord in measure 2 is doubled, but notice further that the third of the V chord in measure 3 is also doubled. Once more the circumstances dictating the exception to the rule are evident: both *G-sharps* are a result of step motion in the soprano and tenor lines.

Ex. 13–24. Praetorius: *Ich dank dir, Lieber Herre.*

The same voice distributions that were discussed in relation to three voices earlier in this chapter apply to four-voice combinations. However, the addition of another part makes possible a greater variety of voices, as well as a fuller texture.

As we also noted earlier, wider intervals appear more frequently at the bottom of a texture than between the upper voices. Intervals greater than an octave are found often between the bass and tenor; they do not appear as frequently between adjacent upper voices, alto–soprano, tenor–alto.

Two basic types of spacing traditionally have been applied to the dispositions of four voices: the term *close* applies to any arrangement in which the three upper members of a chord are in their closest possible positions. In such arrangements the soprano and tenor voices normally lie no more than an octave apart.

Ex. 13–25. Close spacing.

The term *open* is used for distributions in which the three upper parts are not arranged in their closest possible relations. In such arrangements the soprano and tenor notes will usually (though not always) lie more than an octave apart.

Ex. 13–26. Open spacing.

The designations of *close* and *open* are helpful, but they are such general descriptions that many kinds of spacing are not adequately identified by them. We can apply the term *homogeneous* (or *uniform*) to any distribution, close or open, that makes use of approximately equal intervals between the adjacent voices.

Ex. 13–27. Homogeneous spacing.

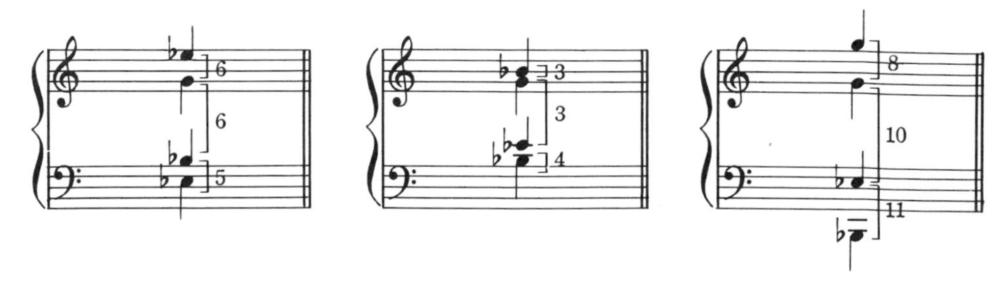

The opposite of homogeneous, *heterogeneous* (or *gapped*), refers to any chord in which the members are spaced with unequal gaps between them. Notice that most heterogeneous spacings are automatically also *open*.

Ex. 13–28. Heterogeneous spacing.

A four-voice texture in which separate pairs of adjacent voices are coupled together (as described in the discussion of spacing earlier) is a *heterogeneous spacing*. These kinds of arrangements are more typical of instrumental textures than of vocal. The use of certain heterogeneous distributions depends upon the available pitch range covered by participating instruments; obviously a combination of piccolo, clarinet, trumpet, and tuba possesses greater potentiality for heterogeneous spacings than do the soprano, alto, tenor, and bass vocal choir.

Ex. 13–29 contains five different settings of the first phrase of "America." Each passage has been written to illustrate a particular distribution of voices. Adoption of some of the spacing principles for this particular passage imposes occasional crudities of texture and voice movement one might wish to avoid. It would be inappropriate, however, to judge the effectiveness of the five settings on their merits alone, for the success of any one could be decided only in terms of its fulfillment of a particular musical need.

Examples 13–29a and 13–29b are similar to choral textures used frequently for this kind of communal song; but the remaining settings might be more appropriate for other uses. Each version should be played by instruments or sung several times (avoid using the piano if possible) followed by a discussion of the various factors that contribute to its musical effect.

Ex. 13–29a. Open homogeneous: chordal distribution.

Ex. 13–29b. Close homogeneous: emphasis on brilliance of sonority.

Ex. 13–29c. Heterogeneous coupling: soprano–alto; tenor–bass.

Ex. 13–29d. Homogeneous: emphasis on low register.

Ex. 13–29e. Open homogeneous: emphasis on individualized lines.

Composers control the spacing of their music with the same care lavished on chord structure, melodic pattern, and rhythmic motion; the appropriate chord could be inappropriate if its spacing were not matched with the desired effect. In this respect, spacing, individual voice range, and dynamics are inseparable factors. Example 13–30 shows a passage in which all three of these factors are combined in a complementary union that creates a sense of placid solemnity. Note that all four voices lie within the lower reaches of their respective ranges, that the spacing is generally homogeneous, and that the dynamic level is *piano.*

Ex. 13–30. Beethoven: *Missa Solemnis,* Gloria.

The excerpt in Ex. 13–31 illustrates the way a single musical phrase might shift quickly from one kind of distribution to another. Here the upper and the lower pairs of voices are coupled; after a beginning that is open, the couplings move together into a tight formation.

Ex. 13–31. Dello Joio: *Song of Affirmation,* Part 1. Copyright 1953 by Carl Fischer, Inc. Reprinted by permission.

The opposite condition—close spacing moving progressively to open—could be equally appropriate in another musical situation. Furthermore, abrupt shifts from one spacing to another are most appropriate when the nature of a passage demands variety rather than unity for its intended effect. In general, however, a single kind of vertical distribution prevails within any musical phrase or passage.

Contrapuntal Considerations (Voice Leading)

Although linear matters are not paramount in homophonic textures, the joining of one chord with another is normally achieved by means of predictable motion from one chord tone to the next. The individual chord members are links in separate unfolding chains of lines, even if those lines are sometimes of negligible melodic interest. In this sense, linear considerations are pertinent.

All lines of a four-voice texture usually do not move in parallel motion, and it is obviously impossible for *all* voices in such a texture to move in contrary or oblique motion in relation to one another. In the usual four-voice homophonic texture a general balance of all of these possible relationships is maintained.

In achieving this balance the following principles hold true:

1. Consecutive (parallel) fifths and octaves usually do not occur between voices, particularly between the outer voices.

Ex. 13–32. Parallel motion.

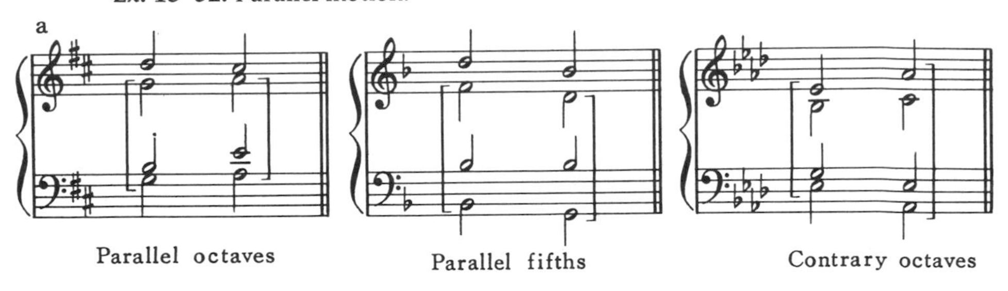

2. Fifths and octaves usually are not approached by similar motion in the same voices, particularly in the outer voices. This occurs occasionally at cadences, but even here one voice almost always moves by step to the cadential sonority.

Ex. 13–33. Similar octaves and fifths.

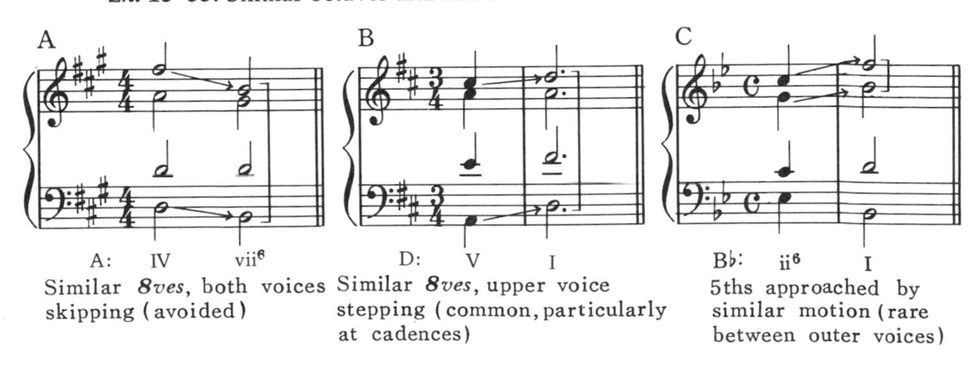

3. A tritone created between two voices normally resolves in the manner established earlier (°5 contracts, the +4 expands).

Ex. 13–34. Resolution of tritones.

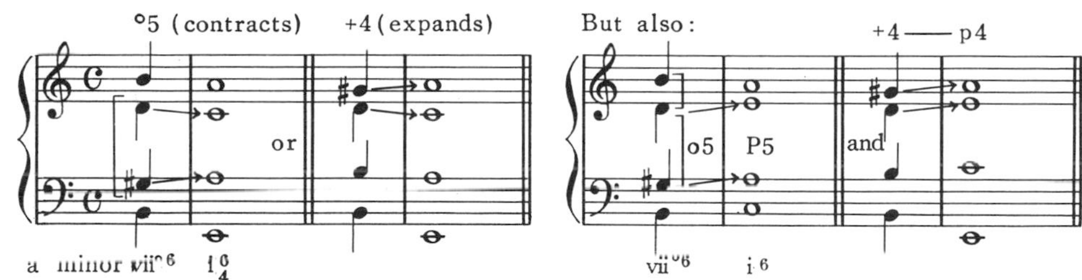

4. Voices usually maintain their range identities by not immediately overlapping the range of adjacent voices. (In Ex. 13–35 the tenor part in skipping upward from *G* to *D* overlaps the alto in its movement from c^1 to f^1.)

Ex. 13–35. Overlapping voices.

5. Outer voices often create an effective two-voice counterpoint, the inner voices in many instances being reduced to subsidiary lines. Note the static line of the alto and tenor voices in Ex. 13–36.

Ex. 13–36. Schumann: *Freue dich, O meine Seele.*

6. When linear considerations do not overrule it, every chord contains a full complement of chord tones, root (or prime), third, and fifth. When this possibility is overruled, a simpler sonority might well result: diad, unison, or octave doubling, etc. (The composer's desire for a particular sonority also can overrule this norm of the complete chord.)
7. When two successive chords contain one note that is common to both (or in some instances more than one), this note is retained in the same voice part unless melodic considerations demand another linkage.

Ex. 13–37. Common tones between chords.

A step-by-step working procedure for the homophonic setting of a melody is shown in Ex. 13–38. The result is only one of many possible solutions to the given problem. These settings are planned as simple choral arrangements without recourse to any procedures that would create more forceful musical statements. The chordal resources deliberately have been limited to diatonic triads.

Ex. 13–38. Working procedure for setting of melody.

(C) Bass voice completed

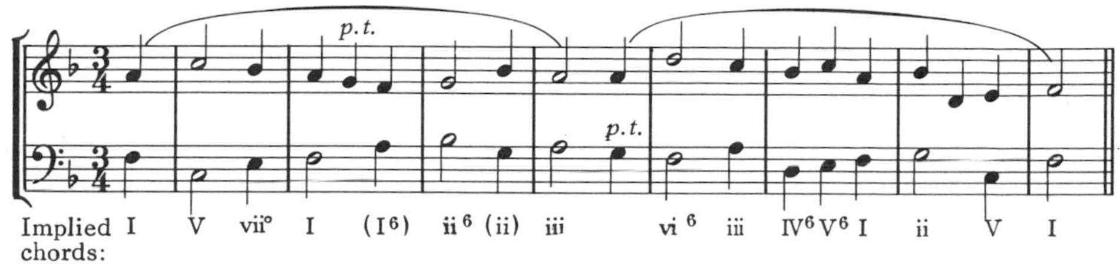

(D) Sketch of pitches for middle voices

(E) Completion of middle voices

(F) Decorative patterns added for more contrapuntal texture

Exercises

For more detailed assignments see *Materials and Structure of Music I, Workbook,* Chapter 13.

1. Plan a three-part rhythmic texture for percussion (clapped hands will suffice for performance if necessary) that consists of three complementary patterns.

Model:

2. Write an eight- to ten-measure passage in which the top voice dominates, and the two lower voices are relatively subordinate and are coupled together in register. Write another passage in which the bass dominates and the two upper voices are coupled.
3. Analyze a number of contrapuntal textures (Bach, Handel, Mozart) for basic pitches in three separate voices. Construct a three-voice basic framework as an abstraction of the texture. Then decorate the resultant framework to create a different composition.
4. Find several examples to illustrate each of the following homophonic textures:
   a. A dominating melody with a chordal accompaniment
   b. Block harmonies with isolated rhythm activity
   c. Two-line texture, the lower outlining chords (similar to Ex. 13–20)
   d. A texture in which contrapuntal and homophonic elements are blended
5. Using the harmonic progression of Ex. 13–37 as a harmonic basis, create piano settings illustrating homophonic textures (a), (c), and (d) of Exercise 4 above.
6. Taking an *F* major triad as a harmonic unit, see how many different four-part arrangements you can devise using customary vocal ranges, doublings, and spacings; do the same with a *d* minor triad in first inversion.
7. Perform each of the versions of "America" appearing in Ex. 13–30 by singing the on-the-beat chords in arpeggiated form (bass up), making suitable octave transpositions in order to fit your vocal range.

Chapter Fourteen

Decorative Patterns as Non-Chord Tones

We now expand our survey of melodic elaboration to encompass harmony as well as melody. At the same time we shall narrow down and make more precise our definitions of the various types of decorative patterns we discussed in Chapter 8.

The clearest way to describe the many types of decorative tones in a harmonic context is to relate them to the underlying chord structure in terms of direction (same, different; up, down) and motion (step, skip). Their common denominator is their *step relation* to one or more of the chord members. The term *non-chord tone* clearly indicates their relationship to the chord they embellish. Non-chord tones serve the same purposes as do all decorative tones—they increase melodic activity, connect, delay, introduce expressive highlights, or emphasize a structural tone. Numerous examples in this chapter will demonstrate that chord tones and even complete chords may also function in a decorative way (cf. the later section on decorative chords). Though all non-chord tones are, by definition, decorative, not all decoration in music is non-chordal in origin.

As voices are added to a musical texture, a greater number of consonant or dissonant interval relationships are formed between the

Outline of Non-chord Tones

Type	*Approached by*	*Left by*	*Direction and other characteristics*	*Rhythmic placement*
Passing tone	Step	Step	Same direction; connects two chord tones. Multiple passing tones fill in wider intervals between chord tones.	Unacc. or acc.
Neighbor tone	Step	Step	Direction changes; returns to same chord tone.	Unacc. or acc.
Appoggiatura	Skip	Step	Direction may or may not change.	Acc. is more frequent.
Escape tone	Step	Skip	Direction may or may not change.	Usually unacc.
Neighbor group	——	——	Pattern is step-skip-step; a figure formed with both upper and lower neighbors of a chord tone.	Unacc. or acc.
Anticipation	Step or skip	Rearticulation	Approached from either direction.	Unacc.
Suspension	Rearticulation or tie	Step	Preparation on weak metric location, suspension on strong, and downward resolution on weak.	——
Retardation	Rearticulation or tie	Step	Same as suspension but with upward resolution.	——
Pedal point	——	——	May be sustained or rearticulated in any voice. Commonly tonic or dominant pitch.	——

various parts. Consonance and dissonance are the most crucial considerations in two voices where interval relationships become the main basis for tension and relaxation. In thicker textures, though dissonances still are formed between a non-chord tone and one or more of the other parts, the effect is partially masked by the consonances formed with still other parts.

The chart on page 214 is a slightly expanded and redefined version of the earlier outline given on page 120.

Passing and Neighbor Tones

We can now view the passing tone as a non-chord tone that is approached by step from a chord member and resolves by step in the same direction to another chord member. The intervallic progression still suggests the *stable–unstable–stable* pattern. The only new aspect of the analytic process is that concerned with the vertical relationship: the members of each successive chord must be identified so that we can distinguish the non-chordal material from the chordal.

Ex. 14–1. Passing tones.

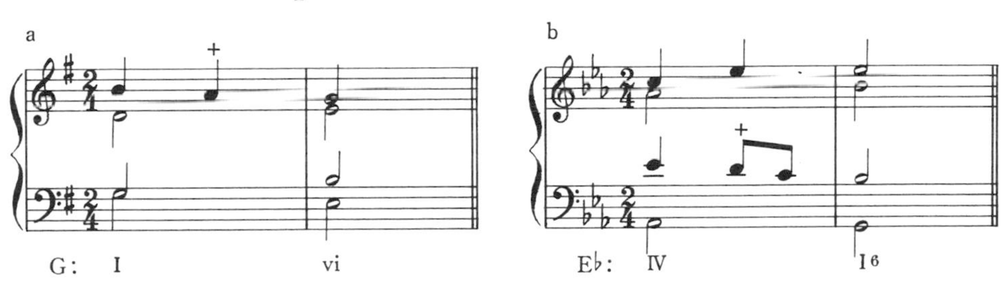

Neighbor tones fufill a similar role in relation to a chord: they are non-chord tones (approached by step from a chord member) that return to the same chord member.

Ex. 14–2. Neighbor tones.

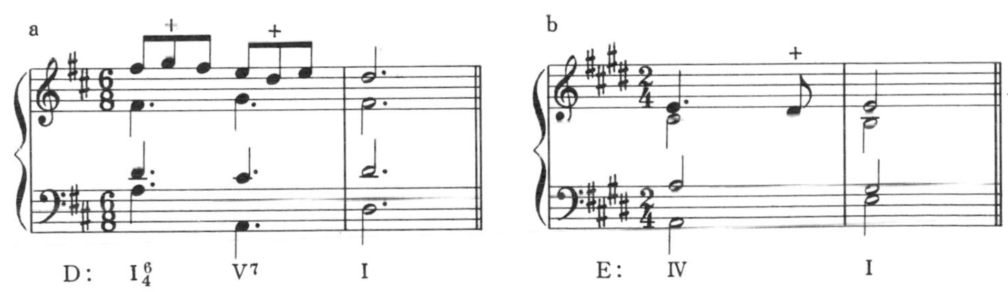

A study of the musical excerpts given next will reveal that, as in two-voice textures, passing and neighboring tones are the most common types of melodic embellishment. Even in a more linear and complex harmonic fabric, decorative pitches are approached or resolved by step. Each independent voice forms a cohesive and meaningful musical line, and the three parts fit harmonically into an intelligible tonal whole.

Ex. 14–3. Beethoven: Quartet in F Major, Op. 59, No. 1, I.

Ex. 14–4. Buxtehude: Prelude in E Minor.

Ex. 14–5. Mozart: Variations on a Menuet by Duport, Var. I.

Ex. 14–6. Hindemith: *Ludus Tonalis,* Fugue No. 8 © 1943 by Schott & Co., Ltd., London. Reprinted by permission.

Sequence, imitation, and other types of pattern-generating procedures depend heavily upon passing and neighbor tones, as in Ex. 14–7. The double passing tones in the upper parts form dissonant relationships against the bass, which moves in contrary motion to them; consecutive dissonances appear on each later portion of beat 3, but each resolves by step to a member of the prevailing harmony, a *d* minor triad. A similar treatment occurs in measure 2, organized this time around an *a* minor triad.

Ex. 14–7. Ockeghem: *Ut hermita solus.*

Ex. 14–8 illustrates a popular three-voice texture in Renaissance vocal music: parallel tenths in the outer voices surrounding a much less active middle part. The harmonic framework of this example is extremely simple, organized around the root progression . The elaborate neighbor and passing tones transform an uncomplicated harmonic framework into an extended contrapuntal passage that is characteristic of the style.

Ex. 14–8. Ockeghem: Motet.

Suspensions in Three and More Parts

All of the suspensions found in two-part music occur in thicker textures too, but some, such as the 9–8 suspension, are more common in three and more voices. Ex. 14–9 is an excellent introduction to the study of suspensions in more complex textures. Its sense of flow is increased by the alternation of consonance with dissonance as well as the introduction of new voices that coincide with suspension resolutions. Measure 11 illustrates another important fact about suspensions in multipart music—that they occur not only against the bass but also against other chord members; this measure contains a 4–3 suspension between the lower voices but also a 2–3 between upper voices. Measure 15 contains one of the less frequent 6–5 suspensions, considered by Renaissance theorists to be motion from lesser to greater consonance.

Ex. 14–9. J.C. Fischer: Fugue in E Major.

The following summary of principles that characterize the use of suspensions should be noted:

1. 4–3, 7–6, 6–5, 9–8, and 2–3 figures occur in three-voice compositions.
2. Suspensions often occur between the two upper voices in conjunction with suspensions above the bass.
3. The note of resolution is not generally sounded against the dissonance on the same pitch level as the dissonance. It frequently occurs in a

different octave. This is always true with 9–8 suspensions, sometimes with 7–6 patterns.

4. Suspended tones are not doubled.
5. Change of bass may occur with the suspension.
6. Suspensions are frequently ornamented by the interpolation of changing tones, which elaborate the suspension figure.
7. Suspensions may occur as diatonic or as altered pitches.

In the hands of some composers (such as Beethoven, for example) the suspension has been more freely treated. Ex. 14–10 incorporates several unusual suspensions in an interesting three-voice texture.

Ex. 14–10. Beethoven: Sonata in A-flat Major, Op. 110, Fugue.

The next two examples present suspensions in four and more voices. As may be seen in Ex. 14–11, the bass suspension provides an effective way of creating dissonance. A complete description of the interval pattern formed here would be $\begin{matrix}5\text{–}6\\2\text{–}3\end{matrix}$; we can simplify this figuration to 2–3, measuring the bass against the upper member of the chord that forms the characteristic dissonance.

Ex. 14–11. Pachelbel: *Nun lasst uns Gott, dem Herren.*

Several suspension types appear in Ex. 14–12. In thicker textures it is pointless to determine all of the intervallic relationships; therefore, we shall refer to most types of suspensions by measuring the suspended tone and its resolution against the bass, less often against an inner part that forms a characteristic dissonance.

Ex. 14–12. Brahms: Violin Sonata in G major, I.

As in two voices, resolutions of suspensions are often elaborated by additional pitches that embellish the dissonance. Ex. 14–13 contains, in measure 2, such an elaboration of the 7–6 suspension in the upper voice. In addition, the third measure illustrates resolutions with change of bass on beats 2 and 4.

Ex. 14–13. Mozart: Piano Concerto in A Major, K. 488, I.

Pedal Point

We considered pedal point briefly in an earlier chapter and now return for more detailed study of this forceful and prominent non-chord tone. As we noted earlier, pedal point is unique among the non-chord tones since it is the *structural* and anchoring element, whereas the other pitches are subordinate and prolong the effect of the pedal with a variety of decorative patterns. Thus pedal point—sometimes referred to as just "pedal" or "organ point"—is one of the simplest, yet most effective, techniques for providing a strong feeling of tonal and formal stability.

Pedals appear with frequency in the world's various ethnic musics and throughout the history of Western music. A drone on the tonic, or tonic and dominant combined, is a common feature of such unrelated cultures as Scottish bagpipe music, Arabian orchestral music, and the *tanbura* that accompanies the music of India.

In its simplest form a pedal consists of a tone that is sustained through a succession of chords, generally in the bass, but occasionally in an inner or upper part. Ex. 14–14 is an early example of pedal point, dating from the Middle Ages. In this style, known as *organum*,[1] the pedal voice sustains while the upper voices move together in strictly measured rhythm.

Ex. 14–14. Perotin: Three-voice Organum, *Alleluia*.

The pedal tone may or may not be a member of the chords that occur with it. In Ex. 14–15 the tonic pedal is a member of both tonic and subdominant triads but is foreign to the dominant (see measure 4).

Ex. 14–15. Haydn: Quartet in B Minor, Op. 64, No. 2, IV.

Pedal tones are not always sustained. Rearticulated pitches produce the same harmonic effect in a slightly "busier" way, as in Ex. 14–16.

[1] The name for the earliest form of polyphonic music, dating from the ninth century.

Ex. 14–16. Haydn: Quartet in D Major, Op. 50, No. 6, I.

Tonic and dominant pitches serve frequently as pedals, particularly in the music of the eighteenth and nineteenth centuries. Whichever pitch is used, the pedal tone has an extraordinary tonal forcefulness and suggests extreme harmonic and tonal stability; the chordal weavings that accompany it function more as decorative patterns that prolong the motion but do not affect real changes in the harmony of the passage.

The tonic pedal often appears near the beginning of a movement (as in the previous example by Haydn) or near the end. Both are locations in which the composer usually wishes to solidly establish the tonic. An examination of the Preludes and Fugues of Bach's *Well-tempered Clavier* will disclose his fondness for the closing tonic pedal. Used in this manner the pedal gives the impression that the harmonic progress of the composition is closing, that the moving voices are merely elaborating previous material in a prolongation of the cadential pattern.

Ex. 14–17. J.S. Bach: Fugue in C Minor (*Well-tempered Clavier,* Book I).

On the other hand, the dominant pedal is used with telling effect as a signal of the return of the tonic key. For obvious reasons, this is often found just prior to a closing section. The following passage contains a pedal on the dominant.

Ex. 14–18. Reger: Toccata in D Minor.

More than one pitch may act as a pedal. Sometimes the tonic and dominant are combined, as in the following example.

Ex. 14–19. Schubert: *Die Winterreise,* "Der Leiermann."

In passages employing pedal, tonal orientation remains unswerving despite the presence of chords quite foreign to the pedal pitch. In this sense chords which move over (or under) a pedal are *decorative chords* (passing chords, neighbor chords, etc.), and as such they prolong the harmonic meaning of the pedal tone and the key it represents.

Even more complicated uses of the same basic technique occur. Ex. 14–20 contains a passage in which two violins arpeggiate a C major triad through three measures, under which viola and cello move in parallel minor sevenths. Note again that it is the unchanging triad arpeggiation, the pedal, that provides the stable element; the moving sevenths form a decorative motion.

Ex. 14–20. Shostakovitch: Quartet, Op. 49, III. By permission of the International Music Company, New York.

Escape Tones, Appoggiaturas, Anticipations

Both the escape tone and the appoggiatura feature a melodic leap, the escape tone in its resolution and the appoggiatura in its approach. Generally the direction of the melodic line will change from approach to resolution, although many exceptions exist. While the escape tone is almost always unaccented, the appoggiatura is frequently accented, and its placement on a strong metric location accentuates the leap by which it is approached. Accented unprepared dissonances are rare in music composed before the nineteenth century.

Ex. 14–21. Escape tones and appoggiaturas.

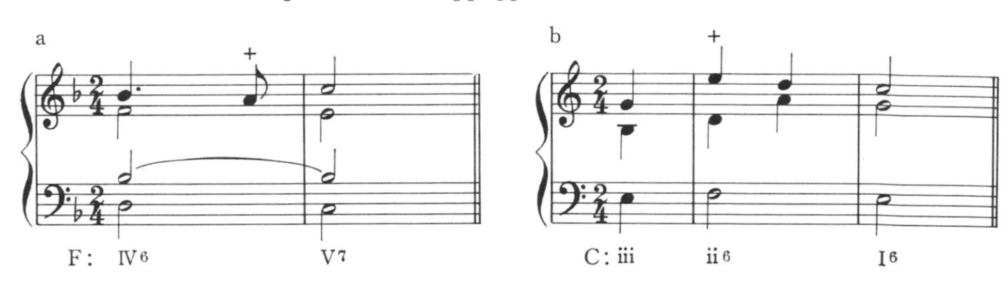

The anticipation, as its name implies, acts as a preview of the subsequent chord tone. Metrically the progression is from weak to strong.

Ex. 14–22. Anticipation.

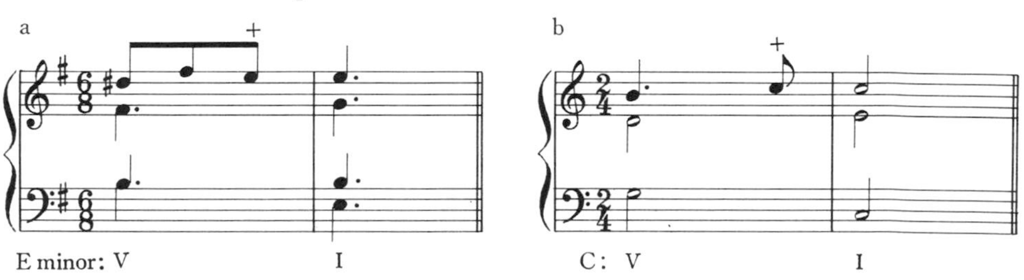

Examples of Escape Tones, Appoggiaturas, and Anticipations in a Variety of Styles

Ex. 14–23. Binchois: *De plus en plus.*

Ex. 14–24. J.S. Bach: Sinfonia in E-flat.

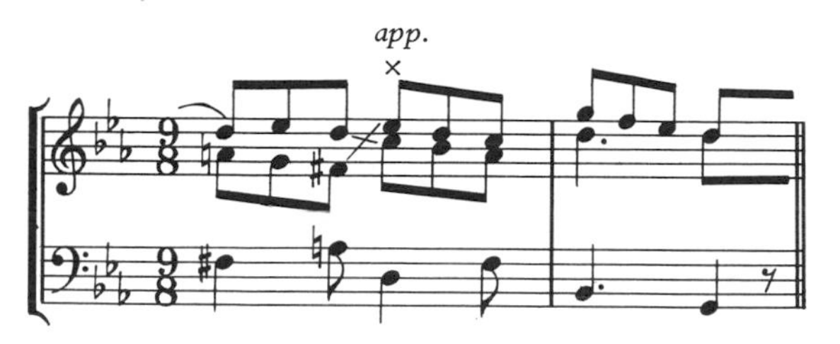

Ex. 14–25. J.S. Bach: Prelude in G Minor (*Well-tempered Clavier,* Book I).

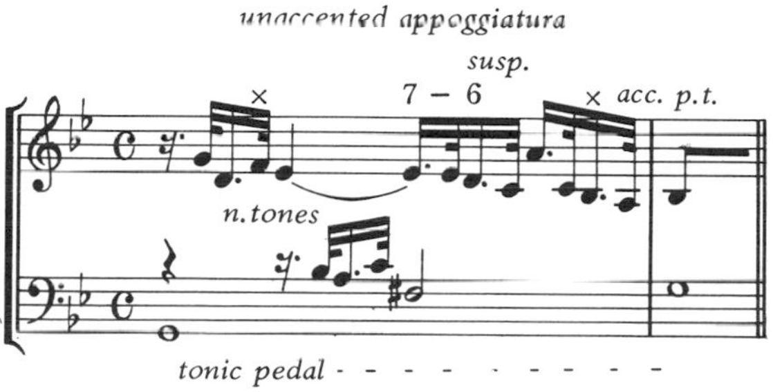

Ex. 14–26. Mozart: *Le Nozze di Figaro,* "Deh vieni, non tardar."

Ex. 14–27. Weber: *Euryanthe,* Overture.

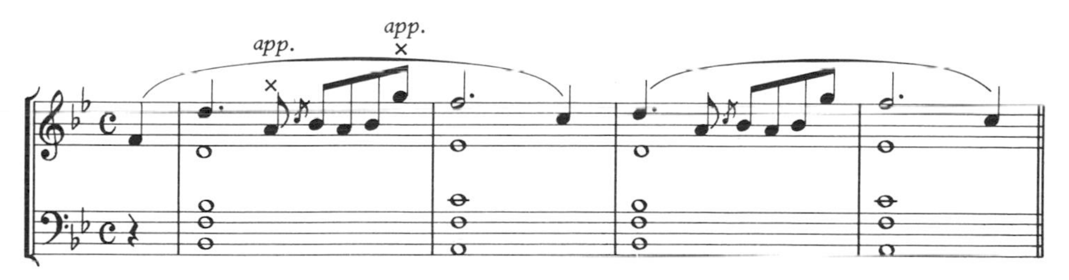

Accented Non-chord Tones

To this point we have generally limited our discussion of non-chord tones to such aspects as approach, resolution, direction, etc. And yet an equally significant feature of their effect lies in their placement in accented or in unaccented locations. *Strong* metric locations always serve to intensify a dissonant tone: accented non-chord tones appear to possess more melodic "thrust" than unaccented ones.

Nineteenth-century harmonic practice featured the use of accented non-chord tones—appoggiaturas, accented passing and neighbor tones, rearticulated suspensions—often combined with one another. The following chorale prelude on a familiar German Christmas chorale exemplifies this highly expressive and intense melodic/harmonic style.

Ex. 14–28. Brahms: *Es ist ein Ros' entsprungen.*

Simultaneous Non-chord Tones

Non-chord tones do not always occur singly. A great degree of mobility can be created when two decorative patterns occur together, particularly when they are articulated simultaneously. The simple combination of an anticipation along with the resolution of a suspension, for example, produces a sharp dissonance colorfully known as the "Corelli clash." (In spite of the name, it was used by other baroque composers as well!)

Ex. 14–29. Corelli: Sonata, Op. 2, No. 4.

Other non-chord tones are frequently combined, particularly when they are of the same type—double passing tones, double neighboring tones, etc. Example 14–30 contains a double suspension. This type of pattern is particularly common when two lines are moving in parallel thirds or sixths.

Ex. 14–30. Mozart: Motet, *Ave verum corpus.*

A more complex combination occurs when an entire chord is suspended above a foreign bass note. In Ex. 14–31 the first beat of the final measure contains a diminished triad suspended over an arpeggiated tonic chord. The third tone (the g^1), unprepared in the previous chord, is added to the upper parts to form a more complete sonority.

Ex. 14–31. Mozart: Sonata in D major, K. 311, I.

A non-chord figure containing a so-called *free tone* (which in terms of melodic analysis would be a secondary pitch) occurs when a pitch that is clearly foreign to the prevailing chord is approached and left by skip. The cadence shown in the following example actually is similar to the bichordal effect illustrated in Ex. 14–31; the lower line is merely an arpeggiated tonic triad, part of which forms dissonant relations with the chord in the upper voices.

Ex. 14–32. Free tone.

Decorative Chords

Complete chords also can fulfill the main decorative functions—passing, neighboring, suspension, and appoggiatura—as illustrated in Ex. 14–33. This example contains, in turn, a neighboring chord (N), a passing chord (P), and a suspension chord (S). The terminology implies, of course, that these are the less structural chords in the excerpt.

Ex. 14–33.

A decorative chord is often a passage's most significant feature. In Ex. 14–34 the contrary motion of the outer parts is clearly the organizing force behind the progression of chords. We may recognize some of the chords as being displaced rhythmically; others as chromatic chords, but the outstanding characteristic of the passage is the *passing role* of chords and bass in relation to one another.

Ex. 14–34. Brahms: Symphony No. 4, IV.

In Ex. 14–35 we find a variety of decorative chords as well as some combinations that are more difficult to describe. The texture of this illustration involves considerable decorative activity in the three upper parts over the cello's dominant pedal point. To appreciate the complexity of the musical decoration, make a piano reduction or play the example at the piano with another student, using four hands.

Ex. 14–35. Beethoven: Quartet, Op. 18, No. 5, III.

Ambiguity in Analysis

In some musical passages it is not easy to make an absolute judgment about what is chordal and what is nonchordal, as in Ex. 14–36, measure 3:

Ex. 14–36. Schumann: *Einsame Blumen* (Waldszenen).

Depending upon one's interpretation of the underlying chord structure, each note of the top line within the brackets could be viewed as nonchordal. Is the chord progression VI–iv, VI–ii$^{0}_{0}$, or does the entire measure outline the iv triad? Considering the basic melodic contour as well as the harmonic pattern, the simplest solution seems to be iv, with the *B-flat* and *A* in the upper voice as consecutive passing tones.

But in this and many other instances, no one has the authority to favor one possible solution over another. All things being equal, the simplest answer is often the best. The ambiguity of melodic/harmonic patterns is at once one of music's greatest assets and one of the greatest challenges to the analyst. Rather than decide upon a single authoritative interpretation for every situation, we recommend the development of a critical tolerance for ambiguous musical situations; after examining all possibilities, a single "correct" answer is frequently misleading and unnecessary.

Non-chord Tones in Twentieth-century Harmonic Contexts

Obviously the identification of non-chordal material becomes more difficult as harmonic language becomes more complicated. Nevertheless, these principles of melodic activity are of value in analyzing the music of our century. As the following example demonstrates, clear passing and neighbor patterns can be discerned despite a more complex chordal structure than in the previous examples. Used judiciously, this analytic approach is still relevant for a great deal of the music of the twentieth century.

Ex. 14–37. Bartók: Improvisations, Op. 20, I. Copyright 1922 by Universal Edition; Renewed 1949. Copyright and Renewal assigned to Boosey and Hawkes, Inc. Reprinted by permission.

Exercises

For more detailed assignments see *Materials and Structure of Music I, Workbook,* Chapter 14.

1. Illustrate in three voices 9–8, 7–6, and 4–3 suspensions in various major and minor keys.
2. Locate examples of ambiguous passages and compare alternate analyses of the non-chord tones they contain.
3. Analyze Ex. 14–28 for non-chord tones; then make a basic melody analysis of the upper line and compare your results to the original tune, found in most hymnals with the text "Lo, How a Rose e'er Blooming."
4. Explore Ex. 14–37 for possible non-chord tones; what factors help in determining the tonal and harmonic basis for this composition?
5. Find examples of pedal point in the following literature: J. S. Bach's *Well-Tempered Clavier,* Mozart's piano sonatas, Haydn's string quartets.
6. Locate all suspensions in Ex. 14–9.
7. As recommended earlier in this chapter, make a piano reduction of Ex. 14–35 and locate examples of various decorative tones and chords.

Chapter Fifteen

Broader Aspects of Harmony

The way chords are linked together is an important aspect of harmony: effective harmony is not just a fortuitous succession of chords.

In this chapter we shall discuss three structural aspects of harmony that influence segments of musical form larger than simple chord-to-chord movement. All three bear upon the mobility and punctuation of a musical texture, whether it be homophonic or polyphonic. Our discussion will relate almost exclusively to music produced between 1650 and 1900.

Harmonic Rhythm

Consider first the rate at which chords change within a passage.

Ex. 15–1. Schubert: Impromptu in A-flat Major, Op. 90.

As in many compositions, the rate of chord change—the *harmonic rhythm*—in this excerpt is periodic: a new chord with each measure. This kind of regular change lends an air of simplicity to any passage; it is predictable and thus provides a solid foundation for other musical events that occur with it. In some music such a consistent rhythm of chord change joins with other elements, such as meter, to control the unfolding of a complete composition.

The piece from which Ex. 15–2 is taken is almost totally organized on the rate of harmonic change established in its initial measures.

Ex. 15–2. J. S. Bach: Prelude in C Major (*Well-tempered Clavier*, Book I).

Strict uniformity of harmonic rhythm is not always the case. In many compositions a single section might retain a generally uniform rate of chord change but with deviations. These deviations may take place to accompany a particular melodic pattern or to intensify a climactic growth through a sense of harmonic acceleration. The passage in Ex. 15–3 is typical of the kind of harmonic acceleration found in some music of the eighteenth century. Observe that the rate of change beginning at *d* is about three times faster than that in sections *a, b,* and *c.*

Ex. 15–3. Mozart: Symphony in G Minor, K. 550, III.

As a rule, increasing harmonic rhythm projects a feeling of greater momentum. And conversely, a relatively plodding rate of change—other factors being equal—suggests a more placid condition.

Tempo and harmonic rhythm usually correspond in a simple way: the faster the tempo, the slower the rate of chord changes. This simple rule must be taken quite seriously when you analyze harmony. In a passage such as Ex. 15–4, chords change on every sixteenth note. Played at a rapid tempo, however, the passage projects only a blurring of harmonic effect. Played very slowly, on the other hand, one might recognize actual harmonic progression from one chord to the next.

Ex. 15–4. Reger: *Kyrie Eleison* (for organ).

Once the prevailing harmonic rhythm of a passage has been determined, then one may draw some conclusions about its importance as an aspect of musical organization, how it might or might not affect other musical properties.

As we mentioned earlier, an increase in the rate of harmonic change can produce a rise in apparent momentum as surely as can increasing loudness or thickening texture. It is not surprising that the rate of harmonic rhythm frequently increases when a passage approaches a cadence. The next two pairs of examples, drawn from compositions of different historical periods, demonstrate this tendency.

Ex. 15–5a. J.G. Walther: Concerto in B Minor (interior passage).

Ex. 15–5b. Same work at a cadence.

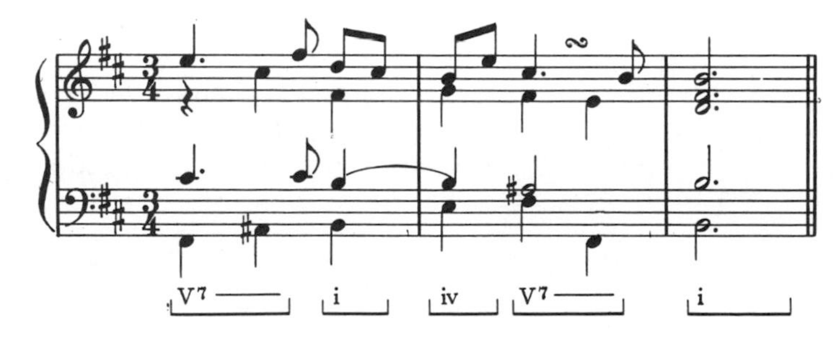

Ex. 15–6a. Franck: Symphony in D Minor (interior passage).

Ex. 15–6b. Same work at a cadence.

We can make still other general observations about how harmonic rhythm affects musical form. Its rate is noticeably faster in sections that are developmental rather than expository in function. Likewise, sections of apparent instability usually contain rapid harmonic change as one means of achieving that instability. Clearly, it is easier to project a clear sense of tonality and to create musical stability if harmonic change is relatively slow. And last, composers frequently define separate formal sections by setting each at its own rate of chordal change. Thus harmonic rhythm can be an agent of form, influencing both thematic and tonal aspects of any passage.

Melodic motion is another property that can influence or be influenced by harmonic rhythm. When melody is the most prominent element of a texture—especially a rhythmically active melody—a slower rate of chord changes is the usual accompaniment. The reason for this is simple: a rapid rate of harmonic rhythm might obscure the free flow of the melodic pitches.

Harmonic Prolongation

It is tempting to think of chords only as simple one-at-a-time congregations of tone, as exclusively "vertical" events within a musical texture. This view must be amended if we are to appreciate the full role of harmony in a lot of music. In fact, composers have developed numerous ways of spinning out a single chord over long time spans. The most obvious way is illustrated in Ex. 15–7, where melodic play "horizontalizes" a *G* major chord.

Ex. 15–7. Simple prolongation of a chord by arpeggiation.

A somewhat less simple example is shown next. In spite of constant side-stepping to brief "neighboring chords," this passage projects a surprisingly placid harmonic rhythm.

Ex. 15–8a. J. S. Bach: Prelude in G Major (*Well-tempered Clavier,* Book I).

Ex. 15–8b. Harmonic analysis of Ex. 15–8a.

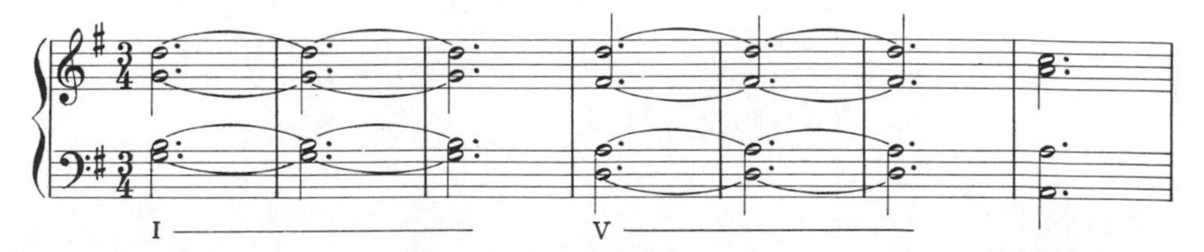

Pedal Point

Prolongations of a single chord over a considerable time span often are rooted in a pedal point that controls the tonal orientation of the texture. Through this process a composer can create a considerable sense of motion, yet motion that ultimately goes nowhere. Distinct chord changes can occur as a harmonic *foreground,* nonetheless remaining solidly anchored in a *background chord* because of the persistence of a single sustained pitch. Note the rhythmic play that weaves through Ex. 15–9, all of this immobilized harmonically by the forceful *E* pedal point.

Ex. 15–9. Buxtehude. Prelude in E Minor (for organ).

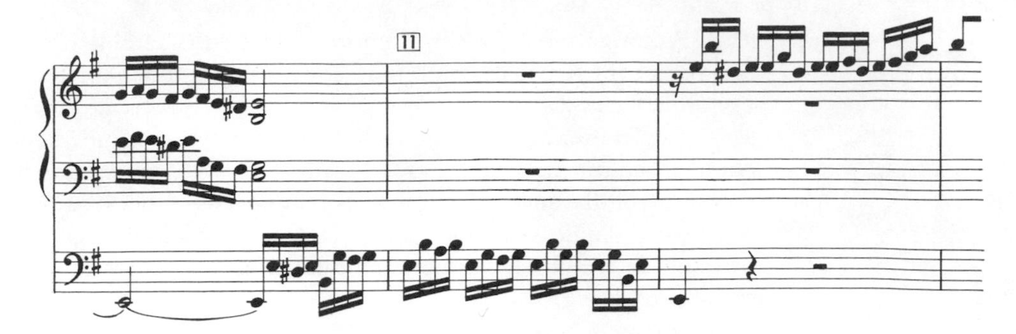

Even greater harmonic change in foreground patterns can be heard in Ex. 15–10. While the Buxtehode excerpt (Ex. 15–9) occurs in the opening of a composition, the passage by Franck spins out the final tonic as a gesture of conclusion.

Ex. 15–10. Franck: Pastorale in E Major (for organ).

This spinning out of a single chord or harmonic function occurs most frequently at formal junctures such as beginnings or endings.

The next excerpt, Ex. 15–11, actually occurs as the linkage between two interior sections, so it is both an ending and a beginning. The second of these two sections (marked by the asterisk) is actually the return of a theme in the tonic key. Observe that this return is prepared forcefully by the persistent rearticulation of *F* in the bass. And thus pedal points are not always sustained; repetition can perform the same function.

Ex. 15–11. Mozart: Sonata in B-flat Major, K. 333, III.

Other Means of Prolongation

Passages of prolongation such as these sometimes are less controlled by pedal point than by other techniques. The next example contains several kinds of prolongation—repeated melodic patterns, arpeggiation, a sustained chord, scale passages, neighbor tones, *and* brief snatches of actual pedal points. Amidst all of this rhythmic motion the pitch *G* lurks in the background as a steadying force. Intensity builds until, by measure 152, the reigning harmonic unit clearly has flowered into a dominant seventh chord, whose anticipated resolution arrives in measure 156. By these means a fourteen-measure passage has prolonged a single chord (*G* major) in order to cast a spotlight on the imminent return of a main theme.

Ex. 15–12. Beethoven: Sonata in C Major, Op. 53, I.

Harmonic Cadence [1]

We have observed many times how a single melodic line can project a convincing cadence through its patterns of rhythm and pitch. Harmony naturally can reinforce or, as the case may be, thwart the cadential effect created by the melody associated with it. In discussing cadences we must always bear in mind that chords alone cannot produce a cadence: melodic and rhythmic factors must be coordinated in special ways for a cadence to occur.

Our task now is to identify cadences more precisely than we did in our discussions of melody in Chapter 4. Our expanded understanding of harmony makes possible this greater precision.

Terminal Cadences

If we consider harmonic content, we find that the cadences we formerly designated only as *terminal* can be found in several subvarieties in music of the seventeenth, eighteenth, and nineteenth centuries. Most common of these terminal subvarieties is the *authentic cadence.* It consists of movement from dominant (V or V_7) to tonic. The following four excerpts illustrate various manifestations of this basic cadential pattern.

Ex. 15–13. Beethoven: Septet, Op. 20, Minuetto.

[1] You may wish to review Chapter Four before studying this chapter.

Ex. 15–14. Mendelssohn: Symphony in A Minor (*Scotch*), I.

Ex. 15–15. Mozart: Symphony in A Major, K. 114, Menuetto.

Ex. 15–16. Mozart: Requiem, Offertory, "Domine Jesu Christe."

Although the chordal content is not exactly the same, cadences in which the leading tone chord (vii°) replaces the dominant also are called *authentic.*

Ex. 15–17. Buxtehude: Instrumental Sonata, *Jesu, Meine Freude.*

A second subvariety of terminal cadences is known as *plagal.* It is produced by movement to tonic from the subdominant chord (IV or IV_7, or iv or iv_7 in minor keys). This root movement of a perfect fourth (or up a perfect fifth) forms the "Amen" at the end of many Protestant hymns. Composers have used it in art music when their intention is to suggest at any point a religious aura.

Ex. 15–18. Brahms: *Alto Rhapsody.*

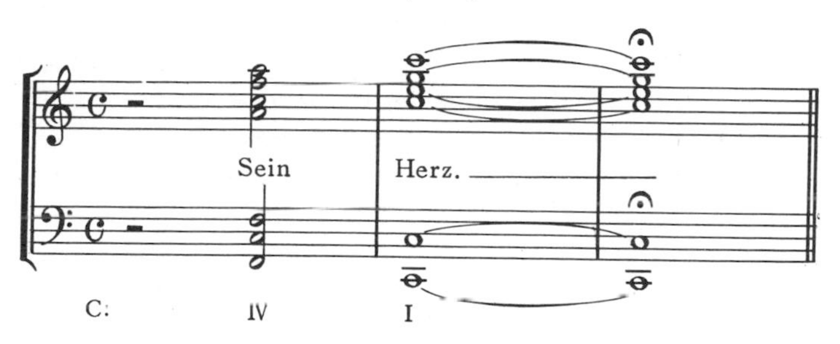

Progressive Cadences

By harmonic means we can classify progressive cadences more precisely too. For example, any cadence that ends with the dominant chord is called a *half cadence.* While any chord might precede the V chord in a half cadence, Ex. 15–19 shows an example that is actually the reverse of the authentic cadence, i–V. Many examples you will hear contain the dominant preceded by IV or ii.

Ex. 15–19. Mass in C Minor, K. 427, *"Domine Deus."*

The so-called *Phrygian cadence* is a special kind of half cadence. It occurs most often in minor keys, less often in major. This cadence type has two essential characteristics: (1) the chord succession iv_6 (or sometimes IV_6) to V, and (2) contrary motion between the two outer voices, those parts expanding or contracting to an octave on the dominant scale degree. Example 15–20 shows a typical example.

Ex. 15–20. Handel: Concerto Grosso, Op. 6, No. 2.

Phrygian cadences occur more frequently at interior phrase endings than at terminal points for whole sections or movements. Occasionally, however, composers of the baroque period used this cadence type at the end of an inner movement, thereby suggesting a tight harmonic connection with the following movement.

The last progressive cadence type we shall discuss here is called *deceptive*. Its deception derives from the fact that the listener expects a terminal cadence to occur, only to be deceived by a progressive harmonic quality. (Sometimes this sense of deception is not terribly dramatic!)

Listen to Ex. 15–21. Note particularly the cadence in measure 8.

Ex. 15–21. Haydn: String Quartet, Op. 76, No. 2, IV.

Actually, Haydn did not write it quite that way. In fact, the cadence he composed for measure 8 provided the phrase with a definite need for continuation by ending with a deceptive cadence on VI rather than i. Note in Ex. 15–22 how Haydn's passage really ends.

Ex. 15–22. Correct version of Ex. 15–21.

The Haydn excerpt is typical of most deceptive cadences in that the two chords are related by roots a second apart. In a majority of deceptive cadences the chord progression is V to vi or, in minor keys, V to VI. Yet there are many deceptive cadences in which the root movement is downward. Example 15–23 contains root movement upward, while 15–24 provides the opposite motion. Both are deceptive.

Ex. 15–23. Bach: Two-part Invention in D Major.

Ex. 15–24. Prokofiev: *Classical Symphony,* II.

Whatever its particular harmonic content, the deceptive cadence has the power of punctuation that can frustrate the listener's expectations. While melodic and rhythmic factors both signal *termination,* the harmonic factor contradicts them by producing a *progressive* effect—and thus deception.

Exercises

For more detailed assignments see *Materials and Structure of Music I, Workbook,* Chapter 15.

1. Study compositions you have performed in the past or are performing currently to find examples of harmonic prolongation.
2. Write an eight-measure phrase (or a two-phrase period) in which the precadence motion is the prolongation of the ii chord.
3. Study the harmonic rhythm of the Scherzo and Trio of Beethoven's Piano Sonata, Op. 2, No. 2. What differences exist (if any do) between the harmonic rhythm of the Scherzo and the Trio? Do the harmonic changes coincide with the metric accents throughout? Compare measures 1–4 and 17–20 of the Trio. Do the harmonic rhythms differ?
4. Determine the harmonic rhythm of the excerpt shown below, then write a four-part vocal composition based on the same pattern. (Use a contrapuntal texture, with or without text.)
5. Examine piano and choral pieces of the 18th century, isolating each cadence to determine its harmonic type (authentic, plagal, etc.) and its function in the form (terminal, progressive, etc.).
6. Practice writing V–I, V_7–I, IV–I, and V–vi cadences in SATB textures in different keys, both major and minor modes.

Beethoven: Piano Concerto No. 4, Op. 58, III.

Chapter Sixteen

Tonic and Dominant Triads; First-Inversion Triads; The Dominant Seventh and the Leading Tone Triad

We observed in Chapter 12 that each scale degree may function as a chord root; the number of a given scale degree identifies the chord whose root is that scale degree. Descriptive names such as *tonic, subdominant,* and *dominant* also are convenient names for designating chords without having to name every pitch in the chord. Thus we can see similar harmonic patterns, even when the actual pitches involved are different. This is the case in Ex. 16–1, where both harmonic progressions are the same *in function.*

Ex. 16–1.

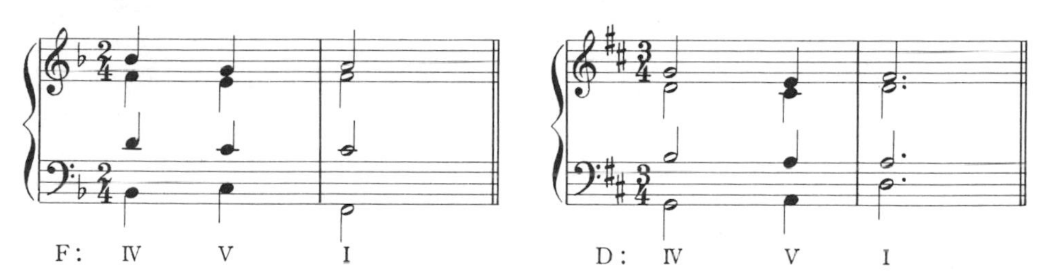

Tonic and Dominant Triads

The tonic (I)-dominant (V) relationship is perhaps the most common in tonal music. It has been said that the V–I (or I–V) pattern is not only the basis for understanding most tonal music but in a more expanded sense the basis for most musical forms of our west European tradition. Before examining specific examples, let us consider the properties of these two chords and the overall effect of their relationship.

Characteristics of the tonic chord: root is the tonal center, creating stability and serving as a starting point and final goal of many progressions.

Characteristics of the dominant chord: root is a perfect fifth above (or fourth below) tonic, creating relative instability; although the dominant chord sometimes serves as a temporary goal, its typical role is to progress to tonic.

Characteristics of the progression dominant to tonic (V to I): instability moving to stability, root movement by descending perfect fifth (or ascending perfect fourth), defining the key and emphasizing the stability of the tonic triad. Melodically, the progression of leading tone to tonic pitch (7–8) complements this harmonic activity. In differing textures, the above features can be seen in Ex. 16–2, Ex. 16–3, and Ex. 16–4.

Ex. 16–2. Schubert: Impromptu, Op. 90.

Ex. 16–3. J.S. Bach: French Suite No. 3, Menuet.

Ex. 16–4. Haydn: Symphony No. 95, Menuetto (towards tonic).

First Inversion of the Tonic and Dominant Triads

Triads are invertible, as discussed in Chapter 12. There are several inverted triads in the next example.

Ex. 16–5. Bach: Chorale No. 365, *Jesu, meiner Seelen Wonne.*

The function of a chord in a key remains unchanged when its root is in a voice other than the bass; however, its harmonic effect and linear (melodic) characteristics are somewhat modified. First-inversion chords often seem richer in sound. They frequently appear following root position arrangements of the same chord, affording variety of voice leading and generating linear connection between the root and the third of the same triad.

Ex. 16–6. Purcell: *Dido and Aeneas,* "Shake the Cloud."

The melodic function of the bass of a first-inversion chord is quite apparent in Ex. 16–7 and 16–8. In these passages the leading tone in the bass emphasizes the tonic by its step movement to it.

Ex. 16–7. Rameau: Rigaudon.

Ex. 16–8. Beethoven: Quartet in E Minor, Op. 59, No. 2, I.

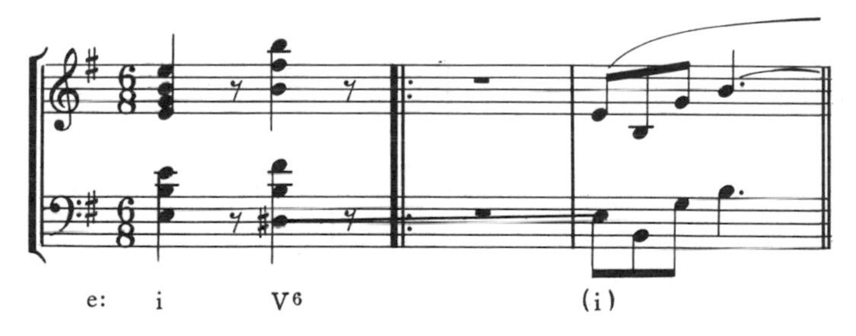

Other Forms of Tonic and Dominant

Until the close of the Baroque era (roughly 1750) composers customarily closed minor compositions with a major triad, a cliché named the *Tièrce de Picardie* (the "Picardy" Third) for reasons that remain obscure. This practice emphasized the conclusiveness and consonant qualities of the major tonic triad.

Ex. 16–9. J.S. Bach: *Orgelbüchlein,* "Puer natus in Bethlehem."

Occasionally the minor dominant chord (v) occurs, as in Ex. 16–10; the subtonic is present instead of the raised leading tone, imparting a modal flavor to the harmony. It is far less common than progressions involving the major dominant triad, especially in music of the eighteenth and nineteenth centuries.

Ex. 16–10. Vaughan Williams: *Mass in G Minor,* Kyrie. Reprinted by permission of the copyright owner, G. Schirmer, Inc.

The Dominant Seventh Chord (V_7)

A significant feature of tertian harmony is the possibility of creating many different types of sonorities by superimposing various types of thirds. We have seen that four common varieties of triads (M, m, °, +) can be created using major and minor thirds. This process can be extended to create more complex sonorities. Generically, any four-note sonority is a *tetrad*; when its components can be arranged to form a series of consecutive thirds, we refer to it as a *seventh chord.* Ex. 16–11 contains several possible combinations.

Ex. 16–11. Tetrads (X = a seventh chord).

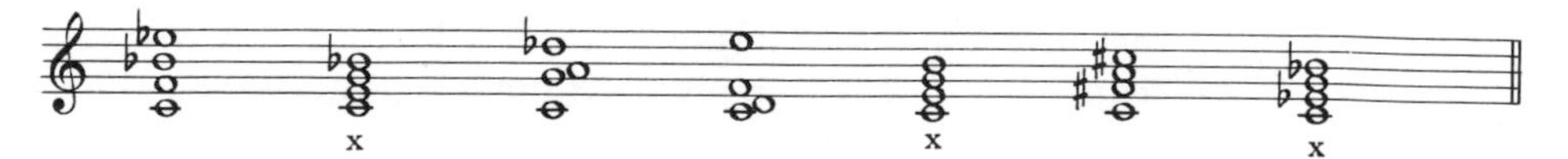

Seventh chords, because of their potential for adding harmonic color and melodic tension, became an important part of the composer's vocabulary in the seventeenth, eighteenth, and nineteenth centuries, reaching peak usage between 1825 and 1900—an age characterized by harmonic color. Throughout this evolution toward greater harmonic complexity, one type of seventh chord was used with greater frequency than all the rest: the "major-minor" seventh chord.

Ex. 16–12 shows a dominant seventh chord in its simplest arrangement. Its name derives from the intervals contained in the chord: a major triad and a minor seventh built on the same root pitch (*D*)—hence the term *major-minor* (Mm) *seventh*. When this chord is built on the dominant, we call it V_7.

Ex. 16–12. Mozart: Concerto in G Major, K. 453, I.

Melodic Tendencies in V_7

The dominant seventh chord contains a strong set of melodic "tendencies." It is characteried both by mild dissonance (the interval of the seventh) and tonal instability (the tritone formed by the third and seventh of the chord). Historically, we can see that composers have often cushioned the effect of dissonance through melodic preparation and resolution. Early examples of V_7, as illustrated in Ex. 16–13 and Ex. 16–14, demonstrate this: the dissonant seventh is approached by step or prepared in the same voice and resolved by descending step.

Ex. 16–13. Tye: *Come, Holy Ghost* (seventh approached by step).

Ex. 16–14. Scheidt: *Allein Gott in der Höh sei Ehr* (seventh prepared in the same voice, suggesting a suspension).

In Ex. 16–15 the dominant seventh is introduced in such a way that the chord's seventh is a chord member rather than a result of linear activity. Its metric location, duration, and approach (by leap) confirm the fact that the seventh is an integral member of the chord and not merely the result of melodic motion.

Ex. 16–15. Monteverdi: *Ohimè, se tanto amate.*

The tritone in the major-minor seventh chord is an equally important factor in the chord's resolution. Traditionally the interval is resolved in one of two ways:

When notated as an augmented fourth, it expands to a sixth.
When notated as a diminished fifth, it contracts to a third.

The usual result is that (1) the leading tone is resolved by a step up and (2) the seventh is resolved by a step down.

Ex. 16–16. Resolution of the V_7.

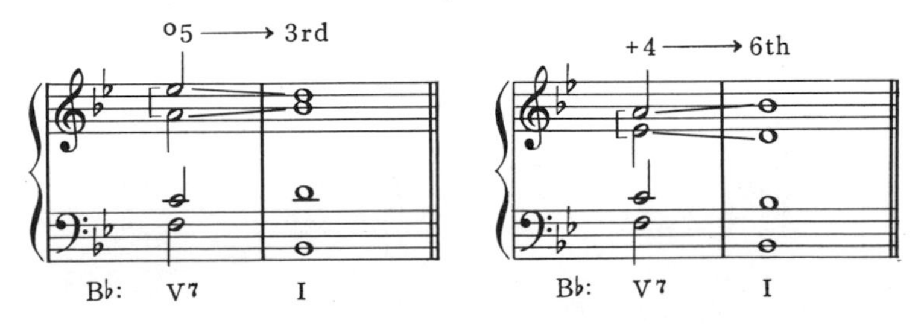

This resolution pattern is sometimes not followed. A composer may resolve the leading tone downward to the fifth of the tonic chord in order to obtain a complete triad on the resolution chord. This is seldom done, however, when the leading tone is in the top or bottom part.

Ex. 16–17. Variant resolution of the diminished fifth in the V_7 chord.

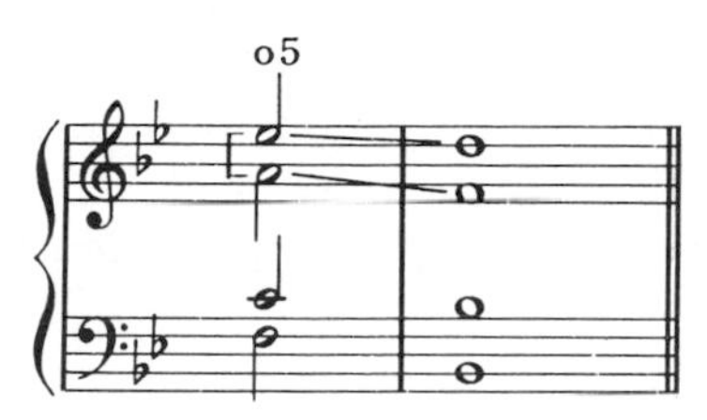

Figuration of V_7 and its Inversions

As with triad inversions, we shall indicate seventh-chord inversions by figured bass symbols. Since we are dealing with a more complex sonority, however, the figurations must be more complete. For the four positions of the dominant seventh (and for all seventh chords in general), we use the following figured bass symbols.

Ex. 16–18. Figuration of inversions of the V_7.

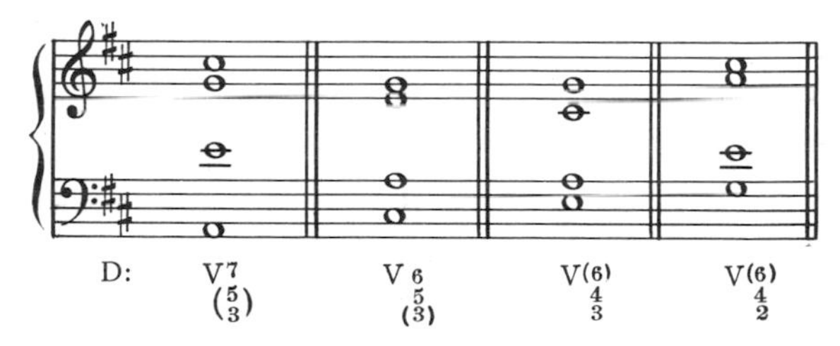

In Ex. 16–18 the figures in parentheses are unnecessary to the identification of the chord and, consequently, are generally omitted both from the figured bass and from the analytical symbols. Note that the numerical relation that represents the interval of the *seventh* (or its inversion, the *second*) is *always* included—$7\text{-}{}^{6}_{5}\text{-}{}^{4}_{3}\text{-}{}^{4}_{2}$, respectively.

Inverted forms of V_7 are usually complete. On occasion, though, V_7 appears with the fifth missing and root doubled. Similarly, when V_7 does appear in complete form, its chord of resolution is often incomplete. Ex. 16–19 contains three typical versions of this progression.

Ex. 16–19.

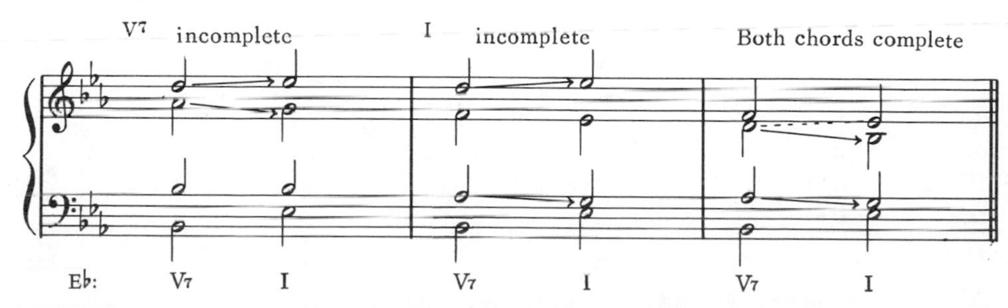

These progressions illustrate the conflict that often exists in music between *harmonic* and *melodic* goals. Completeness of sonority is a prime harmonic goal; likewise, smooth melodic motion and resolution of unstable intervals are important melodic goals. When it is not possible to achieve both of these objectives, the composer must decide in favor of one or the other. In the first two progressions of Ex. 16–19, harmonic values are subordinate to melodic purposes; in the third the tritone is not resolved.

Inversions of V_7

The following examples illustrate typical uses of V^6_3, V^4_3, and V^4_2. Each excerpt should be carefully examined for (1) preparation and resolution of the seventh and (2) resolution of the leading tone.

Ex. 16–20. Haydn: Quartet in D Major, Op. 50, No. 6, I. V^6_5 to I with characteristic tritone resolution.

Ex. 16–21. R. Strauss: *Breit über mein Haupt.* V^6_5 to I with seventh prepared in the preceding chord.

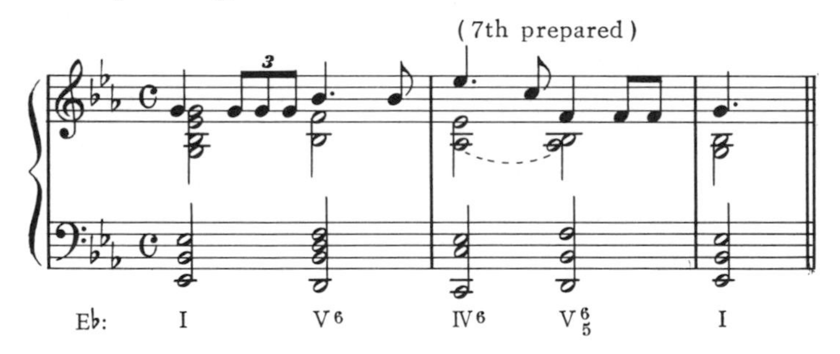

Ex. 16–22. Tchaikovsky: Violin Concerto in D Major, I. V^6_5 as a neighbor chord to I (tritone approached and left by contrary motion).

Ex. 16–23. Haydn: Quartet in C Major, Op. 54, No. 2, II. V^6_5 with delayed resolution to i.

Ex. 16–24. Bruckner: Symphony No. 7, II. V^6_5 with bass note approached by skip.

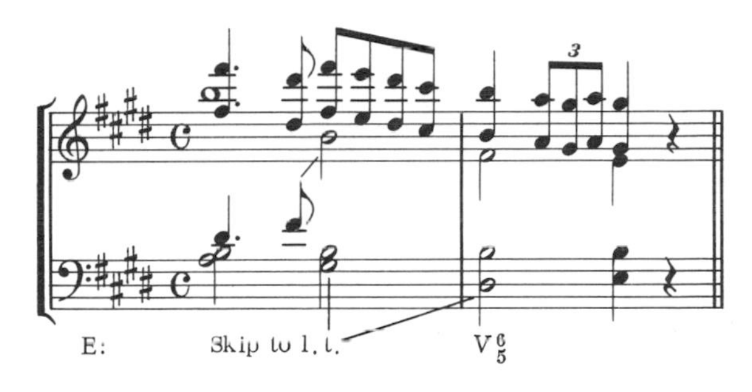

Ex. 16–25. V_7 interpolated between V^6_5 and i.

Ex. 16–26. Mozart: Quintet, K. 516, III. V^4_3 used as a passing chord between I and I_6.

Ex. 16–27. Schumann: Piano Concerto, Op. 54, II. V $\frac{4}{3}$ to I_6 with seventh resolving upwards by step (a common feature in resolutions of V $\frac{4}{3}$).

Ex. 16–28. Brahms: Symphony No. 3, I. V $\frac{4}{2}$ to I_6, the seventh approached and left in the manner of a *neighboring tone.*

Ex. 16–29. Beethoven: *Coriolan* Overture. V $\frac{4}{2}$ with seventh approached and left in the manner of a *leaning tone.*

Ex. 16–30. Pachelbel: *An Wasserflussen Babylon.* V $\frac{4}{2}$ with seventh prepared as a *suspension.*

Ex. 16–31. Wagner: *Lohengrin,* "Ha, dieser Stolz." V $\frac{4}{2}$ with seventh approached and left as a *passing tone.*

Ex. 16–32. Beethoven: Sonata in C Minor, Op. 13, III. V $\frac{4}{2}$ to I_6 with characteristic leap of a fourth in one upper voice.

Summary of Characteristics of V_7

1. It is built on the dominant, resolves generally to tonic, and is often preceded by ii, IV, V, or I.
2. In its resolution, V_7 is more intense and reveals stronger melodic tendencies than V.
3. It is complete when inverted. V_7 is incomplete at times for melodic reasons (fifth omitted, root doubled).
4. Resolution tendencies of the tritone:
   a. When spelled as augmented fourth, the tritone expands to a sixth.
   b. When spelled as a diminished fifth, the tritone contracts to a third.
5. The seventh is commonly approached and left by a melodic pattern that suggests one of the following decorative-tone figures:
   a. the passing tone
   b. the suspension
   c. the neighbor tone
   d. the appoggiatura (infrequent)
6. Exceptions to the downward resolution of the seventh are made
   a. when the resolution occurs in another voice (Ex. 16–3)
   b. when the resolution is decorative
   c. when the resolution is delayed (Ex. 16–23)
   d. when V progresses to I_6 (Ex. 16–27)

The vii_6 Chord

The diminished triad on the seventh scale degree bears a marked resemblance to the dominant seventh chord, since all of its members are also members of V_7. Walter Piston and others have argued that it is actually a *dominant* chord, and that its root is missing (this root would be the dominant). One cannot deny the similarities between vii° and V_7, but we must regard this triad as a separate chord in its own right. As discussed in Chapter 12, we shall regard the lowest member of this chord as its *prime*, for the sonority does not possess a root.

Like most diminished triads, vii° usually appears in first inversion. The bass thus is not a member of the tritone that characterizes this chord. A typical progression involving vii°_6 is shown in Ex. 16–33.

Ex. 16–33. Brahms: Violin Sonata in A Major, I.

The obvious similarities between vii°_6 and V^3_4 account for their frequent interchangeability. Their sounds are virtually identical, creating a problem in distinguishing one from the other. In most contexts vii and V^4_3 are equally appropriate.

Ex. 16–34 and 16–35 illustrate customary doubling in the vii°_6 These apply equally to any diminished triads. When either prime or third is in the soprano, composers have preferred to double the third (the one member that is not a part of the tritone). The fifth of the chord, however, is customarily doubled when it is in the soprano. Particular care should be taken *not* to double the chord's prime—the leading tone—for reasons mentioned in previous chapters. Obviously, melodic considerations can preclude one or the other of these procedures.

Ex. 16–34. Pachelbel: *Aus tiefer Not.*

Ex. 16–35. Buxtehude: *Herzlich thut mich verlangen.*

Despite the similarities between the vii° triad and the various inversions of V_7, composers have preferred to use the dominant seventh in all but one inversion. Ex. 16–36 illustrates the various possibilities and the general preference. Surprisingly enough, there are very few exceptions to these conclusions. It seems likely that the exposed tritone in both vii° and vii°$_6$ is a decisive factor, as well as the greater functional stability of the chord when the dominant tone is present.

Ex. 16–36. Comparison of dominant seventh and vii° inversions.

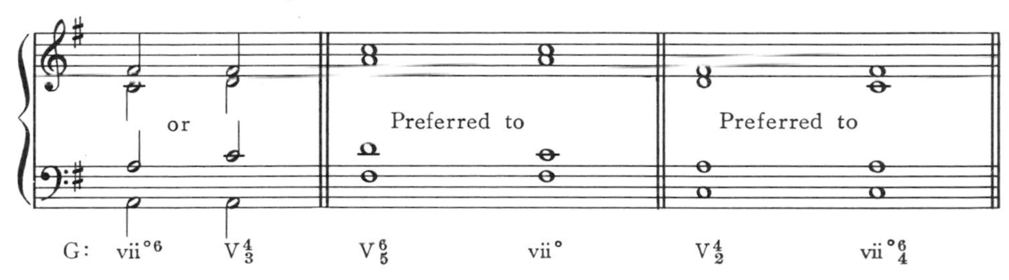

Exercises

For more detailed assignments see *Materials and Structure of Music I, Workbook,* Chapter 16.

1. Practice spelling I, V, and V_7 chords in a variety of major and minor keys.
2. Write an eight-bar melody outlining tonic and dominant triads.
3. Listen to a recording of *Frühlingstraum,* by Schubert, and identify the I and V_7 chords used in the opening section of the song.
4. Ear-training procedures: Continue the following drills from previous chapters.
   a. Recognition of intervals, melodically and harmonically
   b. Recognition of triad quality, soprano and bass factors
   c. Harmonic dictation for roman numeral designation and chord inversion
   d. Harmonic dictation for roman numeral designation and one or both of the outer voices
   e. Melodic and rhythmic dictation with continuation of syncopation and increasing complexity of rhythm

f. Intensive drill in rhythmic reading and sight singing

5. Practice spelling Mm seventh chords on various roots.
6. Write out V_7 chords in four voices, using at least five different spacings; resolve each chord to tonic.
7. Find examples of V_7, V^6_5, V^4_3, and V^4_2 from the repertoire for your instrument. Examine these for (a) preparation of the seventh, (b) resolution of the tritone, and (c) completeness. Find examples of seventh preparation.
8. Spell dominant seventh chords from the bass up, and identify them as to function in various major and minor keys.
9. Sing (from the bass up) dominant seventh chords (root position and inverted).

Chapter Seventeen

The Subdominant Triad; Second-Inversion Triads; The Supertonic Triad

The Subdominant Triad

It has become traditional to explain the triad on the fourth scale degree as a so-called "under-dominant"—the literal meaning of the term *subdominant*. This produces a neat picture of the tonic at the center of all harmonic progression, with dominants both above and below:

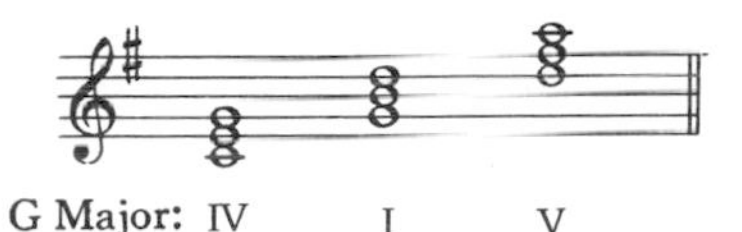

This explanation, unfortunately, is not supported by musical facts. We shall discard this archaic explanation in favor of some observations that can be substantiated through our study of the rate of occurrence of the subdominant triad in music.

Characteristics of IV: a chord that has two important roles, (a) as an "approach" chord to V and (b) as a means of prolonging or embellishing another chord. IV often tends to lead away from the tonic rather than toward it (compare the progressions V–I and I–IV). Thus it too may serve as a temporary tonal goal, often near the end of a composition. Furthermore, the chord is variable in quality (major or minor), especially in nineteenth-century music.

Examples of the Subdominant in Root Position and First Inversion

Ex. 17–1. Haydn: Quartet in E Major, Op. 20, No. 6, I.

Ex. 17–2. Brahms: *Sehnsucht.*

Ex. 17–3. Schumann: Quintet in E-flat Major, Op. 44, II.

Ex. 17–4. Schubert: Sonata in A Major, Rondo.

The following extended example reveals that it is possible to create a substantial composition using *only* I, V, and IV. Through the use of elaboration and embellishment a limited chord vocabulary can form the basis for extended passages.

Ex. 17–5. Schubert: Sonata in G Major, IV.

The first thirty or so measures of Ex. 17–5 are simple and tonally clear, consisting mainly of various positions of the tonic, dominant (or V_7), and subdominant triads. These chords are elaborated by processes such as note repetition, inversion, and melodic figuration.

Tonic and dominant triads occur alternately in measures 1 to 11. In measure 12 a mild digression occurs with movement to the subdominant triad. Note that the two chords (tonic and subdominant) have in common the tonic note itself, *G*, retained in the bass. Similarly, in measures 17 and 25 the subdominant chord embellishes statements of the tonic that precede and follow the IV.

In another typical role the subdominant triad appears immediately before the dominant or I in closure. This common role of the IV (or ii_6 is signaled by rising step movement in the bases, linking the root of IV to V.

The progression that results (IV–V–I or its variant, ii_6–V_7–I) has appealed to composers for a long time (the Renaissance until the present day), perhaps because it involves all the notes of a diatonic scale, or perhaps because of the circle of harmonic motion in a tonality that the pattern I–IV–V–I defines: tonic (stability), subdominant (digression), dominant (leading toward tonic), and tonic (restoration of stability). At any rate, the progression I–IV–V–I is basic to most tonal music, and the study of tonal harmony is in many respects the study of variations and adaptations of I–IV–V–I. The two passages that follow in Examples 17–6a and 17–6b substantiate the preceding statement.

Ex. 17–6a. J.S. Bach: Chorale, *Freu' dich sehr, o meine Seele.*

Ex. 17–6b. Schumann: *Phantasiestücke,* Op. 12, No. 4.

Second-inversion Triads

Triads appear less often in second inversion than in root position or first inversion. A probable reason for this is the intervallic structure of the chord: major and minor triads in root position and first inversion contain at least *one* cadential consonance between the bass and upper parts (specifically, root position contains both a perfect fifth and a third; first-inversion triads contain a third and one decorative consonance—a sixth). Only the second inversion contains *no* cadential consonances above the bass; it contains the sixth and the perfect fourth. Hence it is a less stable sonority.

The perfect fourth, in particular, sets this inversion apart. The fourth has been treated as an unstable interval throughout much of music history and normally has not been used above the bass without some special treatment to cushion its effect (introduction by step, resolution as a suspension, etc.).

Whatever the reasons behind this practice, we find relatively few second-inversion triads, in contrast to a profusion of root position and first inversion. The three uses of six-four chords we will examine are the *cadential* six-four (I^6_4), the *passing* six-fours (V^6_4 and I^6_4), and the *embellishing* six-four (IV^6_4). The latter have particularly contrapuntal treatments.

The Cadential I^6_4

By far the most frequent use of the second-inversion triad is as preparation for an authentic cadence; hence the label *cadential*. In this context the tonic is the only chord found in the $^6_4$ position. Its approach and resolution demonstrate the restrictions composers have placed upon its use.

Ex. 17–7. Mozart: Violin Sonata in E Minor, K. 304, I.

This example of i^6_4 can easily be interpreted as a combination of non-chord tones: the *E* suspended from the previous chord and the *G* an accented passing tone. To continue this line of reasoning we could logically conclude that this is merely an embellished V, that the "real" harmonic progression is from iv_6–V–i.

Not all examples of the cadential I^6_4 are as easily explained. Ex.

17–7 illustrates, though, the salient features found in virtually every instance. One of the most significant of these is the metrical placement of the six-four—usually on a strong beat, resolving immediately to V on the next beat. The notes that form the intervals of the sixth and fourth generally resolve, as they do here, down by step to the nearest tones of V. Another characteristic is the doubling of the bass note (the dominant) in another part. These features are present in Ex. 17–8.

Ex. 17–8. Bach: *The Musical Offering,* Six-voice Ricercar.

Ex. 17–9 illustrates the cadential I$^6_4$ appearing on a weak beat.

Ex. 17–9. Haydn: Quartet, Op. 9, No. 2, Menuet.

The following summary of the characteristics of the cadential I$^6_4$ should be helpful:

1. It usually occurs in a strong metric location.
2. The dominant tone is in the bass.
3. It resolves to V or V_7.
4. The bass is doubled in an upper part (when there are more than three parts).
5. The upper voices, other than the doubled tone, usually resolve down by step.

Passing Six-four Chords

The second-inversion triad is sometimes heard as a link between two more basic chords (basic because of their duration, metric location, or other factors). In such cases, as in Ex. 17–10, the entire sonority may be viewed as an aggregate of non-chord tones or as a decorative chord. It is frequently of very short duration. Passing six-four chords are found on the tonic and on the dominant.

Ex. 17–10. Stamitz: Sinfonia in E-flat Major.

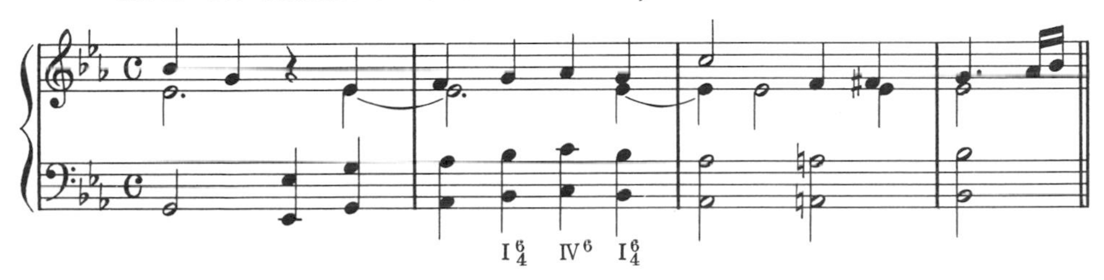

Ex. 17–11 also illustrates a typical passing I^6_4. In contrast to cadential six-four chords, passing six-fours occur most frequently on weak beats.

Ex. 17–11. Corelli: Concerto Grosso, Op. 6, No. 11, Sarabande.

The following two examples (Ex. 17–12a and Ex. 17–12b) illustrate the passing V^6_4. V^6_4 appears between I_6 and I or vice versa. Examples from music literature are not numerous enough to justify detailed conclusions about their doublings and other characteristics, but the general melodic principles governing the use of six-four chords usually are followed.

Ex. 17–12a. Haydn: Quartet in G Minor, Op. 74, No. 3, III.

Ex. 17–12b. Beethoven: Sonata in C Major, Op. 2, No. 3, III.

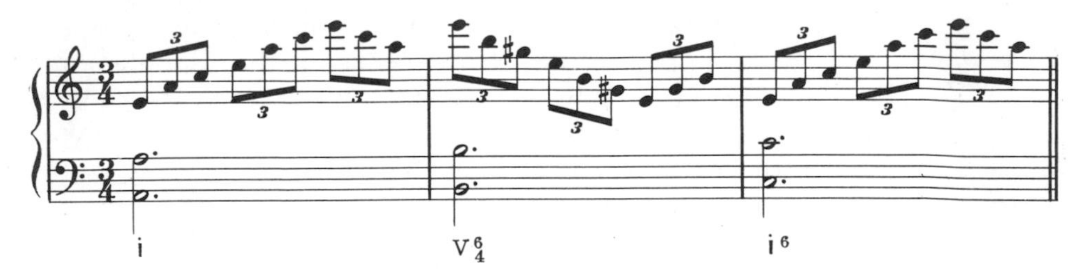

Embellishing Six-four Chords

A third frequent type of six-four treatment is as an embellishing chord, or, described from a linear viewpoint, double neighboring tones grouped over a stationary bass tone. In this context IV $^6_4$ is the only chord that appears with any frequency. As in the final cadence of Ex. 17–13, it embellishes the final tonic chord.

Ex. 17–13. Embellishing six-four chord.

Numerous examples of IV $^6_4$ can be found in works from the classical period. In many of these the chord occurs virtually at the beginning of the movement, as in Ex. 17–14. In this context it helps to focus attention on the tonic note and thus tends to establish solidly the key of the movement. In another sense it occurs above a tonic pedal.

Ex. 17–14. Haydn: Symphony No. 102, IV.

A similar, yet more elaborate, illustration appears in Ex. 17–15. The IV^6_4 occurs briefly in the first measure and again in a more prominent role in measure 3.

Ex. 17–15. Cannabich: Sinfonia in B-flat Major, II.

Other Uses of Six-four Chords

Tonal compositions often exploit the suspenseful effect of I^6_4 as a preparation for the cadenza in instrumental concertos. The orchestral passage that precedes the cadenza customarily ends with a sustained I^6_4, as in Ex. 17–16.

Ex. 17–16. Beethoven: Piano Concerto No. 4, I.

The harmonic progression interrupted by the cadenza is resumed at the end of the cadenza. The soloist usually signals closure with a trill that embellishes V, resolved with the entrance of the orchestra on the I chord. There are, of course, some striking exceptions to this procedure,[1] but they are in the minority.

The appearance of six-four chords can be a useful aid in harmonic analysis, especially in the sometimes difficult problem of determining the key. Since they are relatively infrequent, a six-four chord of even a beat's duration usually appears within a context of tonal stability and often points unmistakably to the dominant of the key. Cadences on six-four chords are not common in tonal music. An unusual example of such a

[1] See Beethoven's Piano Concerto No. 3, I, bar 481, for a brilliant and unusual exception.

cadence occurs in Ex. 17–17 (the cadence is an interior one). It appears to be the result of the extended dominant pedal point in measures 4–6.

Ex. 17–17. Verdi: *Aida,* "Ritorna Vincitor."

In Ex. 17–18 a six-four chord appears at the climax of a section. Although the tonality of this excerpt is not as clear as in eighteenth- and nineteenth-century music, the relationships between the individual chords are, for the most part, by fifth and the chords are mostly major and minor triads. The enharmonic spelling of the six-four chord (*G-sharp* = *A-flat; D-sharp* = *E-flat*) appears to be for organization of the melodic line.

Ex. 17–18. Bartók: Concerto for Orchestra. Copyright 1946 by Hawkes & Son (London) Ltd. Reprinted by permission of Boosey & Hawkes Inc.

The Supertonic Triad [2]

The supertonic triad is minor in a major key, setting it apart from the major triads I, IV, and V. In Ex. 17–19 the second scale degree appears as the bass note in measure 5; it is also the root of the chord. Since *G* is the tonic of this excerpt, the minor triad on *A* is supertonic. However, the relationship of the *A* minor triad to the tonal center is not strongly confirmed until the *G* major triad is heard in measure 8, where

[2] *Supertonic* literally means "above the tonic."

it can be related to *G* and understood as *ii*. The ii chord also contains the fourth and sixth scale degrees, so it can be used to harmonize either the second, fourth, or sixth scale degree.

Ex. 17–19. Beethoven: Piano Concerto No. 4, Op. 58, III.
Vivace

In minor keys the supertonic triad usually is diminished. We have seen that the diminished triad is less stable than either the major or the minor triad, that its characteristic interval, the diminished fifth, usually is resolved to a smaller interval, and that the fundamental of this chord is a *root* in only a broad sense.

In Ex. 17–20, the lowest note, the *prime,* of the chord is doubled after the resolution of *G* in the soprano voice. The diminished fifth (*F-sharp–C*) moves to an octave (*B–b*) in similar motion, making clear that *F-sharp* is in fifth relation with the root *B*. The characteristic resolution pattern of this interval often is not used in minor when the ii° functions in the same way as the ii chord in major, in root relation of a fifth with the dominant chord.

Ex. 17–20. Carl Loewe: *Der Pilgrim vor St. Just,* Op. 99, No. 3.

Its difference in quality distinguishes ii (or ii°) from IV, yet this does not explain the similarity between them. Because of tones in common, ii (ii°) is more closely related to the IV and V chords than to I. It has two tones in common with IV, one tone in common with V.

Ex. 17–21. The supertonic triad.

Like the subdominant, the supertonic chord frequently functions as a "pre-dominant chord," that is, a chord used to approach the dominant. The ii chord frequently appears on an unaccented beat when it precedes V, so V is emphasized both by root relationship and by rhythmic placement. Both of these factors appear at the end of Example 17–22. Note also that ii has two notes in common with V_7.

Ex. 17–22. Mendelssohn: *Songs Without Words,* Op. 85, No. 5.

As its root-position form, the first inversion (ii_6) of the supertonic triad frequently precedes V. In the three-part illustration (Ex. 17–23), the two lower parts move in parallel thirds until the dominant is reached (measure 3) in the lowest part. Note that the fourth scale degree (measure 2) forms the third of the supertonic chord.

Ex. 17–23. Mozart: Quartet in A Major, K. 464, II.

The occurrence of ii_6 ($ii°_6$) is often characterized by the harmonic sixth between the two outer voices, placing both the root (or prime) of the chord and the fourth scale degree in prominent positions. Instead of the characteristic diminished fifth of ii°, an augmented fourth is created between the prime and some other part.

Ex. 17–24. Brahms: Symphony No. 4, IV.

In this excerpt $ii°_6$ moves to i, and the tritone resolves typically. The bass motion in measures 2 and 3 outlines 4–1, supporting an upper voice motion 2–3. The motion by step in the upper voice balances the motion by skip in the lower voice.

Exercises

For more detailed assignments see *Materials and Structure of Music I, Workbook,* Chapter 18.

1. Write an eight-measure melody in *G* major which clearly outlines tonic, subdominant, and dominant chords. Use passing and neighbor tones to decorate basic pitches. Then apply the same procedure to writing a melody in *b* minor.
2. Practice spelling I, IV, and V chords in a variety of major and minor keys.
3. Listen to a recording of *Frülingstraum,* by Schubert, and identify the I, IV, and V_7 chords used in the opening of the song.
4. Write an eight-measure piano piece in *A* major, using an essentially homophonic texture. Write in $\frac{6}{8}$ meter, allegretto, creating two four-measure phrases, both of which illustrate the chord sequence I, IV_7, V_7, I.
5. Make several settings of a bass line consisting of IV–V–I in different major and minor keys. Write for four voices in chordal and contrapuntal textures.
6. Practice writing and identifying V–I and IV–I cadences in different textures.
7. Listen to the slow movement of Symphony No. 39 in E-flat by Mozart. Note particularly the treatment of subdominant and dominant seventh chords.
8. Connect the following chords in a major and then in a minor key. Write in $\frac{4}{4}$ meter, SATB.

   I–IV–V_7–I–iv–I–V–IV_7–V_7I. Use decorative pitches to effect smooth chord connections.

9. In music of various composers, find several examples of the main kinds of second-inversion chords discussed in this chapter (*cadential, passing, embellishing*). Also find examples which do not fit the definition of these three types.
10. Write several textural versions based on the cadential pattern shown below. Do these in major and minor keys and in different meters. Write the two-voice outer framework first for three- and four-voice examples.
    Progression: IV–I$^6_4$–V$_7$–I // *or* ii$_6$–I$^6_4$–V$_7$–I //
11. Write a four-voice homophonic setting for the following chord progression: G minor:

G minor: $\frac{2}{8}$

i iv$^6_4$ i | i^6 | V | i iv i | iv V i | i iv$^6_4$ i | i iv$^6_4$ i ||

12. At the piano, play the following progressions in major and minor keys:
    (a)I–I –I$_6$ (b)I–IV –I (c)IV$_6$–I –V$_7$–I
13. Improvise an arpeggiated melody based on a progression such as the following. Be sure that the lowest note of each arpeggio pattern corresponds with the given inversion. Choose keys that make this comfortable for your own voice.
    Progression: I /IV$_7$ / I$_6$ / V$^6_4$ / I$_6$ / I //
    Sample:

14. Spell, write, play, and sing the chords that could appear on the second scale degree of any diatonic scale.
15. Analyze several of the following, indicating keys, chords, and non-chord tones:
    a. Beethoven: Piano Sonata, Op. 2, No. 3, I (5–8)
    b. Brahms: Symphony No. III, Op. 90, III (1–8)
    c. Chopin: Mazurka, Op. 30, No. 1 (5–8)
       Nocturne, Op. 37, No. 1 (33–40)
       Nocturne, Op. 48, No. 1 (25–32)
    d. Franck: Symphonic Variations, Allegro non troppo
    e. Mozart: Piano Sonata in D Major, K. 311, III (23–26)
    f. Schubert: Symphony No. V, III (1–18)
    g. Sibelius: Symphony No. II, Op. 43, III (Trio) (1–4)

Chapter Eighteen

Formal Archetypes; Ternary Form; Through-Composed Form

We could make a lengthy list of particular musical forms. Yet, in spite of their apparent profusion, it is surprising how few actual organizing principles exist. Basic to all traditions of music are the processes of *repetition, contrast,* and *variation;* they pervade the world's folk and art musics.

Four Basic Form Types

The three principles of musical organization determine the four basic types of musical form we shall discuss. In general, the more sophisticated a piece of music, the more likely that it will possess a form that combines at least two of these basic principles.

Strophic Form

Repetition is the key element in strophic form. This procedure is heard whenever successive verses of a poem are sung to the same music. The strophic form principle is best represented by the alphabetic order *A, A, A, A,* etc., which denotes the repetition of a single musical event.

This strophic principle frequently is combined with one of the other form types to create interesting formal plans. Without a text, the danger of boredom is difficult to avoid, thus its usual association with vocal music.

Additive Form

The opposite of strophic form would be any series of musical sections that contain no repetition. In such a composition one musical event is followed by a contrasting event, and so on. It is a series best represented in simplified form by *A, B, C, D, E,* etc. There is not much music organized exclusively in this way. Used by itself, it might result in a sense of randomness. But combined with another form type, it clearly provides needed contrast.

Return Form

A mixture of unity and variety occurs in many compositions when a contrasting section is followed by the return to musical events that occurred earlier. Any music whose principal sections are organized in this way is an example of the return principle. A work of *A B A* outline, as well as one whose extension encompasses *A B A C A,* is return in form.

Processive Form

A more complicated kind of form is achieved when one musical idea is used as the basis for continuing extension, not repeated but in continually altered or transformed versions. This developmental or variational process is less easily represented by alphabetic symbols; it can be understood as something like A A^1 A^2 A^3, etc., so long as it is remembered that each event is tied to the other only by the presence of the nuclear musical idea, as in a theme with variations. It is not strophic, because each *A* might be dramatically different from any other.

This brief introduction to four basic form types can guide our future discussion of particular musical forms. Now we shall discuss individual pieces whose forms correspond in some way with two of the four types. For the present our attention shall be confined to only *ternary form* (return type) and *through-composed form* (additive type).

Ternary Form

Ternary form involves three distinct sections, each of which may be different (as *ABC*, which would be *additive*), alike (as *AAA*), or partially alike (such as *ABA*). In this chapter we shall discuss the latter, a ternary design characterized by the return of the opening section.

Ex. 18–1 clearly displays a division into three parts. The change of melodic rhythm at measure 5 provides a striking contrast, as does the elaborately "decorated" melody of the second section. Both factors counterbalance the emphasis given to the rhythmic motive of the first section.

Ex. 18–1. Schumann: *Album for the Young,* "Folk Song."

Even though the more active melody in measure 5 catches our attention, other factors also help to produce contrast. The entire composition is in *D*, but the section beginning at measure 5 is in *D* major instead of *D* minor. Another contrasting element is the wider range of measures 5–12 and the linear triadic outlining.

The opening accompanimental figure is used in each section (with some modifications). The retention of the accompanimental rhythm and the retention of the basic pitches of measures 1 and 2 in measures 5 and 6 unify this passage. It is evident that the principal contrast of the *B* section is provided by the change in melodic rhythm, mode, and the scherzo-like character.

The restatement (measures 13–20) is varied by changing the register (measures 13–14) and by doubling the melody in octaves (measures 17–20). This heightens the effectiveness of the return, avoiding the monotony of a literal restatement.

Frequently, however, the third section of a ternary form is a literal repetition of the first. If this is the case, the restatement need not be written out and it is indicated by *da capo* (*D. C.*)[1] at the end of the second section. Sometimes the indication *dal segno* (*D. S.*)[2] is found at the end of the second section, as in Ex. 18–2. This means that the repetition begins at some indicated point (where "the sign" appears) rather than at the beginning. The sign usually looks something like the following: 𝄋

Even though Ex. 18–2 is longer than Ex. 18–1, its form is the same basic *A B A*. Similar relationships delineate the larger sections, but there are notable differences. For example, two distinctive accompanimental patterns are used in the Chopin. The first, measures 1–16, is distinguished by an agogic accent on the second beat in the inner parts. In the second section, measures 17–33, the rhythm is distinguished by a downbeat pattern, as well as a change in the rhythm of the melody. And as a final confirmation of sectioning, contrast between the two sections is achieved by modulation to a new tonal center. In Ex. 18–1 tonal contrast was produced by mutation.

[1] Repeat from the beginning, or "from the head."
[2] Repeat "from the sign."

Ex. 18–2. Chopin: Mazurka in C Major, Op. 33, No. 3.

Texture

Another factor in Ex. 18–2 tends to overshadow the other formal elements: change of texture.

The overall texture of both the Schumann and the Chopin examples is homophonic. We noted in Ex. 18–1 that the pitch range widened in the second section. This increase alters the texture slightly by changing the space between the melody and its accompaniment. In Ex. 18–2 the textural change in measure 17 is more pronounced because the accompaniment changes character and is moved to a different register. The numbers of parts is essentially the same, but spacing starkly distinguishes the textural "top" from "bottom." The motion in parallel sixths and thirds (measure 23 and following) represents still another variation of texture.

Examination of Ex. 18–1 and Ex. 18–2 reveals in both cases basic ternary plans, but a closer look at the structure of each section shows that the processes of unfolding are not the same in both pieces. Thematic material, tonality, rhythm, and total length provide obvious differences.

Another difference is the way each middle section closes and connects with the restatement of *A*. The *B* section of Ex. 18–1 closes with a half cadence that is combined with a definite rhythmic halt. The listener's expectation of a return to the beginning results from the instability of the half cadence and the extreme rhythmic contrast. In Ex. 18–2 the end of the section is not signaled as boldly because the rhythm in the upper parts continues through to the beginning of the restatement. The two sections merge, and it is not until the return is in progress that we become aware of it.

Modified Restatement

Literal restatement of all musical parameters need not occur to create a satisfactory return. For example, in some styles thematic restatement is associated with tonality restatement; in some styles this is not an essential ingredient. The second movement (*Grablegung*) from Hindemith's *Mathis der Maler* illustrates this well. The movement begins in C (shown in Ex. 18–3).

Ex. 18–3. Hindemith: *Mathis der Maler,* II. Copyright 1934 by B. Schott's Soehne-Mainz. Copyright © renewed 1962 by B. Schott's Soehne-Mainz.

The restatement, which overlaps with the close of the middle section, begins in a different key (Ex. 18–4) and in a reorchestrated version featuring brass. An interruption by *B*-section material after only two bars of restatement intensifies the musical drama. After the interpolation of the *B* material the restatement takes up at the point where the interruption occurred.

Ex. 18–4. Hindemith: *Mathis der Maler,* II. Copyright 1934 by B. Schott's Soehne-Mainz. Copyright © renewed 1962 by B. Schott's Soehne-Mainz.

kl. Fl.
gr. Fl.
Ob. 1 2
Kl. 1 2
Fg.
Hr.
Tr. 1 2
Pos
BT
Pk.
Viol.
Br.
Vc.
Kb.
8va
mf
cresc.
f

Unlike the original statement of *A*, which begins in *C*, the restated version begins in *B* then moves to *B-flat* and ends in *F-sharp*. The movement closes with an extended coda in *C-sharp*. Even though the initial tonality does not recur, return is accomplished through thematic, textural, and dynamic means.

And yet, in many ternary movements sectional tonal unity is basic. This departure from convention in Hindemith's music is not disturbing, since the conditions for its presence are not established in any other parts of the movement. What *is* established is a formal process in which each section begins with a tonally simple context, gradually becomes more complex, and then returns to a simpler tonal context.

Each of the preceding musical examples illustrates ternary movements with restatements involving all or most musical parameters, and in which all of the three sections of the design are of approximately the same length. Length in music, however, is as much a psychological response as it is a measurable fact, and sometimes a shorter section (in terms of measures or clock time) may balance a longer section. Similarly, the return effect so essential to *A B A* designs may be satisfactorily achieved by restating only a small portion of the *A* section.

Most of the essential melodic and accompanimental material is heard immediately in Schoenberg's Piano Piece, Op. 11, No. 1, the opening bars of which are shown in Ex. 18–5.

Ex. 18–5. Schoenberg: Piano Piece, Op. 11, No. 1. Used by permission of Belmont Music Publishers, Los Angeles, California.

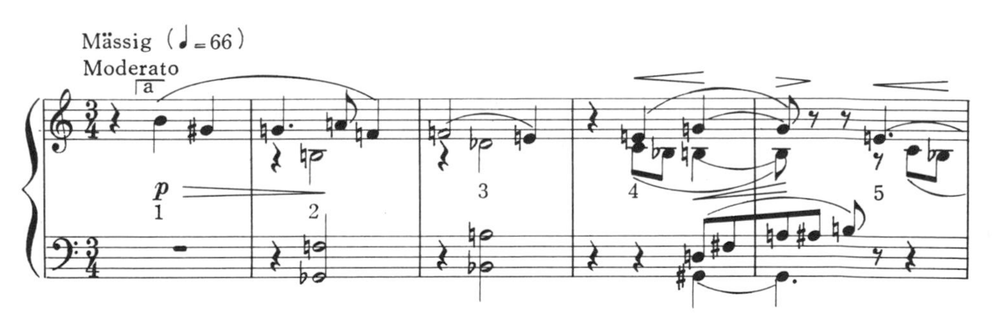

In the much shortened restatement (Ex. 18–6) the opening melodic material is presented at the original pitch level with octave coupling and in a new texture (the accompaniment is now in an arpeggiated form). Only the first two bars of the restatement are of this literal quality, but it is sufficient for us to perceive the restatement.

Ex. 18–6. Schoenberg: Piano Piece, Op. 11, No. 1. Used by permission of Belmont Music Publishers, Los Angeles, California.

Once the return is accomplished, the original three-measure phrase (Ex. 18–5) is extended to six.

Both the *A* and *B* sections are made up of subsections that correspond to phrases and periods of tonal music. Tonality, however, is not an organizing factor. Texture, dynamics, and rhythms are prime sectional delineators; unity results from recurrence of the melodic material in altered versions.

Our discussion has emphasized the overall plan of ternary design, as well as some of the factors that produce contrast between the sectional parts of the total form. As a matter of fact, it is very difficult to describe a piece of music without taking into consideration both the structural plan and the smaller elements that fill out this plan. Many compositions have a ternary structural design, just as many buildings are basically rectangles. However, we know that architects have adapted the rectangular principle to many different designs, and similarly, the ternary principle of statement, contrast, and return has been used in many quite different compositions.

Through-composed Form

There are compositions in which the return of larger formal units does not occur. Broadly speaking, this means that no two parts of such a composition are identical in all respects. If this were adhered to consistently, the composition would be a series of contrasts without any sense of return or rounding off of the whole form.

A unified musical design depends upon many factors; large-scale return is only one of these. Compositions in which each section is essentially different are said to be *through-composed*,[3] to distinguish them from strophic, processive, or return schemes. Through-composed compositions may contain several contrasting parts or sections, with the total length determined by a text or a dramatic situation that might underlie the composition.

In Ex. 18–7 none of the five phrases is precisely like another; even so, it is a balanced structure. Each of the phrases is only externally different; within the separate phrases similarities exist that create unity.

Ex. 18–7. Gregorian Chant: *Sanctus.*

[3] The German form of this term, *durchkomponiert*, appears frequently in books that discuss musical form.

Some of the phrases have similar contours, in some pitch patterns recur (f^2, e^2, d^2, e^1). In addition, the tones focus decisively on *F* as tonic. Thus, even though this melody does not contain repeated or restated phrases, other factors make it a unified whole.

The through-composed form is most often found in vocal compositions. A simple plan prevails. No return to earlier musical material occurs, except in tonal music in which return to the original tonality or area of the key is an integral part of the design. Most through-composed compositions are highly sectionalized; although recurrence of large musical events is not an overriding factor, motives or phrases may recur within each section.

A brief song from a large song cycle is shown in Ex. 18–8. In this song a declamatory style enhances the text (contemplation of the death of a husband), as does the through-composed design. The three sections of the song are delineated by their overall motion; (1) From tonal stability to tonal instability (measures 1–7, from i → V, closing with a Phrygian cadence); (2) from instability to greater stability (measures 8–15, tonality ambiguous → *c* minor); (3) from chromatic to diatonic harmony (measures 16–22) but without a full tonal close. By ending with a half cadence, the V area of the first section is recalled; as such it does provide a framing effect.

Subtle changes in the accompaniment also delineate the sections. One example is the changing metric position of the accented chord (*sf*). In measures 1–7 it occurs on third beats. In measures 8–15 the *sf* accent occurs only twice; in both instances it comes on a first beat with the same word, *leer*. In measures 16–22 *sf* does not occur. These *sf* accents give shape to the overall design in a manner similar to the tonal shaping: their presence adds tension and drama, their absence suggests release, calm.

Ex. 18–8. Schumann: *Frauenliebe und Leben,* "Nun hast du mir den ersten Schmerz getan."

The potentials of the additive design principle are limited only by psychological practicality. It would be possible to create a form in which there is no repetition at any level, motivic, phrase, or sectional. That would be the exception, however, rather than the rule. The distinguishing feature of through-composed design is large sectional contrasts. These gross contrasts often are softened by transferring characteristic patterns from one section to another.

Exercises

For more detailed assignments see *Materials and Structure of Music I, Workbook*, Chapter 18.

1. Listen to and study compositions such as the following. Isolate those

musical elements that play a prominent role in creating the ternary design of each work.

a. Schumann: *Traumerei*
b. Rachmaninoff, *Prelude*, Op. 3, No. 2
c. Debussy, *La fille aux cheveux de lin*
d. Mozart, "E amor un ladroncello" (*Cosi fan tutte*)

2. Write a short three-part (*A B A*) composition for a combination of four different instruments. Create a middle section that does not rely upon tonality change to provide contrast.
3. Make a detailed analysis of Ex. 18–8. What other patterns than those mentioned in the chapter are used to unify the composition?
4. Write a sixteen-measure through-composed composition for piano that uses a key scheme such as the following: G-flat major, parallel minor, G-flat major.
5. Locate, sing through, and analyze several through-composed compositions.

Chapter Nineteen

Submediant and Mediant Chords; Mutated Chords

Some of the musical examples in preceding chapters contain chords we have not discussed. The roots of these chords are in most cases the third and the sixth scale degrees. They represent the only two diatonic triads, iii and vi, not yet studied.

The quality of both the mediant (iii) and submediant (vi) triads in major keys differs from that of I, IV, and V, thus making possible an immediate distinction (minor as opposed to major). Other differences will become apparent as we examine iii and vi in various contexts.

The Submediant and Mediant Chords

The submediant chord contains 6, 1, and 3 of a scale and often is used to harmonize any of the three in a melody. The mediant chord contains the 3, 5, and 7 scale degrees.

In Ex. 19–1 the repeated *G* (the third scale degree) in the upper part is harmonized by both I and vi. Use of the two roots with the melodic *G* results in a more mobile harmony than if only the tonic chord had been used.

Ex. 19–1. Beethoven: Piano Concerto No. 2, Op. 19, II.

In Ex. 19–2 the overall harmonic motion of the phrase is I → IV. The mediant connects I to IV in measures 1 and 3, and connects V with IV in measure 4.

Ex. 19–2. Brahms: Symphony No. 4, III.

The primary organizing principle of Ex. 19–2 is contrary motion. Fewer chords could have been used to support the melody; however, the contrapuntal chords are a basic characteristic of the rhythmic-tonal drive of this phrase. Even though we can isolate a mediant chord in measures 1, 3, and 4, its role is as much melodic as harmonic in measures 1 and 3.

Mediant and Submediant in Minor Keys

In minor keys the submediant and mediant triads are major. Like its counterpart in major, VI is frequently associated with melodies that contain successive repetitions of the tonic note. As a consequence, VI frequently follows i. In Ex. 19–3, VI alternates with i in measure 2, maintaining the harmonic rhythm of the preceding measures. The harmonic succession *I–VI–iv* is a typical phrase progression involving the submediant.

Ex. 19–3. Schumann: *Dichterliebe,* "Die alten, bösen Lieder."

The appearance of both VI and III in the second phrase of Ex. 19–4 suggests the relative major, B-flat, creating a distinctive contrast with the first. The root movement of VI–III is similar to iv–i, so we can say that the iv–i of measure 3 is a sequence of vi–iii, that is, a harmonic pattern repeated at a different pitch level.

Approach to V

In major or minor keys the submediant and mediant chords often occur in progressions moving to the dominant. The V_7 in m. 4 of Ex. 19–5 is emphasized by the preceding root motion by a fifth from the ii chord. Note that vi is similarly related to ii. Each of the chords in measures 1–4 is related to the next with at least one common tone, and root relationships by fifth occupy most of the phrase.

Ex. 19–4. Mozart: Requiem, K. 626, *"Domine Jesu Christe."*

Ex. 19–5. Haydn: *The Creation*, "Now Vanish Before the Holy Beams."

The III chord appears between i and i $^6_4$ in Ex. 19–6. The melody at this point could have been harmonized with i, III or V. Using III enhances the harmonic color. Notice that the resulting root movement outlines the tonic chord, thereby confirming the tonality.

Ex. 19–6. Brahms: Sonata in C Major, Op. 1, II.

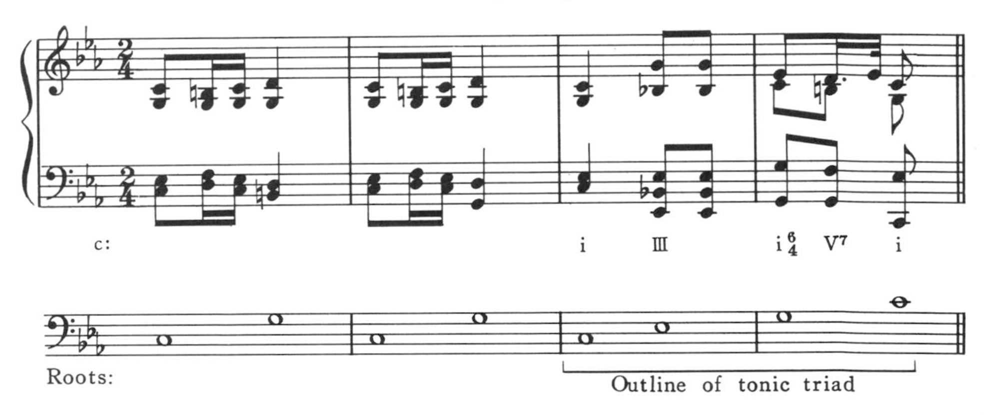

Root Motion By Thirds

In Ex. 19–7, IV appears between vi and ii, producing root movement by thirds. As a consequence, each chord in measures 1 and 2 has two notes in common with its immediate predecessor. Compare this progression with the first three chords of Example 19–1.

Ex. 19–7. Wagner: *Parsifal*, Grail motive (Act I).

Sometimes the iii chord precedes tonic in a cadence, especially in music of the late nineteenth century. The two tones of the iii chord that are common to I (root and third of iii = third and fifth of I) create a smooth relationship that borders on chord repetition. The leading tone in the iii chord is the factor that most clearly marks such a pattern.

Ex. 19–8 and Ex. 19–9 illustrate terminal cadences involving iii–I. Both examples are similar in cadential effect, but there is a notable difference: in Ex. 19–8 the I chord is melodically outlined, while in Ex. 19–9 the iii chord is melodically outlined. So even though the harmonic pattern is the same in both excerpts, the motion of each melody has a different character because of chordal outlining.

Ex. 19–8. R. Strauss: *Ein Heldenleben,* Op. 40.

Ex. 19–9. Brahms: *Intermezzo,* Op. 10, No. 3.

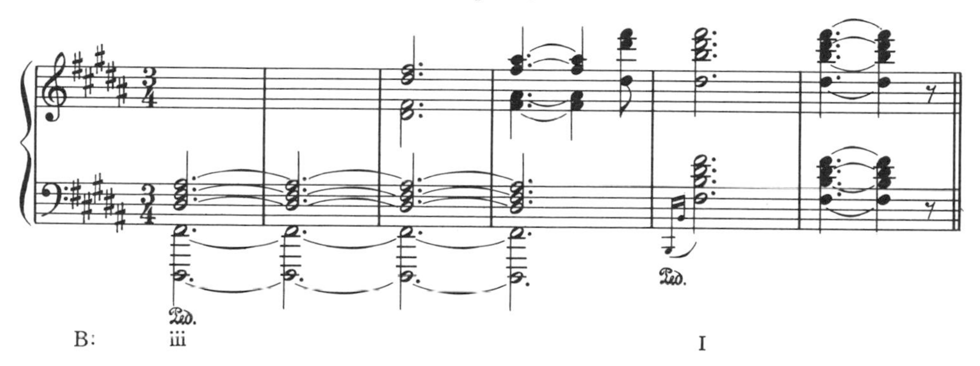

The submediant chord also appears in the role of a neighbor chord, creating root movement by a second. Ex. 19–10 shows vi as a neighbor to V, clearly indicated by its durational relation to V. Notice that the resultant step motion in the bass adds variety to the phrase.

Ex. 19–10. J. S. Bach: *Ermuntre dich, mein schwacher Geist.*

Deceptive Functions of VI and IV

In some contexts vi appears to substitute for I. The melody note marked (*) in measure 2 of Ex. 19–11 could be harmonized with the I chord. The change causes the bass line in measure 2 to relate sequentially to beats 2 and 3 of measure I, as well as adding harmonic color. The vi chord, better than the I, helps to project the passage forward.

Ex. 19–11. J. S. Bach: *Aus meines Herzens Grunde.*

The appearance of vi as a cadential chord can create a particularly striking effect. It ends the second phrase (measures 5–8) in Ex. 19–12. The earlier harmonic and melodic activity of this phrase predicts that it will probably close on tonic, as did the first phrase. Furthermore, we have already heard the melodically outlined V_7 move to tonic in measure 4, so we expect the same resolution of the V_7 chord in measure 8. Since the expected harmonic pattern is evaded, harmonic deception results.

Ex. 19–12. Beethoven: Trio in B-flat Major, Op. 11, I.

A deceptive cadence usually is followed by motion to tonic. In Ex. 19–13 a cadential vi appears in measure 8. Here the deception intensifies the expectation of I, as well as enhancing the immediate repetition of previous material. Unlike the major-minor relation formed in a major key, the deceptive cadence in minor involves two successive major triads.

Ex. 19–13. Haydn: Quartet in D Minor, Op. 76, No. 2, IV.

V and vi being a second apart, they share no common tones. Therefore, V–vi, like the succession of all chords whose roots are a second apart, generally involves contrary motion. The third of the vi chord (the tonic note) usually is doubled when it is preceded by V or V_7; the root obviously can also be doubled. In minor the root of VI is usually not doubled when it is preceded by the dominant, because the leading tone would then resolve to a tone an augmented second lower. Ex. 19–14 gives usual doublings for both major and minor.

Ex. 19–14. Doubling in deceptive resolutions.

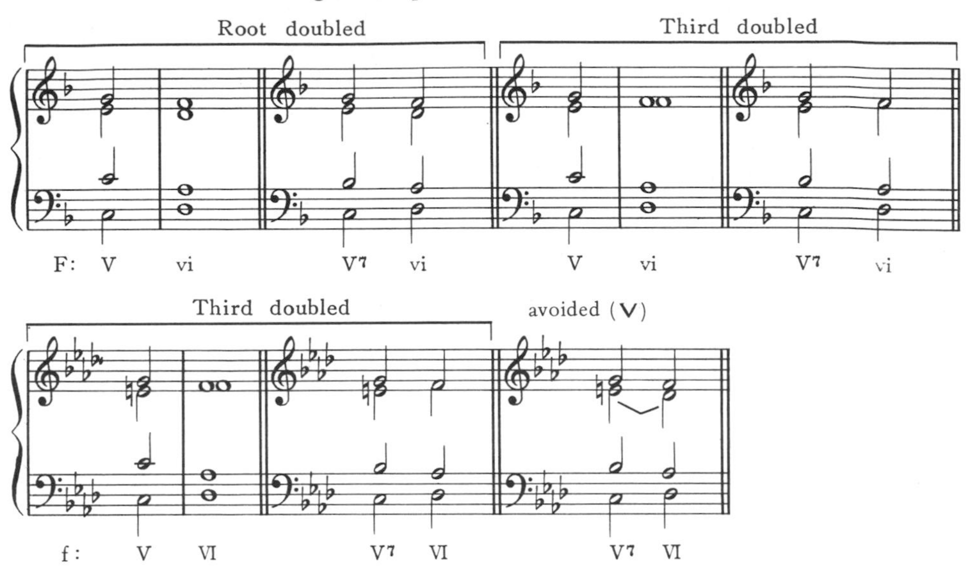

In Ex. 19–15 the vi chord ends the first phrase. Here vi is preceded by V_7, which harmonizezs the seventh degree and resolves to tonic. The fifth of the V_7 is part of a descending line (tenor part) and also moves to the tonic note. Consequently the third of the vi chord is doubled.

Ex. 19–15. Schubert: Symphony No. 5, II.

Augmented Mediant (III+)

When it occurs, the augmented mediant is usually found in positions similar to III. Any differences are produced by the augmented triad's distinctive quality. As we observed in previous chapters, the inclusion of augmented or diminished intervals in tonal music implies greater tension, because resolution to a point of stability seems imminent. Since the leading tone is a member of the III^+ triad, it usually resolves to chords that contain the tonic note.

In Ex. 19–16 the III^+_6 chord is approached by contrary motion between the two outer parts. A logical chord at this point would have been

III_6, but instead the tenor voice moves from *A* to *G-sharp*. This forms the augmented version of the chord, and it also directs attention to the *A* that follows on the second beat.

Ex. 19–16. Bach: *Herr, ich habe missgehandelt.*

As in most unstable chords, the notes doubled in the III^+ chord are those that do not suggest resolution. The third (the note *E* in the previous example) is most often doubled.

First Inversions of vi and iii

The first inversions of both the vi and the iii chord are treated similarly to their root-position counterparts. Since the root of the chord does not appear in the lowest part, the resulting harmonic change is weakened. For example, if vi_6 follows tonic, the same pitch remains in the bass voice, reducing somewhat the effect of the harmonic motion. The result resembles more an embellishment of the I chord than a decisive harmonic change.

The first inversions of both iii and vi are often used in passages that unfold by sequence. In Ex. 19–17, iii_6 appears between vi and IV. Its use here coincides with the established pattern that alternates root position and first-inversion chords. So even though the roots change in every measure, the harmonic rhythm, because of alternating inversions and root positions, consists of greater and lesser accents.

Ex. 19–17. Mozart: Piano Concerto in F Major, K. 413, I.

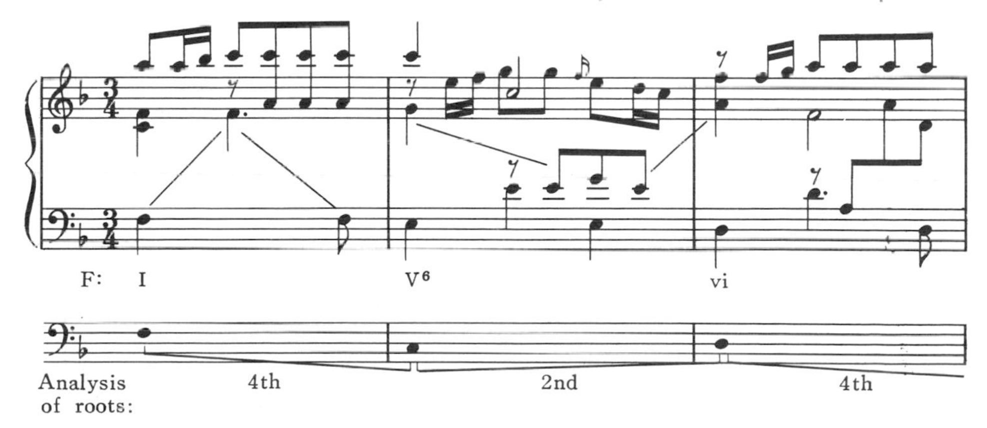

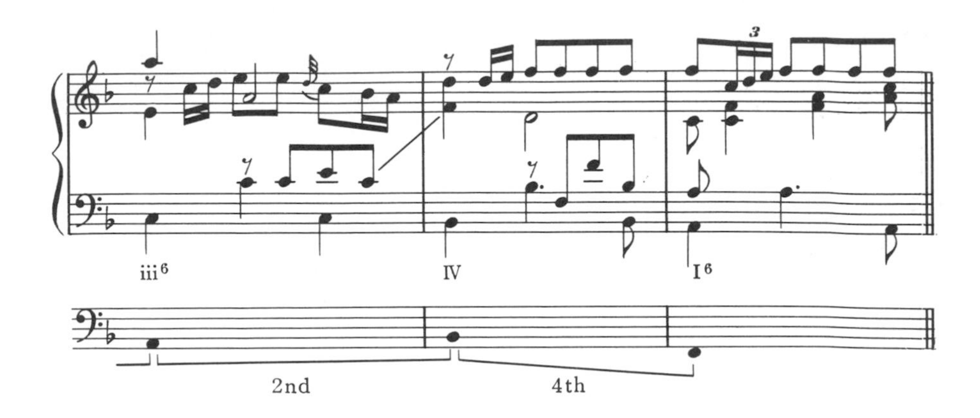

Ex. 19–18 has two important features. The first is the sequence formed over a tonic and then dominant pedal in measures 1 and 2. Along with this strong root relation of I–V is a *harmonic sequence* that accompanies the melodic sequence of the top voice.

Ex. 19–18. Massenet: *Manon* (Act III, Scene I).

Notice that the succession of I–vii$^{\circ}_{6}$–vi$_6$ in the first measure is followed by its sequence *at the dominant level* of V–IV$_6$–iii$_6$.

Mutated Chords: ♭III and ♭VI

Earlier in this chapter we saw how the mediant and submediant enrich the harmonic palette. Harmonic color is further expanded by using chords of chromatic inflection, such as the minor tonic and the minor subdominant in a major key. These chromatically inflected third and sixth scale degrees give the impression of mixing elements of major and minor modes. The resulting chordal and melodic digressions are regional, or "coloristic," in effect; structurally, they prolong harmonic activity.

Frequently the progress of a composition is enhanced when a repeated phrase is mutated as in Ex. 19–19. The effect is that of juxtaposed modes, but the total impression is a blending that does not distort or change the structural relationships. On the contrary, the mixture increases the available tonal possibilities within a given key.

Ex. 19–19. Haydn: Quartet in B-flat Major, Op. 64, No. 3, I.

It is probably realistic (although somewhat confusing) to designate compositions in which elements of both major and minor systems appear consistently as *major-minor*. Since the third and the sixth scale degrees determine the major or minor mode of a given key, chords constructed on them are often referred to as *modal*, and their roots are sometimes called the *modal scale degrees*.

Like its diatonic counterpart, the ♭VI chord often is used to create a deceptive cadence. The marked difference between it and diatonic vi is the result of two main factors: (1) a major triad replaces a minor triad, and (2) the root motion is by half step rather than by whole step.

In Ex. 19–20 this replacement of vi by ♭VI occurs between two elided phrases. The deceptive cadence in measure 4 is intensified by the appearance of the *B-flat* major chord, which is a mutation of the diatonic vi made by lowering the root and fifth by semitones.

Ex. 19–20. Haydn: Quartet in D Major, Op. 64, No. 5, III.

Chromatic Third Relation

When ♭VI occurs outside a cadence, its harmonic function is the same as that of the diatonic chord it replaces. If ♭VI is directly preceded by I, as in Ex. 19–21, two versions of 3 are mixed. The resultant root movement is a major third, and this, combined with the chromatic inflections, produces a *chromatic third relation.*

Ex. 19–21. Brahms: Symphony No. 3, II.

Third-related chords are present whenever two chords' roots are a major or minor third apart. If they have two notes in common, a *diatonic* third relation exists (*e.g.*, vi–IV); if the chords involved have only one tone, or no tones in common, a *chromatic* third relation exists.

In Ex. 19–21, ♭VI both prolongs the influence of the tonic pitch and focuses attention on the plagal cadence. In part, this attention is a by-product of the lowered sixth scale step, both as root of ♭VI and as the third of iv in the cadential pattern.

The ♭III chord is also used in ways similar to its diatonic equivalent. In it, both the root and the fifth of the mediant triad are lowered by half steps. When ♭III precedes V or V_7, a cross relation may be created by the mixture of both the diatonic and the mutated seventh scale step, as in the second measure of Ex. 19–22.

Ex. 19–22. Dvořák: Quartet in A-flat Major, I.

The ♭III chord bears a chromatic third relation to both I and V (one tone in common with each). The ♭III also bears an interesting relation to ♭VI because of their root relation by fifth and their one common tone.

The purely coloristic roles of ♭VI and ♭III are sometimes less notable than their structural roles. In Ex. 19–23 the cadential activity is heightened by introducing ♭VI_6 as a delay of tonic.

Ex. 19–23. R. Strauss: *Die Nacht.* By permission of the International Music Company, New York.

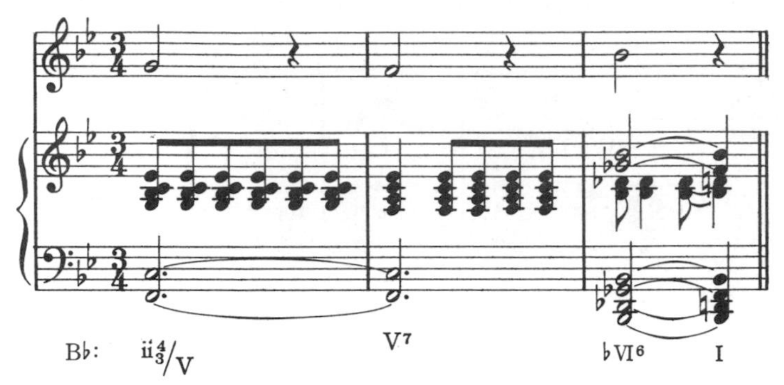

Simultaneous Mutation

Earlier in the chapter we stated that consistent use of mutated chords produces the effect of mixed major and minor. The process we have seen thus far has always involved juxtaposition. In more recent music the mixing involves both juxtaposition and superposition.

Ex. 19–24. Stravinsky: *Symphony of Psalms,* I. Copyright 1941 by Russischer Musikverlag, Renewed 1958. Copyright & Renewal assigned to Boosey & Hawkes Inc. Revised Version Copyright 1948 by Boosey & Hawkes Inc. Reprinted by permission

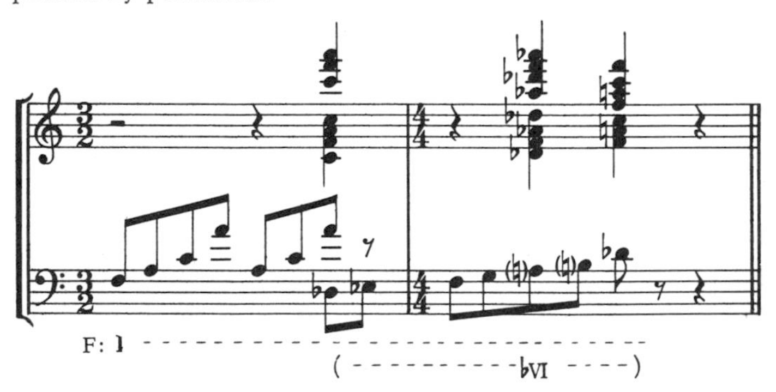

In Ex. 19–25 a harmonic groundwork of *A* major is clearly outlined by the cello chords. Above this is the pattern of the violins that moves within the lower fifth of the *a* minor scale.

Ex. 19–25. Bartók: Quartet No. 2, I.

The following is a chart of common harmonic progressions.

——→ — — — — — — — — — — — — — — ——→

TONIC		PRE-DOMINANT (subdominant)	DOMINANT	TONIC
I, i	vi, VI	IV, iv	V, V_7	I, i
	iii, III, III+	ii, ii°	vii°_{6}	(vi, VI)
		Secondary Sevenths,	(iii_6, iii	
		Secondary Dominants	III)	

The harmonic cycle may begin at any point.
Any step in the cycle may be omitted.
Any step or steps may be retraced before direction is resumed.

Exercises

For more detailed assignments see *Materials and Structure of Music I, Workbook,* Chapter 19.

1. Sing and spell the mediant and submediant chords in all diatonic keys.
2. Use the melodic material from measures 1 and 2 of Ex. 19–11 as the motivic basis for a sixteen-measure piano composition in ternary form.
3. Reduce Ex. 19–15 to a two-voice framework. Then elaborate this basic frame to create a "new" four-phrase work.
4. Reset the melody of Ex. 19–5 with a "faster" harmonic rhythm. Incorporate all of the diatonic chords into your setting.
5. Write a composition that uses a preponderance of chords other than tonic, subdominant, or dominant.
6. Write a three-phrase vocal composition. Use the following plan: first phrase, only root-position chords; second phrase, parallel first-inversion chords; third phrase, alternating root-position and first-inversion chords. Close the example with a mediant-to-tonic cadence.
7. Spell and sing mutated chords (i, iv, ♭III, ♭VI) in all major keys, first establishing tonic clearly.
8. Listen to compositions such as Brahm's *Rhapsody,* Op. 119, No. 4. Discuss the use of mutated chords.
9. Create various harmonic patterns that could be treated sequentially. Use one of the examples in this chapter as your model.

Chapter Twenty

Secondary Dominants

As we have seen, chromatic notes in a passage may indicate one of several things: alterations of decorative tones (non-chord tones), usual altered degrees of the minor scale, mutation, or change of key. Practically any page of music contains accidentals—either flats, sharps, or natural signs—which indicate inflections of notes within the diatonic scale system. Many such alterations result from the composer's desire to exploit and extend one of music's strongest harmonic relationships, that of dominant–tonic.

In Ex. 20–1 the *D-naturals* that appear in the seventh measure create a half-step (leading-tone) relation with *E-flat.*

Ex. 20–1. Mozart: Symphony in E-flat Major, K. 543, II.

The *D-natural* is part of a melodic sequence begun in measure 6 that rises to *E-flat*, the dominant of *A-flat* major. The last chord in measure 7 is a Mm 7 chord on *B-flat*, the V_7 of *E-flat*. Mozart here heightens the effect of the cadence by preceding the dominant with its own dominant seventh chord. In other words, he employed a *secondary dominant*[1] (more precisely, a *secondary dominant seventh*), the symbol for which is V_7/V.

Using this example as a point of departure, we may generalize about secondary dominants as follows:

1. Any diatonic major or minor triad may be embellished by its own "dominant."
2. Such embellishment creates harmonic color and strengthens linear motion (leading-tone effect), thereby heightening resolution.
3. The presence of a secondary dominant is sometimes indicated by the presence of one or more chromatic tones.
4. The secondary dominant *seventh,* because of the added dissonance and the resolution tendency of the members of the tritone, stands in stronger relation to its "tonic" than does the corresponding secondary dominant *triad.*
5. Secondary dominants and secondary dominant sevenths appear in inversions as well as in root position.

[1] In this sense, the dominant of a key might be regarded as the *primary dominant.*

6. In four-voice textures the root of the secondary dominant triad is frequently doubled, while the secondary dominant seventh usually appears in complete form; if not, the root is doubled.
7. Secondary dominants resolve *regularly* (to their "tonics"), *deceptively* (to a chord whose root is a step above that of the secondary dominant), or *irregularly* (to a variety of other chords.)

It is easy to overlook the *melodic* significance of secondary dominants, since their *harmonic* effect is so pronounced. To do so is to ignore one very important aspect of their use. Ex. 20–2 (late sixteenth century) contains patterns of harmonic relation identifiable as secondary dominant in function. Through the use of the chromatic inflections *G-sharp, C-sharp*, and *F-sharp*, the composer has heightened the melodic drive to *A, D*, and *G*, respectively.

Ex. 20–2. Gesualdo: *Io pur respiro.*

In Ex. 20–3, composed some two centuries later, chromatic alterations are again used for line inflection, resulting in a secondary dominant chord function.

Ex. 20–3. Mozart: *Eine kleine Nachtmusik*, K. 525, Menuetto.

At the cadence in measures 3–4, perform either the viola or cello line as written, then perform it with *C* substituted for *C-sharp*. Obviously, either arrangement is possible; however, it is apparent that the original version drives more forcefully to *D*, the dominant. Stressing the progressive nature of this cadence, the composer cancels out the leading-tone effect of the *C-sharp* by the use of *C*s in the following passage, which ends on tonic.

It is worth noting that secondary dominants are usually used to embellish and emphasize structural chords within a tonal framework. Consequently, their appearance is usually predictable. For example, you can expect to find V_7/V used with considerable frequency before the V chord in authentic cadences.

Ex. 20–4. J. S. Bach: Cantata No. 140, *Wachet auf.*

Dominant of the Dominant (V/V; V_7/V)

In major keys the appearance of the V/V or V_7/V is suggested by the raised fourth degree of the scale. In such instances the chord will be the regular ii, except for the altered fourth scale degree, the third of the chord. As a matter of fact, it is helpful to think of the V/V in two ways: as a major triad built on the second degree of the scale, and as a variant (raised third) of the supertonic chord.

In minor keys the V/V is created by two chromatic alterations, the raised fourth and sixth degrees of the scale. The principles of resolution of the V/V and V_7/V are not different from those of the V and V_7. The usual resolution is to their "tonic," that is, to a major chord whose root is a fifth below. The raised fourth degree, the "secondary leading tone" in V/V, usually progresses to the fifth degree. In other words, it follows the tendency of the chromatic inflection. One exception occurs when the third of the chord (the chromatic note) proceeds to a note a third below, that is, to the fifth of the chord of resolution. This usually occurs in one of the inner voices in order that the chord of resolution be a complete triad. Further, the notes of the tritone in the V_7/V usually resolve as do those of the V_7; that is, augmented fourth expands stepwise and diminished fifth contracts stepwise:

The V/V frequently is used in transient-terminal cadences. Here the secondary dominant often appears in root position and progresses to the dominant, which also is in root position.

Ex. 20–5. Mozart: Symphony in E-flat Major, K. 543, III.

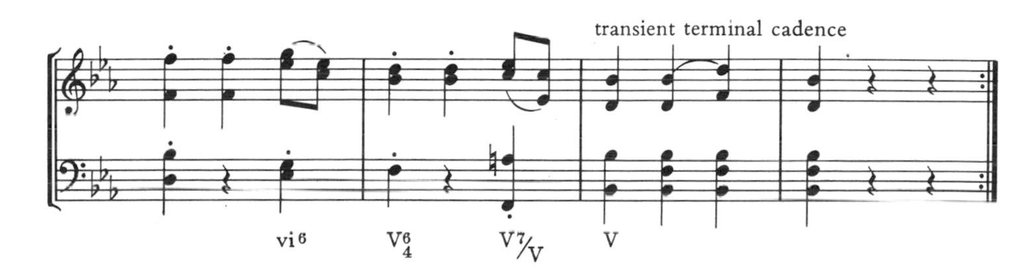

Within a phrase, V/V frequently resolves to an inverted form of V. Note that in Ex. 20–6 the V/V is preceded by ii, its diatonic counterpart.

Ex. 20–6. Wagner: *Tannhäuser,* Overture.

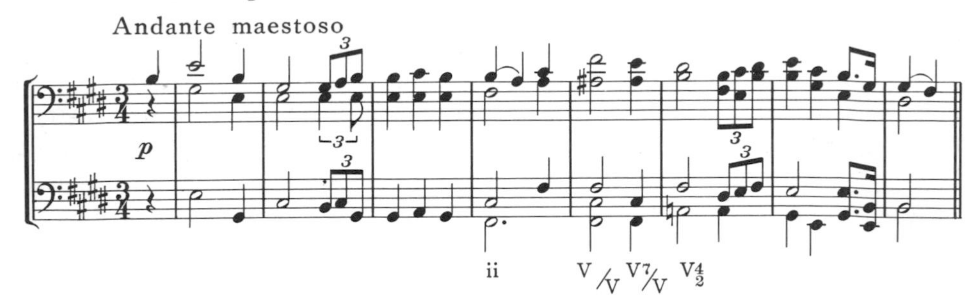

There are no major differences in the use of V/V in minor. However, it is sometimes used in minor to embellish the *minor* dominant chord. This is the case in Ex. 20–7, in which the minor dominant is introduced unexpectedly as the transient-terminal cadence chord of a passage in which the major dominant has prevailed. The effect is that of a brief modulation to the dominant minor key.

Ex. 20–7. Beethoven: Piano Concerto No. 3 in C Minor, Op. 37, III.

When working with V/V and V_7/V in minor, take care to avoid augmented intervals in vocal lines containing the chromatic inflections. In instrumental performance these intervals are not as difficult to produce accurately.

Dominant of the Subdominant (V/IV; V/iv)

The harmonic thrust of a secondary dominant moving to a cadential V chord can be further strengthened by the addition of other secondary dominants, such as V/IV. This dominant of the subdominant chord is a major sonority, whose root is the tonic scale degree.

Ex. 20–8. Mozart: Sonata in C Major, K. 279, II.

On the other hand, the V_7/iv also occurs as in Ex. 20–9 *at the beginning* of a section before tonic has been established.

Ex. 20–9. Chopin: Mazurka in E Minor, Op. 41, No. 2.

The V_7/IV is often used to counterbalance emphasis on the dominant and, in many such instances, appears toward the close of a phrase, period, or section. Ex. 20–10 shows only the last phrase of the second period of a theme whose first period ended with a transient-terminal cadence, V/V–V. Through V $\frac{4}{2}$/IV, the subdominant is emphasized at the climax of the phrase.

Ex. 20–10. Haydn: Sonata in D Major, III.

Because of the common pitch shared by I, V_7/IV, and IV (root, root, and fifth, respectively), these chords often appear in conjunction with a tonic pedal. The pedal offsets the weakening of tonality that can result from V_7/IV. In Ex. 20–11 V_7/IV is preceded by tonic in a passage with a rearticulated pedal. The harmonic movement to IV is heightened by the seventh, *A-flat*.

Ex. 20–11. Schubert: Octet, Op. 166, II.

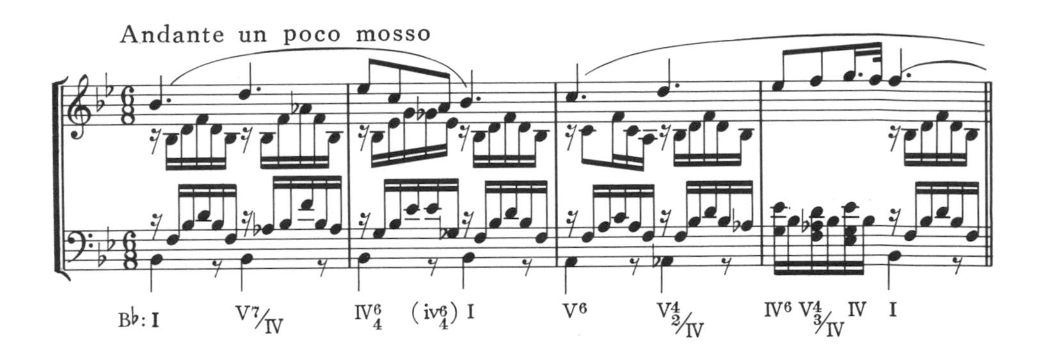

There are many other uses of this chord in various types of music. Obviously, any appearance of a subdominant can be embellished by its dominant. Consider one final use, the standard "blues progression" of jazz whose first phrase cadences on V_7/IV.

Ex. 20–12. Arlen-Mercer: *Blues in the Night.* Copyright 1941 by Remick Music Corporation. Used by permission.

Dominant of the Supertonic (V/ii)

The V/ii usually occurs in major, for the supertonic chord in minor is diminished and thus does not function satisfactorily as a "temporary tonic." Its root is the sixth degree of the scale, and its presence is suggested by the raised first degree of the scale ("leading tone" of 2) that usually resolves upward.

Ex. 20–13. Brahms: *Ein deutsches Requiem,* "Herr, du bist würdig."

Noteworthy exceptions are illustrated in the next two examples. In Ex. 20–14, V_7/ii serves as a climactic cadence chord (measure 4).

Ex. 20–14. Chopin: Prelude in A Major, Op. 28, No. 7.

And, in Ex. 20–15, a V_6/ii chord appears as the opening chord, the beginning of a sequence that is completed by V_6–I.

Ex. 20–15. Mozart: Sonata in B-flat Major, K. 281, III.

The V/ii is often used to prolong the ii chord, as in the beginning of the second phrase of Ex. 20–16. In this passage V$^4_3$/ii appears between occurrences of the ii chord. This treatment parallels the first three measures of the first phrase, where I and I$_6$ are linked by V$^4_3$.

Ex. 20–16. Beethoven: Sonata in D Major, Op. 10, No. 3, III.

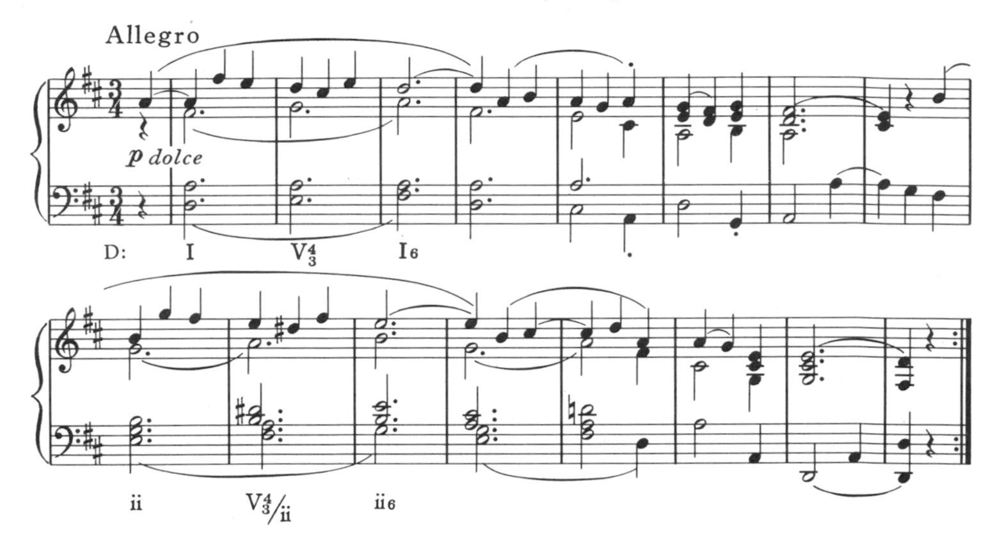

Dominant of the Submediant (V/vi; V/VI)

There are two basic forms of the submediant chord—vi in major and VI in minor. Each has a related secondary dominant whose root is the third degree of the scale. The V/vi (major mode) requires that the fifth of the scale be chromatically raised. The *C-sharp* in Ex. 20–17 is the third of a major-minor seventh chord whose root (*A*) is dominant of the submediant.

Ex. 20–17. Dvořák: Symphony in D Minor, Op. 70, II.

In minor mode no chromatic alterations are required for the triadic form V/VI, but the seventh chord (V_7/VI) necessitates the lowered second degree of the scale. For example, in measure 6 of Ex. 20–18, the *B-flat* creates the seventh of a V$^6_5$/VI chord.

Ex. 20–18. Mendelssohn: *Songs Without Words,* Op. 19, No. 2.

The V_7/vi resolves the same way as each of the secondary dominants discussed earlier. Let us consider some typical uses of this decorative chord.

The progression of tonic to submediant is common, particularly at the beginning of a phrase. The V$^4_3$/vi frequently serves as their connecting link.

Ex. 20–19. Wagner: *Lohengrin,* Prelude to Act III.

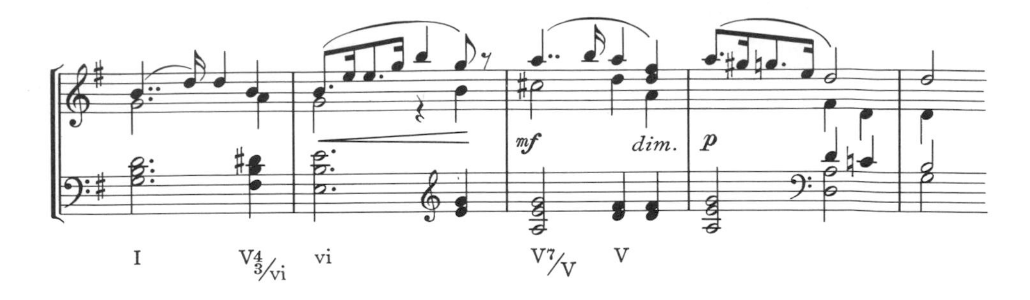

The V/vi, in the interior of a phrase, is usually preceded by tonic, as the previous excerpt illustrates. In Ex. 20–20 V_6/vi is approached through the dominant and prepares the way to the transient-terminal cadence.

Ex. 20–20. Verdi: *Aida,* "Su ! Del Nilo," Act 1, Scene 1.

Dominant of the Mediant (V/iii; V/III)

As is true of the submediant chord, the mediant chord usually appears in one of two forms, iii in major and III in minor. Each has a related secondary dominant whose root is the seventh degree of the scale. A V_7/iii (major mode) requires raising the second and fourth scale degrees a semitone. Ex. 20–21 contains a passage in which V_7/iii follows V_6. Notice that this particular progression uses the common tone between the two chords as a repeated bass.

Ex. 20–21. Brahms: *Ein deutsches Requiem,* "Wie Lieblich."

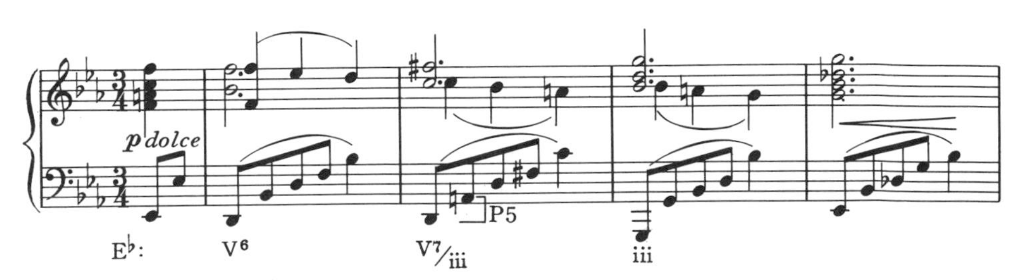

The root of the V/III in minor is the subtonic scale degree. In Ex. 20–22 a V_7/III is used in the approach to the cadence on III in measure 4, producing a transient-terminal cadence.

Ex. 20–22. Beethoven: Piano Concerto No. 4 in G, Op. 58, II.

Example 20–23 shows a typical phrase in which the iii chord is embellished by its secondary dominant (V^4_3/iii). Here the progression consists of a brief harmonic/melodic sequence, measures 3–4 being the duplication one step higher of the pattern of measures 1–2.

Ex. 20–23. Beethoven: Quartet in F Major, Op. 18, No. 1, III.

As we have noted, one of the common functions of a secondary dominant is to reinforce various kinds of cadential patterns. Such a use of the V_7/iii may be found in Ex. 20–24. The period closes with a transient-terminal cadence on iii. Compare the treatment of the first and second phrases. Also note that the V_7/iii appears in root position, thereby creating a decisive cadence to the iii chord.

Ex. 20–24. Haydn: Symphony No. 88, IV.

In minor the V_7/III is the same chord as the V_7 of the relative major. It frequently is used to exploit this duality. In Ex. 20–25 the V_7/III supports a transient-terminal cadence on III at the end of measure 4. The harmonic resources of *g* minor have been expanded by this exchange between these two closely related keys; each tonic is in turn supported by its own dominant. Since the passage begins and ends in *g* minor, the fleeting focus on *B-flat* is more a prolongation of the mediant than a modulation.

Ex. 20–25. Beethoven: Sonata in G Major, Op. 79, II.

Dominant of the Subtonic (V/♭VII)

Our survey of secondary dominants would not be complete without brief mention of the V/♭VII in minor. Since the leading-tone chord (vii°) is diminished and therefore never functions as a temporary tonic, its secondary dominant is not used. However, a major triad built on the lowered seventh degree (subtonic) may be embellished by its dominant, $V_7/^{\flat}VII$.

In Ex. 20–26 observe that the $V_7/^{\flat}VII$ is used in a sequence that begins in measure 3 and ends in measure 6. Observe also the jolting effect in measures 6–7 of the root relation (tritone) in the progression $V_7/^{\flat}II$–V_7/V, in spite of the very smooth motion of *G-flat–G-natural* in the melody. As you can see, this passage is a virtual lexicon of secondary dominants.

Ex. 20–26. Chopin: Mazurka in G Minor, Op. 67, No. 2.

Thus far our discussion of secondary dominants has been concerned primarily with "regular" resolutions. By definition, a secondary dominant stands in a fixed harmonic relationship to its "secondary tonic," a root relationship of a perfect fourth up or perfect fifth down. Its harmonic function is determined by the realization of this relationship (i.e., by its regular resolution). When the resolution is irregular but the resolving chord is still diatonic (or a clearly related chord, such as another secondary dominant) the embellishing sonority may still be considered a secondary dominant.

Perhaps the most obvious irregular resolution is that in which the secondary dominant resolves deceptively (root progression up a second), as illustrated in Ex. 20–27.

Ex. 20–27. Prokofiev: Classical Symphony, III. Copyright 1926 by Edition Russe de Musique. Copyright assigned to Boosey & Hawkes Inc. Reprinted by permission.

This is a particularly interesting example because it illustrates simple chords in chromatic relationships. Note especially the deceptive resolutions of the secondary dominants, V_7/vi–IV and V_7/ii–I in measures 3–4 and 7–8. The progression in measures 1 and 2 is a succession of major triads whose root line is *D–C–B* and whose outer voices are organized in contrary motion.

In many ways Ex. 20–28 serves as a summation of irregular resolution, at least for the harmonic materials thus far presented. It contains six irregular progressions: (V_7–vi)—deceptive; (V_7/vi–V)—root movement up a third; (V–iv_6), (V_7/iii–vi_6), and (V_7/V–I_6)—root movement down a second; (V_6/V_7/iii)—root movement down a third. An important feature is the contrary motion between the outer voices in the long melodic descent in measures 1–5.

Ex. 20–28. Wagner: *Lohengrin*, Prelude.

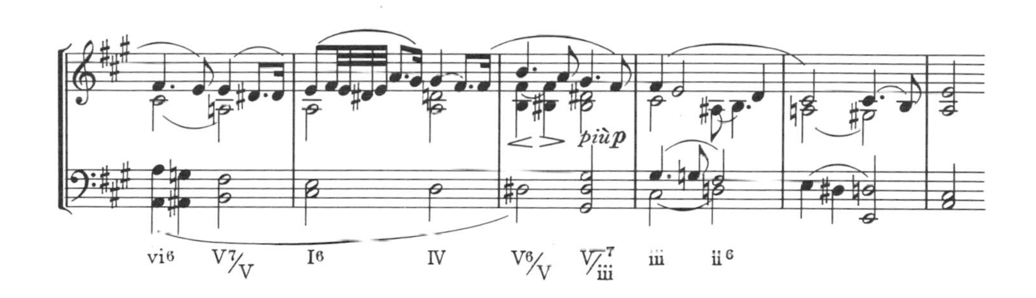

Sequential Secondary Dominants

We have seen that secondary dominants frequently occur in sequential passages. These passages sometimes unsettle the tonality, thus posing the option of returning to the original key or proceeding to a new one. The powerful unity of the sequential pattern itself sets up a propulsive force that continues to an appropriate cadence, either in the original or in a new key.

Certainly a sequence of secondary dominants in which each "tonic" successively becomes a "dominant" of the next chord weakens tonal stability. This is especially true if the sequence is maintained for long. This very factor made the harmonic sequence a popular modulatory device, especially in the classical period. A pattern of chord motion could be established and maintained until the original tonality had been obscured. Upon arrival at the desired new tonic a cadence would establish its supremacy.

In Ex. 20–29 a modulation from *C* to *A* takes place. The original key is clearly established (mm. 1–4). An imitative pattern begins and continues past measure 8 (where *C* is reaffirmed) to measure 14, where a sequence begins, making use of various secondary dominants. This sequence is maintained to measure 18, then interrupted in preparation for the cadence on V of *A*. From measure 8 the key is *a* minor. However, the chain of secondary dominants creates an uncertainty that is not resolved until the arrival at the cadence on the dominant. Test this fact by substituting the optional cadence (No. 2) to force a return to *C* major.

Ex. 20–29. Beethoven: Quartet in A Major, Op. 18, No. 5, IV.

Exercises

For more detailed assignments see *Materials and Structure of Music I, Workbook,* Chapter 20.

1. Spell the indicated chords from the bass up:

a. V^4_3/vi, *A*	d. V^6_5/VI, *b-flat*	g. V^6_5/V, *c*	j. V^4_3/IV, *G*
b. V^4_2/iii, *E*	e. V_7/vi, III, *d*	h. V^4_2/ii, *E*	k. V^6_5/ii, *A-flat*
c. V^6_5/♭VII, *C.*	f. V^4_2/vi, *D-flat*	i. V^4_3/iv, *d*	l. V^4_2/V, *B*

2. Using the following harmonic progressions as models, create two different settings of each, one for piano, the other SATB. Use different harmonic rhythms, textures, and keys for the two settings.
   a. I ii_6 V V^6_5/vi vi V^4_2/iii iii_6 V^6_5/IV ii V
   b. i V^4_3/VI VI iv_6 V^6_5/♭VII ♭VII III_6 V^4_3/III III i^6_4 V_7 i
3. Analyze a number of the following, indicating keys, chords and non-chord tones.

Haydn:	*Symphony No. 85 (La Reine),* II. (1–8)
Beethoven:	*Symphony No. 1,* Op. 21, I. (1–21)
	String Quartet, Op. 18, No. 3, III (63–74)
	String Quartet, Op. 59, No. 1, IV (1–18)
	String Quartet, Op. 59, No. 2, IV (179–209)
Schubert:	*Der Erlkönig* (87–96)
	String Quintet in C Major, Op. 163, III (11–17)
Mendelssohn:	*Nocturne (Midsummer Night's Dream)* (91–100)
Chopin:	*Mazurka,* Op. 56, No. 2 (33–44)
	Mazurka, Op. 59, No. 1 (38–42)
	Mazurka, Op. 67, No. 2 (1–16)
Schumann:	*Symphony No. 2,* Adagio (1–9)
Liszt:	*Les Preludes* (70–80)
Wagner:	*Lohengrin,* Prelude, Act III (1–16)
Verdi:	*Requiem,* "Requiem and Kyrie" (8–11)
Brahms:	*Variations on a Theme by Haydn,* Op. 56a (1–10)

4. Assuming that each of the following secondary dominants is to be resolved deceptively, spell the chord of resolution of each from the bass up.

a. V^6_5/V, *E-flat*	b. V^6_5/iv, *b*	c. V^4_2/III, *c*
d. V^4_3/vi, *D*	e. V_7/V, *e*	f. V^4_3/IV, *B*

5. Write an instrumental and choral setting of each of the following progressions. Use different textures and harmonic rhythms for each.
   a. I vi_6 V_7/V iii vi_6 V^6_5/ii V^6_4 V_7/V V
   b. i V_6 V^4_3/VI iv_6 ii°_6 V V_7 VI V^4_3/III V V_7 i
6. Using a three-part texture similar to that in measures 4–13 of Ex. 20–30, develop an example employing imitation of short motives, using secondary dominants in regular and deceptive progressions or in other irregular resolutions. Arrange for oboe, clarinet and bassoon.
7. Using the sequence pattern (V^6_5/ii–ii) (V^6_5/V–V) (V^6_5–I) (V^6_5/IV–IV) construct a phrase in which motivic treatment is a characteristic feature, and arrange for two trumpets and two trombones.

Chapter Twenty-One

Modulation; Tonal Shift; Mutation

In this chapter we shall turn again to an important aspect of pitch organization, change of key or tonality. Key change is one of the principal means for creating variety in tonal music, past and present. As such, it represents a primary agent of form.

Tonality change may be accomplished in a smooth, almost imperceptible way, concealing the actual point of change, or it may result from an abrupt and decisive shift from one tonic to another. The former process is called *modulation*, the latter *tonal shift*.

A tonality change may or may not be indicated by a new key signature, but it may be recognized in notation by the appearance of "new" accidentals. In fact, key changes within short sections are seldom indicated by a new signature. In Ex. 22–1 a modulation from *c* minor to *A-flat* major takes place without a change of signature.

Ex. 21–1. Schubert: *Erstarrung.*

The principal key of the song is *c* minor, and the change that occurs is a modulation to the *submediant* of *c*, *A-flat*. Schubert might have changed the key signature at measure 5; that he did not emphasizes the subsidiary relationship of the new key, to *c minor*. The note *D-flat* occurs as an accidental, and *B-flats* replace *B-natural*, the leading tone in the original key of *c*.

Relationships of Keys

Subsequently we shall deal with several of the processes by which key change is accomplished. But first it is helpful to review the system of keys, and note some of the relationships that exist between them. *Relationship*, although usually expressed in terms of the interval between the tonic notes of two keys (perfect fifth, third, etc.), means simply this: the number of notes in common. Thus, the more common notes between two keys, the *closer* the relationship.

Near-related keys are those whose key signatures differ by no more than one sharp or flat; hence their diatonic scales differ by no more than one pitch class. A major key and its relative minor (natural form) share identical pitch classes and thus the same key signature.

By returning to the circle of fifths (shown earlier on page 45 as a spiral), we can see a graphic representation of key relationships. The twelve steps on the circle represent the twelve notes of the octave, arranged in a series of perfect fifths—the only such arrangement that will exhaust all twelve pitch classes before returning to the octave. Clockwise and counterclockwise movement around the circle produces the conventional order of flats and sharps in traditional key signatures. A shift of three places aligns major keys with their relative minors, as shown on the inside of the circle in lower case letters.

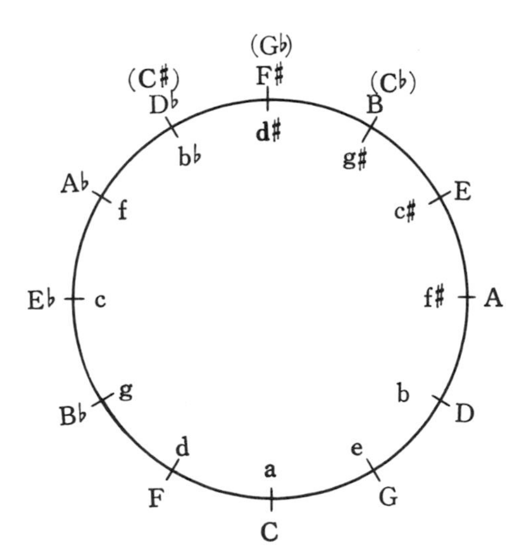

The notes of a major scale are projected as any seven adjacent steps on the circle; note the arrangement of the various scale degrees in the following projection of C major.

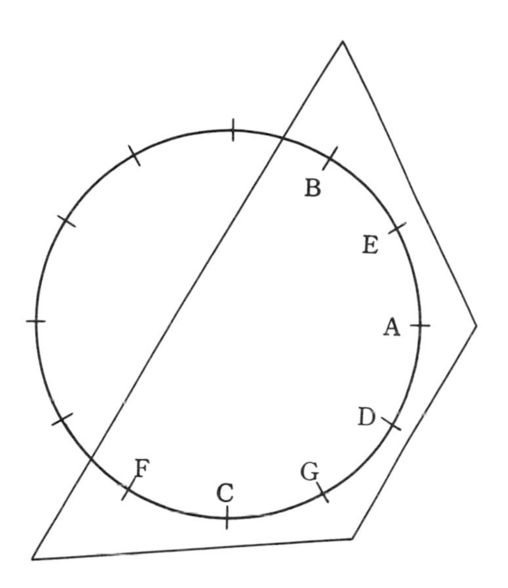

Shifting the set of notes one step counterclockwise produces the notes of *G* major, adding one note (*F-sharp*, the leading tone) and discarding *F*, the old subdominant. Similarly, movement clockwise—to the flat side—would add a new subdominant and discard the previous leading tone.

The key of *G* major projected on the circle of fifths:

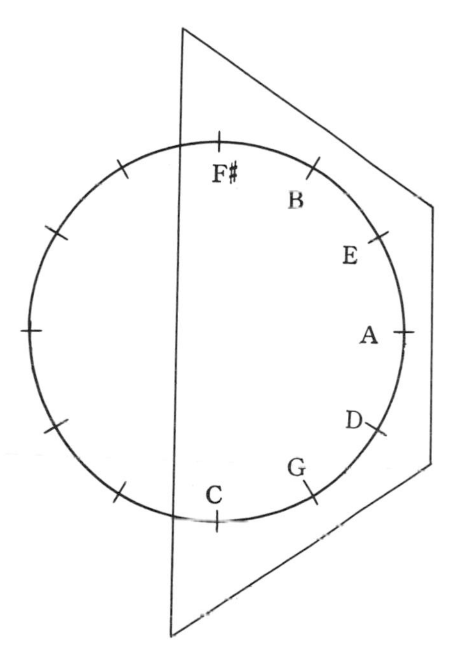

The circle of fifths and key signatures in terms of the number of flats or sharps:

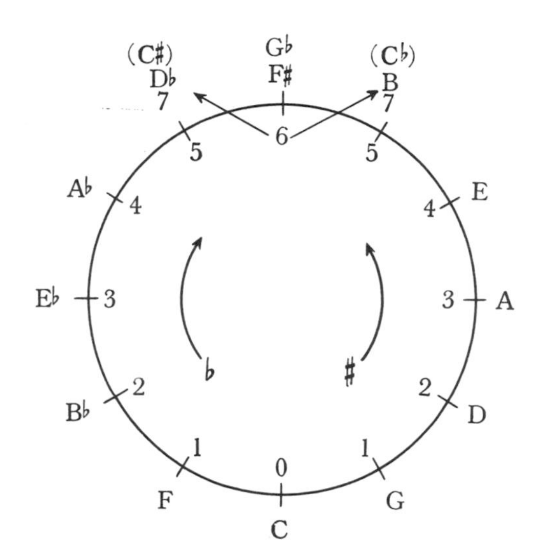

In terms of the above diagrams, near-related keys are those that require a shift of no more than one step in either direction on the circle of fifths.

It should be noted that the keys that stand in this near relationship to another key are not always near-related to each other: *d* minor and *e* minor are each near-related to *C* major but not to one another. Nor does near-related imply close intervallic distance between tonic pitches; it merely denotes a close relationship of keys based on shared notes.

Several illustrations of near-related keys follow. Determine the keys involved and the resulting scale changes that occur.

Ex. 21–2. Chopin: Mazurka in B-flat Major, Op. 17, No. 1.

Ex. 21–3. Beethoven: Mass in C Major, Op. 86.

Ex. 21–4. Bach: Three-voice Invention in G Minor.

The key relationships incorporated in this group of excerpts, which feature a variety of textures and styles, are as follows:

Ex. 21–2 from *B-flat* major to the dominant major (*F*)

Ex. 21–3 from *C* major to the submediant minor (*a*) and back again

Ex. 21–4 from *B-flat* major to the mediant minor (*d*)

Less Common Key Relations

Composers have by no means limited their choices to near-related keys. Virtually any combination or sequence of keys may be found. Compositions written after the eighteenth century sometimes use relationships that bring into play many or all of the members of the chromatic scale. Consistent with the use of more distant key relations is the lessening of key stability and reduction of key duration. Sudden *shifts* of key, in contrast to the more gradual process of modulation, create tonal uncertainty that both broadens the tonal perspective and weakens the listener's feeling of principal tonic.

The *chromatic third relationship* describes a more distant key relationship where the tonic pitches of the two keys are a major or minor third apart, as in *C* major and *E* major. A common tone usually connects the two tonic chords (*E*), and a cross-relationship (*G*/*G-sharp*) provides tonal contrast.

The change to a third-related key often occurs as a sudden shift rather than as a gradual change. Ex. 21–5 illustrates a chromatic third relation (between *D* major and *F* major) with the pitch *A* as the common link between the two tonic triads.

Ex. 21–5. Beethoven: Symphony No. 8, III.

Major and minor keys a half step apart constitute the key relation in Ex. 23–6, in which a new key is introduced on the leading tone of the original key.

Ex. 21–6. Wolf: *Spanish Songbook*, 1, No. 4.

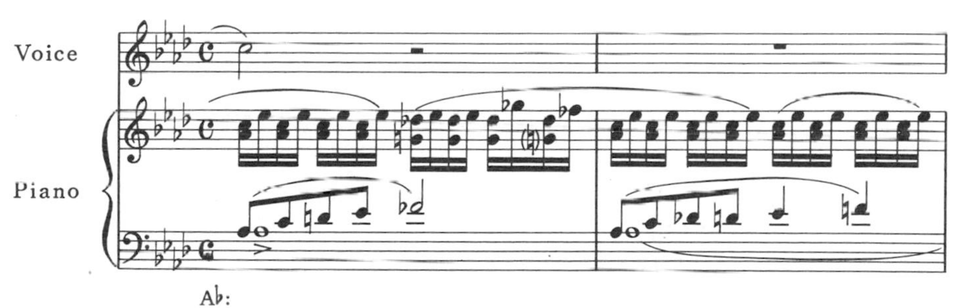

Since the system of keys is most prevalent in music written between the seventeenth and the beginning of the twentieth centuries, it is natural that we begin the study of tonality changes with this music.

The Process of Modulation

Now our objective is to examine *how* a modulation is accomplished. The most frequent techniques include modulation by *pivot chord*, by *pivot tone*, by *chromatic inflection*, and by *enharmonic change*; their common characteristic is a linkage between the two keys—either a common element (note or chord) or a direct movement to the new tonal goal.

Modulation by Pivot Chord

One of the most frequent modulation procedures establishes the relationship between the two keys by means of a specific chord that they possess in common. The agent of modulation, then, is a chord that can be interpreted in both the old key and the new key. This process capitalizes on the fact that a single chord can possess identity in more than one key.

Ex. 21–7 illustrates concisely the pivot-chord modulation technique, in this case involving two distantly related keys, which is not an uncommon relationship in nineteenth century music.

Ex. 21–7. Schubert: *Die Winterreise,* Muth.

From measure 8 the tonality is clearly *E* major; therefore, we must look immediately before this location to see the actual point of shift. The major triad on *E* in measure 7 is clearly V in *a* minor, *if we look no further.* In retrospect, however, we see that it also can be interpreted as I in *E* major. This triad is thus the pivot chord between these two keys; it is analyzed as shown on the example.

We can perceive this type of modulation only by looking back from the point at which the new key has been firmly established. Since any chord is capable of a number of interpretations in any number of keys, we would be in a constant state of confusion if we were always conjuring up the many possibilities of each chord we hear. Fortunately, although we do make guesses as to the possible outcome of a musical situation, we interpret each chord only in the light of the current key, *until this key clearly has been abandoned.*

Apply the same process to Ex. 21–8.

Ex. 21–8. Haydn: Quartet, Op. 64, No. 2. Menuetto.

Once a change of key has taken place—as by measure 8 of Ex. 21–8—it is possible to identify the dual role played by the pivot chord. Each modulation usually contains a *signal* that the former key is no longer in effect. This signal is an accidental foreign to the old key but diatonic to the new key, often a new leading tone. Occasionally, as in Ex. 21–8, the modulatory signal is not merely an accidental but a chord that is clearly foreign to the first key: the Mm_7 on *A* in measure 6 is the first indication that *b* minor no longer obtains. The last chord in measure 5 is thus the pivot chord: i in *b* minor becomes vi in *D* major.

The general rule can be stated as follows: The pivot chord is generally the chord that precedes the signal, as long as it can be interpreted in both the old and the new key.

Pivot-Chord Possibilities

Any chord—diatonic or chromatic—can act as a pivot chord, and a situation may result in which a chromatic chord in the old key becomes a diatonic chord in the new key or vice versa. The V_6/ii chord in *D* major, for instance, can function as V_6 in *E* minor or major. Usually, however, the pivot chord is diatonic to both keys. The diatonic pivot-chord possibilities are easily determined by pairing off the appropriate chords in the two keys involved, as in Ex. 21–9. If, as in this case, the modulation is to the dominant major key, the V will pair with I, vi with ii, and so forth.

Ex. 21–9.

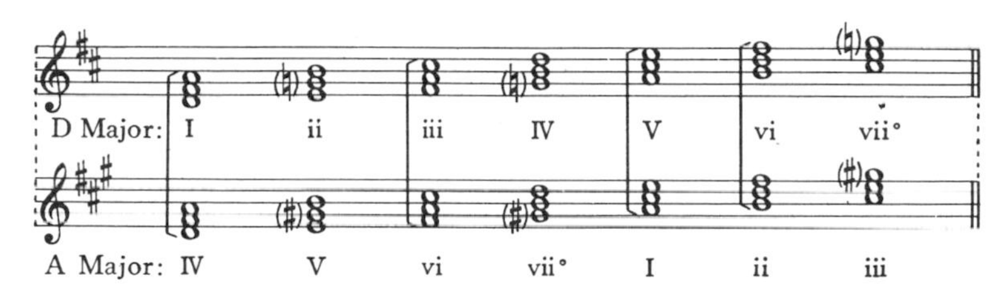

We can rule out several of these chord pairs: ii (a minor triad) will not serve as the chord equivalent of V (although V/V will); IV and vii° are likewise incompatible, as are vii° and iii. Four pairs remain: I and IV, iii and vi, V and I, vi and ii—all equally possible. It is obvious that the primary criterion is identity of chord quality.

Different pairs of keys display widely differing pivot-chord potentials. In certain key relationships, as illustrated in Ex. 21–10, the possibilities are more limited than in Ex. 21–9.

Ex. 21–10.

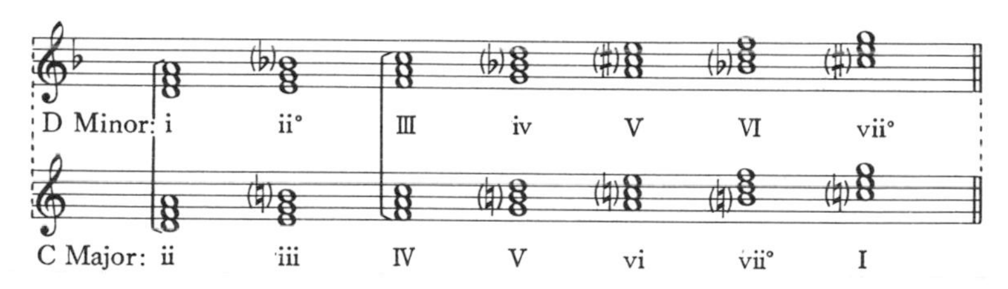

Common-chord modulation does not require a texture of block chords. Ex. 21–11 is clear in its modulatory implications: *F* major is confirmed (although briefly) in measure 7; I becomes IV in the previous measure.

Ex. 21–11. Beethoven: Trio, Op. 97 ("Archduke"), Scherzo.

Ex. 21–12 contains a clear pivot-chord modulation between two keys that are not near-related, but the process is not complex. The pivot chord occurs immediately before the first departure from C major: IV in C becomes V in *B-flat* major in measure 17.

Ex. 21–12. Schubert: Symphony No. 9 in C Major, Scherzo.

Pivot-Tone Modulation

In some modulations the link between the two keys is a single pitch or pitch class. Ex. 21–13 contains a pivot-tone modulation between the keys of *F* major and *D-flat* major; the sustained tone *F* (introduced in m. 5) acts as a link between the two keys. Note that the harmonic motion is from the tonic of the original key to the tonic of the new key. Pivot-tone modulation became more frequent in the nineteenth century than formerly, often as a link between distant-related keys.

Ex. 21–13. Beethoven: Trio, Op. 1, No. 3 Finale.

This principle is equally apparent in Ex. 21–14. The pivot tone here is the reiterated *G* in the viola parts; its role changes from dominant in *C* major (in m. 8) to mediant in *E-flat* major. Here the change is better described as a tonal shift than as modulation because of its abruptness.

Ex. 21–14. Shostakovitch: Quartet, Op. 49, I.

Modulation by Chromatic Inflection

In another modulation the relationship between two keys is established by melodic inflection—a voice that moves up or down a chromatic minor second, leading directly to a diatonic pitch in the new key. This procedure is particularly useful for modulation between keys that are a second apart, and the chromatic inflection is often placed prominently in one of the outer voices. Ex. 21–15 contains such a modulation in the fourth and fifth measures, with the bass moving from the tonic of the old key (*F*) to the leading tone (*F-sharp*) of *G* major, the new key.

Ex. 21–15. Mendelssohn: Symphony No. 3 (*Scotch*), I.

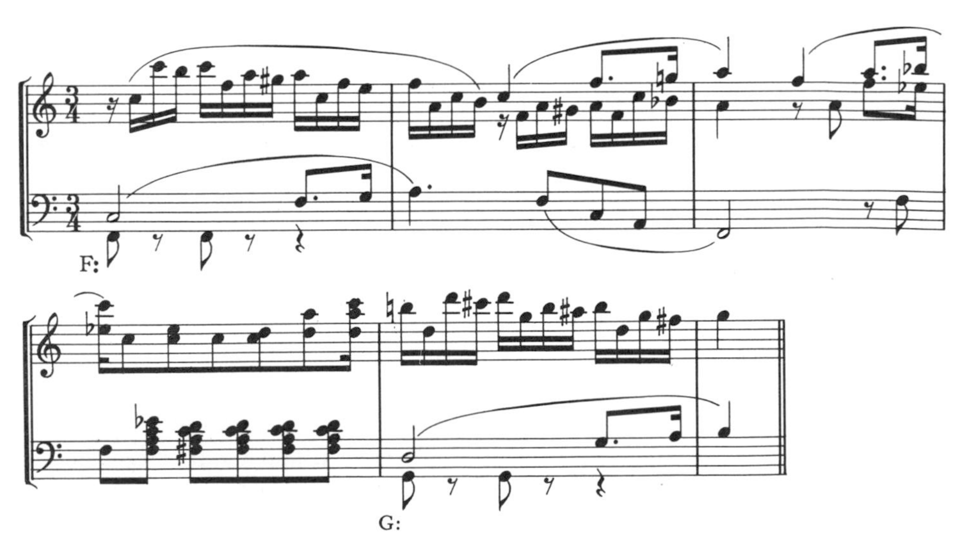

A twentieth-century version of this technique may be seen in Ex. 21–16, in which the two tonics (*F* and *C*) are connected by the *d-flat* minor triad in measure 126. No less than three lines, forming parallel minor triads, participate in the stepwise downward movement.

Ex. 21–16. Bartók: Concerto for Violin, No. 2, I. Copyright 1938 by Hawkes & Son (London) Ltd., Reprinted by permission of Boosey & Hawkes Inc.

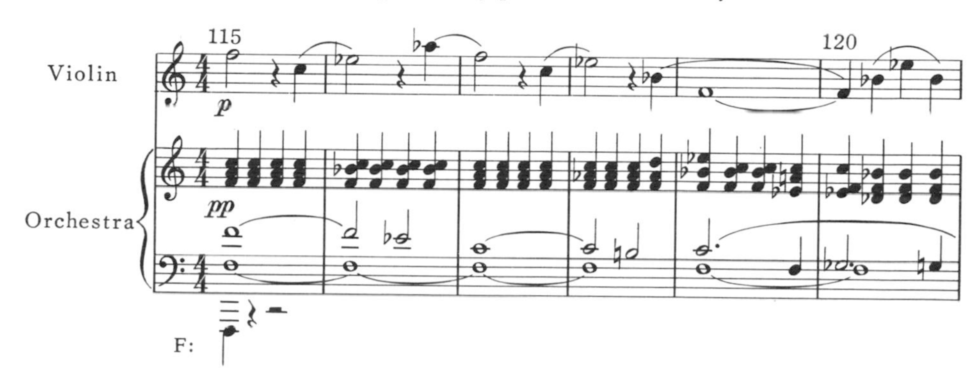

Modulations by chromatic inflection frequently involve the dominant as one of the chords. Composers often have modulated to the supertonic or submediant keys by this procedure. For example, the raised tonic pitch of a key becomes the leading tone of ii; the raised dominant becomes the leading tone of vi.

Ex. 21–17 contains a further example of this type of modulation, in this case involving a chord that is not diatonic to either old or new key. The upward chromatic inflection in the bass at measure 6 leads our attention from i in *f* minor to V^6_5/V in *c* minor.

Ex. 21–17. Purcell: *Dido and Aeneas,* Prelude, Act I, Scene 2.

f:

c: V^6_5/V V ———— i_6

Enharmonic Modulation

Composers occasionally have found it necessary to relate two keys through enharmonic spelling. This does not necessarily imply a remote modulation, however, since the enharmonic spelling is often used merely for the performer's convenience. The keys *F-sharp* major and *D-flat* major seem distantly related at first glance, but they are in fact no more distant than *C* major and *G* major. Most people find *D-flat* major easier to read than *C-sharp* major, because of the notational complications of the latter.

The modulation in Ex. 21–18 is not between keys as closely related as *F-sharp* and *D-flat,* but it does demonstrate that convenience of spelling can take precedence over notational consistency. Measures 5 and 6 of the voice are actually notated in *F-flat* major, although the accompaniment appears in the enharmonic key of *E* major. The pivot chord is also unusually interesting, for it is not diatonic. In the last half of measure 4, V in *A-flat* major becomes V/iii in *F-flat* major and resolves deceptively to the tonic of this new key. However, a more musical interpretation of this modulatory relationship would recognize the common pitch bond between the two keys; *A-flat* (tonic) of the initial key becomes mediant of the new key.

Ex. 21–18. Schumann: *Frauenlieben und Leben,* "Helft mir, ihr Schwestern."

Chordal texture is absent from the enharmonic modulation from *e-flat* minor to *b* minor *in* Ex. 21–19; the change of key is brought about solely by the change in function of the pivot tone: *G-flat/F-sharp* (3 in *e-flat* minor-5 in *b* minor). Schubert cleverly blurs the recollection of the previous key with the running chromatic scale in the piano.

Ex. 21–19. Schubert: Trio in E-flat Major, Op. 100, I.

Tonal Shift

Disguising a change of tonic has not always been the composer's goal. A sudden shift of key can produce a stunning effect, one that many composers have obviously considered desirable at times. We will not dwell on the manifold effects of this procedure except to note that this lays bare the relationship between the two keys, emphasizing their contrast, particularly when they are not near-related.

In addition to the highly chromatic modulatory progression of measure 2–8, Ex. 21–20 contains an abrupt shift of key: from the dominant of *c* minor in measure 11 to *E-flat* major in the next measure. Despite the cross-relation created by this chord succession (*B*/*B-flat*), the effect is one of no more than mild surprise, since each of the two chords has such a clear and logical tonal identity in its respective key.

Ex. 21–20. Haydn: Quartet, Op. 64, No. 6, I.

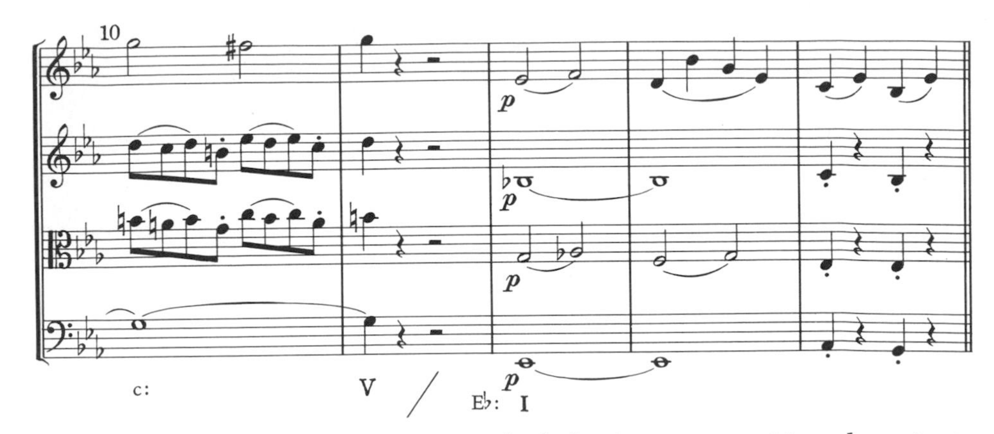

Ex. 21–21 contains a tonal shift—in measure 10 and again in measure 14—that is both more abrupt and more distant in terms of key relationship. The *E-flat* major triad in measure 10 (the new tonic) is totally unprepared and emphasized by the dynamic stress that accompanies it.

Ex. 21–21. Brahms: Symphony No. 4, III.

Ex. 21–22 represents the ultimate in abrupt tonal shifts. The key areas in this excerpt (*E-flat, D-flat,* and *C* major) succeed one another by parallel motion of their respective tonic triads.

Ex. 21–22. Beethoven: Symphony No. 3 (*Eroica*), I.

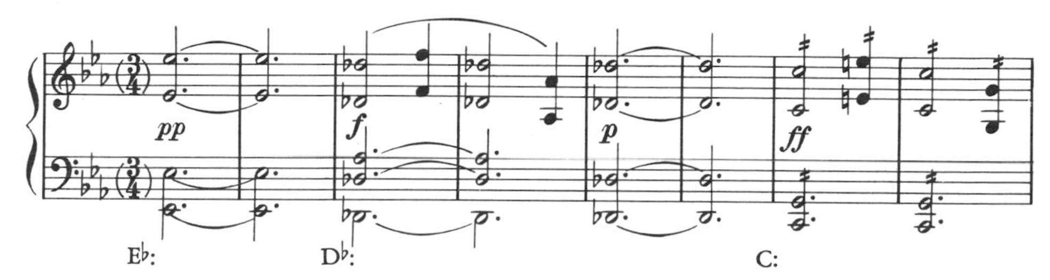

Mutation

We recall that modulation requires an actual change of tonic. The process of *mutation* a change in *mode* retains the same tonic. Although many aspects of one key are changed through mutation, one important factor, the tonic pitch, remains unchanged. Mutation's primary effect is a change in the "color" of the key from predominantly major to minor, or vice versa. Such a passage occurs in Ex. 21–23.

Ex. 21–23. Brahms: Intermezzo, Op. 118, No. 2.

Although not in itself modulatory, mutation often serves as an easy vehicle for modulating to more remote keys. The following diagram demonstrates that when the tonic triad is altered through mutation, a variety of new near-related keys are made readily available.

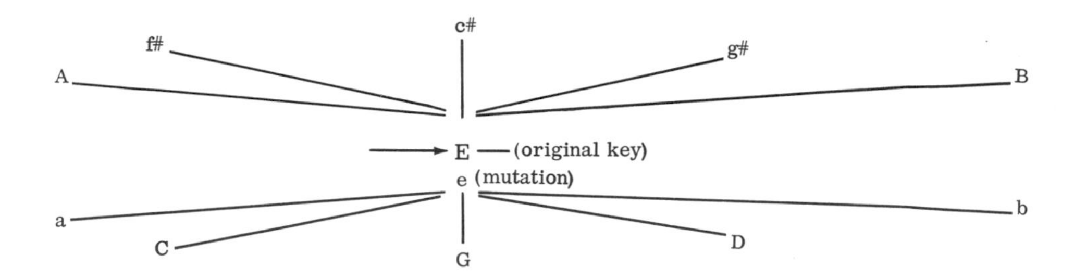

In Ex. 21–24 Schubert twice uses mutation to initiate relatively remote modulations: *A* modulating to *F* major through *a* minor, and later *F* modulating to *D-flat* major through *f* minor. In each case the second form of the chord undergoing the mutation is the pivot chord, i in the old key becoming iii in the new.

Ex. 21–24. Schubert: *Sehnsucht.*

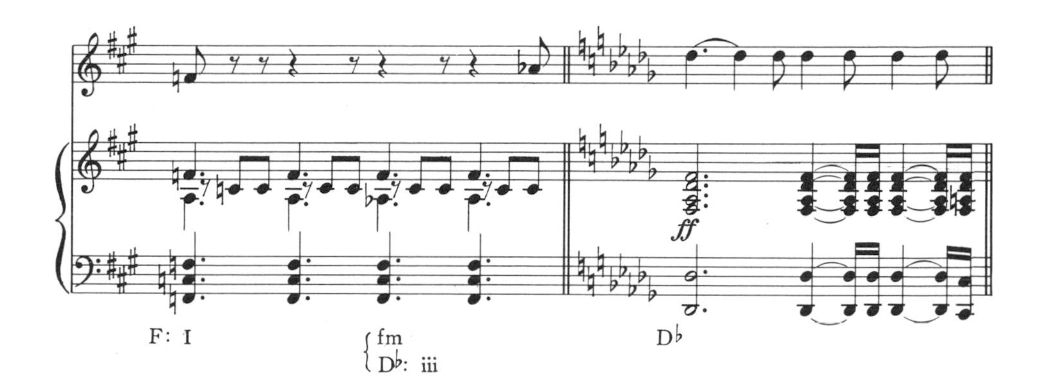

Exercises

For more detailed assignments see *Materials and Structure of Music I, Workbook,* Chapter 21.

1. Explore the diatonic pivot-chord possibilities of the following pairs of keys:
   a. *E-flat* major and its supertonic minor
   b. *A* major and its mediant minor
   c. *F* minor and its subdominant minor
   d. *F-sharp* minor and its submediant major
2. What are some possible pivot tones between the following pairs of keys? Write a melody containing such a modulation.
   a. *C-sharp* minor and *C* major
   b. *A-flat* major and *D* major
   c. *E* major and *A-flat* major
3. Using Roman numerals, plot a modulation from a major key to a near-related key. Improvise at the keyboard, or vocally, a melody that fits this harmonic pattern. Such a melody could be a simple arpeggiated version of the chords, or a more complex line.
4. Find other examples illustrating the various types of tonality changes illustrated in this chapter.

Chapter Twenty-Two

Binary Form

A two-section (*binary*) formal plan is one of the most significant structural designs in music history. From the early days of monophonic music until recent times, one can find compositions demonstrating this two-section pattern of organization. Medieval composers favored a grouping of dances in pairs: pavane-galliard, passamezzo-salterello, and others. One must conclude that a convincing and satisfying psychological basis must exist to account for the popularity of the binary principle over such a great span of time.

In the world's major ethnic musical traditions, we find numerous examples of binary formal types. Perhaps the most important of these is the combination of a slow, improvisatory opening movement with a faster, more rhythmic and organized movement. This pattern, which we might call *free-strict,* is found in the musics of India and Japan, as well as other regions of the world. Much the same effect is generated, though, by traditional combinations of movements in the western European tradition—the *prelude* and *fugue,* the *recitative* and *aria,* the *French overture* of the baroque, and the slow-fast sequence of sections that characterizes the concert overture in the eighteenth and nineteenth centuries. Clearly this pattern satisfies a very basic need in the human experience of musical creation.

Early Examples

Two examples from early medieval song demonstrate various aspects of the binary principle as it later developed. "O Roma nobilis," sung by the traveling Goliard scholars, is an example of the *bar* form (diagrammed *A A B*)—an important early manifestation of the binary pattern. Its characteristic is the repeated first section, followed by a contrasting final strain, often a chorus, or *refrain.* Frequently in many verses, or strophes, this type of song was sung as a dialogue between a soloist and a group. Despite the clear divisions in both the text and music, there is little thematic contrast between the two sections.

Ex. 22–1. Eleventh-century Goliard song: *O Roma nobilis.*

Reuental's "Mayenzeit"—a song describing the beginning of the month of May—contains a similar repeated first section; but it also contains an almost literal repeat of the first section in its final seven measures. The pattern in this case is *A A B A.* Therefore, "Mayenzeit" is an ancestor of the type that usually is called *rounded binary.*

Ex. 22–2. Neidhart von Reuenthal (d. ca. 1245): *Mayenzeit.*

More Recent Examples

Binary organization is equally prevalent in the later history of Western music, both in the form of complete movements and as the pattern for internal *sections* of compositions. Variation movements, for example, frequently are based on a binary theme, as in Ex. 22–3. The subsequent variations on this melody retain the structure, harmony, and melodic outline of the passage illustrated.

In this later version of the binary design, *both* sections are designated to be repeated. The second section thus forms both a logical answer to and a continuation of the first section. We can diagram this pattern as *A A B B*—slight but perceptible contrasts in rhythm, contour, harmony, texture, and phrase structure define the two sections.

Ex. 22–3. Beethoven: Sonata in F Minor, Op. 57, II.

Baroque Binary Form

The form that we call *baroque binary* dominated music during the baroque era. This design is significant not just because it was *the* prevailing small form for more than two-hundred years; it was also the direct ancestor of the *sonata form,* which dominated the concert music of the following century and a half. Binary form is found in the separate movements of the dance suite (*allemande, courante, sarabande, gigue, bourrée, menuet,* and similar stylized dances) as well as in the various movements of instrumental sonatas and concertos.

Many of our observations on the nature of this form will apply equally to other compositions in two-part structure. It should be understood, however, that these specific descriptions are based upon baroque binary compositions such as Ex. 22–4.

Two general aspects are almost always present in this type of form: an obvious parallel between the two sections in the order of themes and an absence of strong contrasts such as those found in ternary movements. A certain basic sameness of themes, texture, register, tonality, etc. often characterizes the two sections of binary form. Both of these attributes are clearly demonstrated in Ex. 22–4, a keyboard sonata by Domenico Scarlatti.

Ex. 22–4. D. Scarlatti: Sonata in B Minor, L. 263.

tr
tr
15
tr
tr
20
25
30
tr
35
tr
40

45
tr
tr
50
tr
tr
tr
55
tr
tr
tr
60
65
70
75

In many respects the previous example is quite similar in its organization to Ex. 22–3. Like the earlier example, its binary design is confirmed visually by the double bars and repeat signs at the end of each section.

The Thematic Design

An understanding of any formal design is eased by extracting the important thematic fragments. The fragments (or "motives") shown in Ex. 22–5 are not complete *themes,* but they constitute the significant musical ideas in the first section (measure 1-47), and they recur in the second section in recognizable form. A comparison of the thematic outlines of these two large sections will make clear the similarities (and differences) between them.

Ex. 22–5. Significant thematic fragments from Scarlatti: Sonata in B Minor.

The thematic outlines of each section are similar. Fragment *a* occurs in much the same form at the beginning of each part (measures 1 and 48). Similarly, fragment *d* is the basis for the last part of each section (measures 35 and 75). The principal difference between the two halves of the form is the order of appearance of fragments *b* and *c*; they are reversed in the second section. Compare measures 7 and 67 and also measures 29 and 62.

From this analysis we can conclude that the two sections of this binary movement are quite similar—almost parallel in many cases. The interchange of position of the two middle motives in this example is not typical of the form, although other examples of the same arrangement do exist. Our analysis has not accounted for every melodic fragment, but it has been thorough enough to disclose the basic thematic similarity of the two sections.

The Tonal Design

Before leaving the Scarlatti movement, we must consider the tonal organization, an equally important factor in the complete analysis. We can chart the tonal progress of the composition as follows:

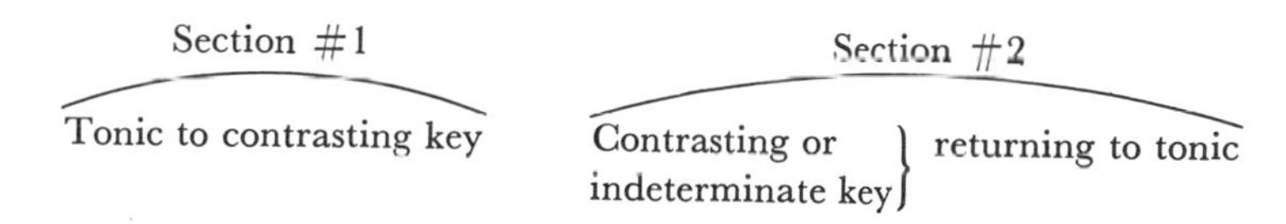

It is apparent that the key scheme of the two sections does not duplicate the same neat parallelism of the thematic design. Section 1 begins in the key of *b* minor, changes to *D* major in measures 25 and 26, and remains in that key until the double bar. The tonality at the beginning of section 2, however, is not clearly defined (*G* major and *D* major are both possibilities). It becomes stabilized in *b* minor, arriving there in measure 55 and remaining until the end of the sonata. The tonal direction of the second section is reversed, in a sense.

The apparent tonal instability at the beginning of the second section is present in most Baroque binary movements. In the analysis of compositions showing this characteristic tonal ambiguity, it is sufficient to point out the general key area.

The relationship between keys is somewhat different when the composition begins in a major key. In that event the contrasting key is almost always the dominant (for example *D* major to *A* major). The minor-key-to-relative-major-key progression of the Scarlatti is the rule, however, when the basic key is minor.

Other Formal Considerations

Our foregoing discussion hardly exhausts the list of possible factors that contribute to the form of this or any other composition. Changes of texture and register, cadences, phrase structure, contrapuntal factors, sequences, melodic contour, harmonic implications, and many other features affect our mental image of the structure of a piece of music. These may not all be of equal importance in any given composition, but all of them—along with countless other factors not mentioned—contribute in some degree to the total experience of musical form.

Among the other significant form-producing factors in Ex. 22–4 is texture. A change of texture is often the signal that a new formal or thematic unit has begun, as in measures 29 and 62. The addition of the octave in the right hand against the continuous sixteenth notes in the left hand marks an important change from the previous texture and attracts attention in both locations.

Cadences play an important role in defining the breaks between sections. An obvious example occurs in measure 34 and again in measure 75, each bringing the previous material to a terminal cadence. These mark the points of arrival for the keys in which each of these sections concludes.

An element that is not readily apparent often serves as a unifying device. Such is the case in measures 1–10, where the left-hand part is an *ostinato*, repeating the same two-measure fragment again and again. Similar figures appear in at least two other locations in each section, particularly near the final cadence. Notice also the use of augmentation in measures 7 and 8; both hands play the same melodic fragment but in different note values.

Binary and Ternary Forms Contrasted

The characteristic features of these two prominent formal types are summarized next. Where the external evidence is not clear, enough of these distinctions should be present to enable one to place the composition in the appropriate category.

BINARY	*TERNARY*
1. In two sections, each set off by double bars and repeat signs.	1. In three sections, the third of which is a literal repeat of or is similar to the first.
2. Each of the two sections ends in a different key from that in which it begins.	2. Each of the three sections usually ends in the same key in which it begins.
3. There is little thematic contrast between the two sections.	3. There is considerable thematic contrast between the first two sections.
4. In the conventional binary, the opening thematic material does not recur in the tonic key.	4. The opening thematic material invariably returns in the tonic key—at the beginning of the final (*A*) section.

Rounded Binary

A basic element of many musical forms is the return, or restatement, of opening material near the close of a composition. This element, prominent in the ternary design, is absent (except in terms of key return) from the binary form we have described. In the Scarlatti sonata, the opening theme does not return intact in the tonic key. The only reprise of this opening pattern appears at the *beginning* of the second section.

After the baroque era many composers began to incorporate short or partial reprises in their binary movements, similar to the organization of Ex. 22–2 and diagrammed similarly. Ex. 22–6 is a clearcut example of *rounded binary* organization; the *recapitulation* (or reprise) occurs at measures 92–93.

Ex. 22–6. Haydn: Quartet in C Major, Op. 76, No. 3, III (Trio).

65
70
f
f
f
75
pp
pp
pp
pp
80
85
90
93
p

The first three of the four criteria suggested earlier apply to this composition. Significant alterations have been made, however. The two sections are not approximately the same length as in the Scarlatti sonata; the second section here is more than four times the length of the first. We also find a restatement of the opening material in measures 93–100, where the mutation of the parallel major key returns to minor. In contrast to measures 56–64, these measures are not modulatory but remain solidly in *a* minor. Tonal instability occurs following the double bar at measure 64. This additional factor contributes to the recognition of the binary structure. The rounded binary form, of which this composition is a typical example, must be viewed as a hybrid form. Although it reveals traces of the ternary form, notably in the restatement it contains, it belongs clearly to the binary category.

Exercises

For more detailed assignments see *Materials and Structure of Music I, Workbook,* Chapter 22.

1. Listen to a recording of Ex. 22–4, noting each formal change and comparing the two large sections. Analyze further for the following details:
   a. Examples of repetition, sequence, imitation, phrase extension, motivic development
   b. Cadence types
   c. Points of contrapuntal interest
   d. Points of contrapuntal sterility
2. Play Example 22–6 from the score at the piano. Analyze for the following points:
   a. In what ways does this example exhibit principles of effective counterpoint?
   b. Analyze for phrase and period construction; analyze and label each cadence by key, Roman numerals, and cadence type.
   c. Make a harmonic analysis of measures 76–92.
   d. Discuss the intervallic structure of the theme in measures 1–8 and how this is developed in the remainder of the trio.
   e. Find examples of stretto and of imitation.

3. Follow a recording of Beethoven's String Quartet, Op. 18, No. 5, II. After listening to the full movement at least twice, make a diagram of the form. Try to incorporate the broad details at first, then perfect by noting smaller details. Listen once again and check for accuracy. Then answer the following questions:
   a. Are there contrasts of homophonic and contrapuntal textures? If so, where do they occur?
   b. Are there examples of sequence, melodic inversion, and repetition? Where do they occur?
   c. Where do the main cadences occur and what types are represented?
4. Following exercise 3 above, study a score of the movement, taking note once again of the above points. Then make a harmonic analysis of selected passages.
5. Write a brief composition for piano that is cast in simple binary form. Make each section no longer than sixteen measures, and retain a simple texture of two voices throughout (prominent top line, accompanimental bass voice).

Index of Musical Excerpts

C

D

N

O

P

R

S

Index

Note: *Italic* type indicates pages on which the definition of a subject appears.

D

E

F

G

H

I

K

L

M

N

O

P

R

S

T

V